Black Protest Thought and Education

Studies in the
Postmodern Theory of Education

Joe L. Kincheloe and Shirley R. Steinberg
General Editors

Vol. 237

PETER LANG
New York • Washington, D.C./Baltimore • Bern
Frankfurt am Main • Berlin • Brussels • Vienna • Oxford

Black Protest Thought and Education

WILLIAM H. WATKINS

EDITOR

Foreword by James D. Anderson

PETER LANG
New York • Washington, D.C./Baltimore • Bern
Frankfurt am Main • Berlin • Brussels • Vienna • Oxford

Library of Congress Cataloging-in-Publication Data

Black protest thought and education / William H. Watkins. [editor].
p. cm. — (Counterpoints; vol. 237)
Includes bibliographical references and index.
1. African Americans—Education—History. 2. Black power—United States—
History. 3. African American radicals—History. 4. United States—Race relations—
History. I. Watkins, William H. (William Henry), 1946- II. Series: Counterpoints
(New York, N.Y.) ; v. 237.
LC2741.B53 2005   370'.89'96073—dc22   2004027261
ISBN 0-8204-6312-4
ISSN 1058-1634

Bibliographic information published by **Die Deutsche Bibliothek**.
Die Deutsche Bibliothek lists this publication in the "Deutsche
Nationalbibliografie"; detailed bibliographic data is available
on the Internet at http://dnb.ddb.de/.

Cover art credit Azikiwe Crowe
Cover design by Lisa Barfield

The paper in this book meets the guidelines for permanence and durability
of the Committee on Production Guidelines for Book Longevity
of the Council of Library Resources.

Printed in the United States of America

Contents

JAMES D. ANDERSON

Foreword

On September 25, 1969 the African American revolutionary, George Jackson, writing from Soledad prison to his younger brother Jonathan, gave him the following advice regarding his high school education:

I hope you are involved in the academic programs at your school, but knowing what I know about this country's schooling methods, they are not really directing you to any specialized methods. They have not tried to ascertain what fits your character and disposition and to direct you accordingly. Decide now what you would like to specialize in, *one thing* that you will drive at. Do you get it? *Decide now*. There are several things as a revolutionary group that we need badly: chemists, electronic engineers, surgeons, etc. Choose one and give it special attention at a certain time each day. [1]

Expressing little faith in schooling to guide his brother toward a productive career and certainly not toward something that would serve the liberation of African American people, Jackson viewed public schooling as a counter to a liberating education for Black youth. His remarks about his brother's schooling represented a particular instance in a long historical process of Black radical critiques of the role of established education in shaping the consciousness of African American youth. Education in the formal and informal sense appeared repeatedly in the writings of George Jackson. By grasping the role of consciousness in Black liberation struggles, revolutionaries like Jackson worried incessantly about the capacity of African American workers, citizens, and intellectuals to identify the source of their oppression and to imagine an alternative society of freedom and equality. Hence, they challenged the educational establishment, but no less did they challenge various segments of the

Black community, including integrationists, nationalists, feminists, and capitalists, depending on the social foundations of their educational thought. Jackson, for example, waged a persistent struggle against capitalist consciousness, arguing that African Americans would never understand the source of their long-standing exploitation without recognizing the role of capitalism in structuring the whole edifice of social oppression, including the repressive role of public education in shaping the consciousness of young people. "It was the capitalist infrastructure of Europe and the U.S. which was responsible for the rape of Africa and Asia," argued Jackson.[2] Regarding African Americans who embraced capitalism as "the most unnatural and outstanding example of man against himself that history can offer," he proclaimed, "a diagnosis of our discomfort is necessary before surgery."[3] The "diagnosis" was education and "surgery" the liberation struggle; thus Blacks could not hope to topple racism and inequality until they substantially transformed their consciousness of capitalist political economy.

Jackson's thinking about education and capitalist social relations represents only one strand in the Black radical tradition. Especially during the nineteenth and early twentieth centuries, exceptions not withstanding, Black nationalists, many of them embracing capitalism, challenged the established educational system on different grounds. Focusing less on the economic foundations of slavery, racism, and oppression, they emphasized African American claims to a separate nationality based on their subterranean life through two and one-half centuries of slavery and the decades of racial oppression that followed emancipation. From the vantage point of nationalists, African Americans were Americans and yet an ethnic group apart from the dominant Anglo-American society. For nationalists, African American ethnicity derived from two underlying forces: a separate and distinctive experience that persisted for over centuries of oppression based on race; and a particular culture produced by that experience, one that served as a passageway for survival as well as a mechanism for resistance to racist oppression. Hence, Black Nationalism constituted the only politically realistic hope of transcending the heritage of slavery and accommodation and building a movement for equality and freedom.

The adherence of so many African American intellectuals to one or another wing of Black nationalist movements evidences the extent to which they believed that the Black experience produced a common polity, a coherent and unique sense of peoplehood, a distinctive culture, and a sense of common destiny. All that was needed to forge a Black nation was a culturally based ideology capable of unifying the leaders and commanding the allegiance of the masses. But once again schools stood in the way because they denied, misrepresented, distorted, or simply refused to teach the masses the truth about their history and culture. Black nationalists viewed established schooling as counter-revolutionary in the sense that it denied to African American children the most important education, knowledge of self and from whence they came. As Malcolm X put it, "A race of people is like an individual man; until it uses its own talent, takes pride in its own history, expresses its own culture, affirms its own self-hood, it can never fulfill itself."[4] Consequently, the nationalists struggle for control of the definition and understanding of the Black experience compelled them to make education a central tenet of their social thought. The great question absorbing Black nationalist concerns about education and intruding itself into the center of their social thought was the failure of public schools to teach Black history and culture, to direct an understanding of racist oppression, and to produce a sense of pride and optimism in Black youth. In a 1974 volume of Harvard Educational Review, *Education and the Black Struggle*, radical intellectuals, many of them nationalists, called attention to the "the struggle over the control of the black experience." Convinced that "the Black community had no future if it did not act responsibly to define for itself and others the nature of its own past and present," they called for a "struggle in the arena of ideas between colonizer and colonized."[5] The call for a struggle in the arena of ideas was fundamentally a call for a struggle over the purpose and function of education, both formal schooling and popular culture.

Although we know a little about the political and social ideas of Black radicals, their thoughts about education remain virtually unknown to scholars and the general public. Many scholars have focused on the origins and development of African American social thought, but with few exceptions (e.g. the Washington-DuBois debate regarding liberal versus industrial education) scant attention has been paid to the place of education within the Black radical tradition. Yet, with respect to issues of curriculum, culture, and training for work and citizenship, Black radicals have always focused heavily on the role of formal and informal education in the socialization of African American youth.

This book brings the historical neglect of Black radical thinking about the role and purpose of education to a close. Although not until extensive work in the future will the full extent of education as a core tenet in the social thought of Black radicals be understood, this is an excellent beginning that is long overdue. Indeed, one of the book's accomplishments is its stimulation of original thinking about a wide range of educational theories and policies in the Black radical tradition. Rarely has the relationship between Black political thought and education been explored so specifically and varied as in this book. Topics range from a new look at Black nationalism and education from the American Revolution through the antebellum era; from an intriguing analysis of Black Marxist and radical critiques during the Progressive Era to a critical analysis of the Mississippi Freedom schools; from a study of the unique but powerful impact of the Black Panthers' educational programs to Black nationalist teachers and school reforms in Chicago during the 1960s; from radical Black feminist pedagogy to critiques of education in the new Millennium and the role of Critical Race Theory in identifying White supremacy in education and countering its hegemony. This anthology brings together the most important research and writing on education and the Black radical tradition to date. Without question, it will spawn a new field of interrogations into the place of education in the social thought of Black radicals and their historic struggles to define and control the education of African American children.

James D. Anderson,
Gutsgell Professor of Education Policy Studies
University of Illinois at Urbana-Champaign

Notes

1. George Jackson, *Soledad Brother: The Prison Letters of George Jackson* (New York: Coward-McCann, 1970: 1994 edition by Lawrence Hill), 195.

2. Ibid. 236.

3. Ibid. 236, 253.

4. Malcolm X quoted in George Breitman, *The Last Year of Malcolm X* (New York: Schocken Books, 1968), 110–11.

5. Institute of the Black World (editor), *Education and the Black Struggle: Notes from the Colonized World*, Monograph Number 2 (Cambridge: Harvard Educational Review, 1974), 1. 31.

Acknowledgments

As always I would first like to thank the ancestors on whose shoulders we stand. More specifically, this project is dedicated to those who suffered, sacrificed and gave their lives in the ongoing battle for equality and justice.

We owe a debt of gratitude to the many prominent scholars, warriors and scholar-warriors who have contributed to the treasury of emancipatory thought and action. Karl, Frederick, Vladimir, W.E.B., Harriet, Malcolm, Patrice, Ho, Mao, Fidel, Ernesto and Nelson P. are exemplars for us all. We owe an even bigger debt to those ordinary people in our families, schools and communities who have nourished us.

Drawing from our intellectual inheritance, the authors in this book have crafted essays that celebrate the radical tradition in education and social thought. They are to be commended for their originality and perseverance.

I especially want to thank our series editors, Joe Kincheloe and Shirley Steinberg for their assistance and encouragement; young gifted artist, Azikiwe Crowe of RK. Design, Chicago, for his cover artwork; Christine Olson, University of Illinois computer support department for her technical assistance, and the many friends and colleagues who provided informed feedback and criticism for this text.

William H. Watkins

WILLIAM H. WATKINS

Introduction

Oppression and protest are inextricably linked. The long history of involuntary servitude, labor expropriation, discrimination and brutality in the United States has given rise to nearly 400 years of protest. While the ruling and propertied classes have squeezed all racial and ethnic groups in their never ending quest for money and power, African Americans have, over time, been among the most exploited and oppressed. From the slave ships to the cotton fields to the housing projects, Black protest has ranged from silent prayer to urban warfare.

Human beings are social creatures. All people desire interaction, exchange and the transmission of ideas and culture. Communication, cultural expressions and some form of education, informal or formal, are integral components of societal life. A central feature in the 400-year history of oppression has been the denial and subsequent control of education. Hence, education has been at the heart of Black protest thought and activism from the plantation to the demand for integration onward to the demands for equity and access. Black educational protest has taken many forms including demands for inclusion, quality, equal funding and culturally sensitive delivery systems.

Nation-states and their hegemonic groups are deeply invested in brokering ideas whether through mass education, the media or other means. Those ideas are often inimical to the interests of marginalized and non-propertied groups who possess their own ideological agendas. Education and the curricula are flashpoints for dialogue and contention.

Black protest literature in the United States generally explores the ideological and organizational response to slavery, oppression and unequal treatment. Black educational protest literature focuses more narrowly on the quest for integration and the splinter movements for community control. The guiding theory of this book holds that education is politics. Education is about ideas and contested social knowledge. Ideas translate into action. The battle of ideas is at the core of social and political discourse. All human history revolves around the battle of ideas.

This work emerges at a critical juncture in history. Globalization, deindustrialization, remilitarization and the new imperialism have impacted all social institutions. Public education is being politicized as never before. Every mayor, governor and president has taken a position. Unprecedented federal legislation is jolting the system at its foundations. Unfulfilled promises and rising societal expectations combined with the new political and economic realities now surround public education. It may be argued that indeed the future of mass education is problematic.

This book is interdisciplinary and intentionally crosses many borders. It acknowledges the marriage of education, politics and protest. It is about the perennial struggle of power and ideas. Most of all it is about the quest for equality and social justice.

The chapter contributions provide a political sociology of Black educational protest. The essays look both into the classroom and at the larger power and racial dynamics. Although the book is not intended as a historical treatment, several chapters look to the past for explanation. Each chapter explores a critique of American education from an ideological lens found in the larger protest arena.

In chapter 1, radical Pan-Africanist political historians Richards and Lemelle brilliantly link education to Black liberation throughout the diaspora. They demonstrate that educational reform politics have been a key ingredient in advancing racial and political and revolutionary consciousness among subject people. Their analytical examination of the educational views of President Julius Nyerere, activist Audre Lorde, revolutionary Ernesto "Che" Guevara and Marcus Mosiah Garvey illustrate the connection of education to social movements.

Educational historian and sociologist Daniel Perlstein presents an examination of the "progressive" roots of Civil Rights–era educational activism both in the freedom schools of the south and the more militant Black Panther schools that followed. His unique work looks at both the pedagogy and content of the militant challenge to the public schools. He shows the overwhelming challenges faced by "progressive" educators in a system that dishonors liberatory education.

In chapter 3, educator Haroon Kharem and racial theorist Eileen Hayes look at 200 years of Black Nationalist criticism of American education. After exploring the foundations of Black Nationalist thought, they illustrate the role of 19th-century African Americans in shaping a critical theory and discourse in both sociopolitical and educational discourse. They find the assimilation or separation issue being shaped by a growing Black consciousness. Their review of the literature helps us understand the deeply embedded feelings of nationalism among Blacks.

In her larger body of work, Black educational theorist and feminist-womanist Annette Henry has long argued that women's contributions, classroom practices, discourses and ways of knowing and being are overlooked in traditional educational criticism. While helping us untangle the racial, social-class and definitional complexities of feminism and womanism, chapter 4 expands and politicizes (Black) feminist ideology and pedagogy. Henry argues that Black feminism in education is inextricably connected to activism and social change. She points us to literature and outlooks focused on social justice, equity and community building.

Next, drawing from the literature on Black Marxism, Social Reconstructionism and critical theory, political sociologist and curriculum theorist William Watkins looks at the critique by Black Marxists on public education in the United States. Whereas that topic is underresearched in the conventional literature, this ambitious essay offers a definitive illustration of Marxist theory while attempting to (re)join the Marxist critique to Black protest theorizing in education.

In chapter 6, education historian Joy Williamson provides an in-depth study of the powerful educational critique and program of the Black Panther Party. She locates the Party's efforts within the community-control movement then erupting in several large urban areas. She illustrates how the Party tried to wed Marxian class struggle to Black history and education reform. Like Perlstein, Williamson concludes that this effort at liberatory education ran into monumental challenges.

Veteran curriculum theorist Beverly Gordon looks at Black protest, educational criticism and the crisis of leadership since "9–11." She sees profound changes in the sociopolitical landscape. The hegemonists are now attempting to supply "safe" Black leadership with muted voices, i.e., non-movement people. She looks at "community-nominated" versus appointed leaders of disenfranchised Black people. Gordon demands a new dialogue and reconstruction of the curriculum in public schools.

In chapter 8, educational historian, Dionne Danns presents a much-needed case study of educational protest in Chicago during the Civil Rights era. Chicago and New York, then and now, lead the nation in educational "reform." Danns's force-field analysis examines the roles of conflict, race and ideology in educational reform. Like other theorists, she demonstrates the tremendous, often insurmountable, odds in undertaking democratic and radical school change.

Finally, critical race theorist David Stovall explores the contentions of Critical Race Theory (CRT) in its criticism of public education in America. Adapted from legal studies, CRT, he argues, brings new dynamics to the table. For him CRT is about praxis. Additionally, CRT introduces a deep and thorough explication of racism within the school curriculum. This essay joins contemporary voices with extant educational criticism and protest.

These scholars and activists provide a literature of reviews and analyses that contribute immensely to our understandings of protest thought and educational criticism. Collectively these essays offer rich and textured analyses of ideology within the dynamics of Black protest. More specifically, we gain new understanding of the centrality of education as a purveyor of ideas and a vehicle of uplift.

Chapter One

SANDRA RICHARDS
AND SIDNEY J. LEMELLE

Pedagogy, Politics, and Power

ANTINOMIES OF THE BLACK RADICAL TRADITION

Introduction

In his groundbreaking book *Black Marxism*, Cedric Robinson (2000) examined radical thinkers who emerged from what he termed the "Black Radical
Tradition." As viewed by Robinson, this tradition was an accumulation of collective intelligence gathered from generations of struggle and resistance to slavery, segregation, and exploitation by "racial capitalism" (Robinson, chap. 1).
Further, Robinson theorizes that this tradition, although originating in Africa
and borne across the Atlantic in the holds of slave ships, evolved from New
World revolts and maroonage to a more direct critique of the West and colo-
nialism. Out of this rose a segment of the colonial petty bourgeoisie, the Black
Radical intelligentsia, whose unique position made them "internal aliens"
(Robinson, p. 182) in their own societies. Robin Kelley argues that

> Their contradictory role as victims of racial domination and tools in the empire, as
> Western-educated elites feeling like aliens among the dominant society as well as
> among the masses, compelled some of these men and women to revolt, thus produc-
> ing the radical Black intelligentsia. (Kelley, quoted in Robinson, xiv)

For such individuals, the purpose of the struggles became one of confrontation "to overthrow the whole race-based structure" (Robinson, xxxi).

Robinson focuses his analysis on three individual members of the Radical
Black intelligentsia: W.E.B Du Bois, C.L.R. James, and Richard Wright, but
he also acknowledges that this tradition "extends into cultural and political ter-
rains far beyond [his] competence to relate" (Robinson, xxxii). In this essay,
we will add the important terrain of education, more specifically the emergence

of a Black Radical Tradition in education. Using Robinson's insights, we will also explore some of the political and revolutionary strands that have emerged within the pedagogical and ideological realms of Black liberation. The following sections explore the educational philosophies of Marcus Garvey, Julius Nyerere, and Audre Lorde within the historical context of their lives and work in the Black Radical Tradition, both nationally and internationally.

Within the Black Radical Tradition we can identify individuals who sought to establish a distinctly Black education that would liberate the minds of African men and women, and "uplift the race" from the throes of White supremacy. These individuals, while they may not have agreed upon specific methods of educating Black people, all recognized the important interrelationship between education, language, consciousness, and politics. The connection between a people's ability to speak and think for themselves, act on their collective knowledge, and become agents in their own liberation are themes echoed by some of the key figures in the Black Radical intelligentsia. These individuals understood the dialectical relationship between education and liberation movements, what Walker (1981) describes as "the revolutionary potential of education," and its corollary, "the educational potential of revolution" (p. 120).

The notion that education is a political act, and that the ideological realm is inextricably tied to larger social, economic, and cultural contexts is certainly not a new idea. In fact, others have written about the ways in which education and political/revolutionary movements are intimately connected. Two of the most widely acknowledged revolutionary pedagogues—Che Guevara and Paulo Freire—focused not only on issues of literacy, but also used education as a means of changing the material conditions of those who were oppressed. According to Löwy (1997), central to Che Guevara's philosophy was a belief that "the only pedagogy that is liberating is one that enables people to educate themselves through their revolutionary practice" (cited in McLaren, 2000, p. 79). In his work, *Che Guevara, Paulo Freire, and the Pedagogy of Revolution,* Peter McLaren (2000) points out that Freire was "one of the first internationally recognized educational thinkers who fully appreciated the relationship among education, politics, imperialism, and liberation. In fact, he clearly understood that they unavoidably abut to one another as well as flash off each other" (p. 141). Furthermore, Freire believed that "educational change must be accompanied by significant transformations in the social and political structure in which education takes place" (McLaren, 2000, p. 148).

The work of Freire and Guevara has been well documented and has contributed to an understanding of the connection between education and revolutionary social change in the so-called "Third World." However, little attention has been given to the ways in which leaders who are of African descent have framed issues of education within Black Liberation Movements and used education as a tool of revolutionary practice. It is time to acknowledge the multiple voices that have been present in the struggle for liberation pedagogy, and to recognize those who either directly or indirectly, through their role in revolutionary movements, emerged as leaders in defining Black education.

Here we begin to explore the pedagogical work of three such leaders: Marcus Garvey, Julius Nyerere, and Audre Lorde—individuals who, in different ways, significantly influenced the sensibilities of the Black Radical Tradition in education throughout the Diaspora. In addition to the significant contributions made by these individuals, our selection of Garvey, Nyerere, and Lorde is a conscious decision to focus on radical Pan-Africanist leaders who have not been widely recognized for their role as "educators." Despite the scarcity of information in educational literature about these individuals, all three were indeed educators and have contributed to the core of knowledge that continues to influence beliefs about the role of education in the lives of Black people and the strategies that should be used in acquiring access and equity within (and without) traditional educational systems.

While many others have been involved in the struggle for liberation and have used education as a strategy in that effort, a thorough analysis of all of these movements and the philosophies of their primary leaders is beyond the scope of this paper. Rather, we are concerned with providing a glimpse, from a historical standpoint, into the making of a Black Radical Tradition in education. Each of the revolutionaries examined here offers a distinct perspective into this tradition throughout the African Diaspora, spanning a time period that begins in the early decades of the twentieth century—with the formation of the Universal Negro Improvement Association (UNIA) in Jamaica and then in the United States, within the context of the New Negro era—and continues into the final decades of the century with the nascent presence of a Black Lesbian Feminist voice in Pan-African–liberation efforts.

Let us first turn to the work of Marcus Garvey, who framed a model of emancipatory education based on race consciousness and Black Nationalism. We move on to examine the philosophies and ideologies of Julius K. Nyerere, whose vision of "education for self-reliance" and *Ujamaa*, or Tanzanian socialism, attempted to create a counter-hegemonic response to the colonial system of education. Finally, we analyze Audre Lorde's literary and activist struggles for the liberation of all people from oppression—but in particular women throughout the African Diaspora. Demonstrating the connection between ideology, language, and survival, Lorde's work opens the possibility for a revolutionary pedagogy that confronts interlocking systems of oppression and creates new visions for social change.

Marcus Garvey: The Emergence of a Pan-African and Black Nationalist Tradition in Education

> *For man to know himself is for him to feel that for him there is no master. For him Nature is his servant, and whatsoever he wills in Nature, that shall be his reward. . . . If 4,000,000,000 Negroes can only get to know themselves, to know that in them is a sovereign power, is an authority that is absolute, then in the next twenty-four hours we would have a new race, we would have a nation, an empire, resurrected not from the will of others to see us rise, but from our own determination to rise, irrespective of what the world thinks. (Excerpt from M.M. Garvey's 1923 essay "Man Know Thyself," cited in A.J. Garvey, 1986, pp. 38–39)*

Garvey's Universal Negro Improvement Association (UNIA) has been described as "the most dynamic mass movement across territorial borders among the African peoples [during] this century" (Campbell, 1991, p. 171). James (1998) also described it as "the largest and most powerful Black Nationalist organization the world has ever known" (p. 136). It is almost inconceivable to speak of organized mass movement within the Black experience without acknowledging the influence and work of Marcus Garvey and his intellectual mentors, including the Sudanese-Egyptian leader of the Pan-African Movement, Duse Mohammed Ali; leader of the "New Negro" radical tradition, Hubert H. Harrison; and the father of Black industrial education, Booker T. Washington. It is through the work of these individuals and others that Garvey's allegiance to "race first," global organizing, Black political movement, self-determination, and economic self-help were first conceptualized.

Garvey met Duse Mohammed Ali while studying at Birbeck College in London in 1912, and found in him a teacher and mentor for African history, politics, and Islam, who shaped his Pan-Africanist discourse. At the time, Ali was one of the foremost members of London's Muslim community and was recognized as a leader in the Black Radical Tradition. He was best known for his journal, *The African Times and Orient Review*, which also had a profound influence on the Pan-Africanist Movement. Ali's Islamic and Pan-Africanist teachings were a primary source of Garvey's understanding of African global connections and cultural identities, which provided the political impetus for establishing a "universal confraternity" (Garvey, n.d., p. 206) among Blacks, and for necessitating an educational program of race consciousness.

Of particular importance to Garvey's emerging ideologies was the Islamic emphasis on two interrelated concepts—signification and identity (Turner,

1997). Both concepts point to the issue of naming and renaming as both acts of control in an imperialist world order and acts of liberation. According to Turner:

> Signification was part of the ambiguous heritage of the Enlightenment. On the one hand, people of color were categorized, stigmatized, and exploited for the purposes of economic and political hegemonies, but on the other, egalitarianism and the universality of humanity were affirmed by Enlightenment thinkers. The Black American community was signified during this period as inferior to the dominant group in America. Since slavery, however, Islam has undercut this signification by offering Black Americans the chance to signify themselves, giving them new names and new political and cultural identities. Thus, signification was both imposed and self-affirmed. (p. 3)

Within the context of Islam, signification was seen as a revisionist and transformative process. Blacks could emerge from the trappings of colonial mentalities and feelings of racial and cultural inferiority, and look toward the possibility of a new identity carved out of the African past—the possibility of naming themselves. The concepts of signification and identification, as defined within Islamic religious teachings, were compatible with Garvey's search for a new politics and religion that would provide cultural strategies for liberation. The influence of "global Islam" created a counter-hegemonic force to the existing imperialist order, bringing "together Pan-Africanists from Asia, Africa, and the United States, Europe, and the West Indies as they creatively reformulated Black cultural and political identities around the issue of self-determination" (Turner, 1997, p. 81). Through the counter-hegemonic influence of Islam, a new language of self-determination emerged that is inherent in the religious, political, and educational discourse of the UNIA.

Garvey's political and educational ideology were also greatly influenced by the work of Hubert Harrison, who sought to combine socialist theory and a race-first approach into a program of Black radicalism that was based on both class consciousness and race consciousness. Harrison served as the "founder and intellectual guiding light" of the New Negro Movement—"the race-conscious, internationalist, mass-based, autonomous, radical, and militantly assertive movement for political equality, social justice, civic opportunity, and economic power" (Perry, 2001, p. 5). With the founding of the Liberty League and *The Voice* in 1917—the first organization and newspaper of the New Negro Movement—Harrison became "a major inspiration for two powerful and seemingly incompatible currents of Black radicalism": *revolutionary socialism* and *radical Black Nationalism*, which became undercurrents in the work of Garvey and members of the UNIA (James, 1998, p. 126). Harrison adopted the phrase "Race First," which was later recognized as the essence of the Garvey movement, in response to Woodrow Wilson's "America First" and the socialist slogan of "Class First" (Perry, 2001, p. 16). Speaking to the failure of socialism to adequately engage concerns of the Black race, Harrison (1920) vowed, "We say Race First, because you have all along insisted on [White] Race First and class after, when you didn't need our help" (cited in Perry, p. 109). Advancing a race-first agenda, and advocating protests and militant strategies, Harrison encouraged a more radical approach, within the Black political movement, compared to the politics of other Black leaders of the early twentieth century, including Booker T. Washington and W.E.B. Du Bois. Harrison was particularly critical of Booker T. Washington and described his philosophy as "one of submission and acquiescence in political servitude" (cited in Perry, p. 14).

Pointing to the conservatism of Black politics during this era, Harrison (1914) woefully admitted that, "Radicalism does not yet register to any noticeable extent the contributions of our race in this country" (cited in Perry, p. 42). Harrison also criticized the "elitist" educational strategy set forth by W.E.B. Du Bois in his theory of the "Talented Tenth." In contrast to the philosophies of both Washington and Du Bois, Harrison believed that Black equality necessitated an intellectual renewal of the masses. Harrison provided the inspiration for a radical Black nationalism that included notions of race consciousness and self-determination—notions that became part of a revolutionary program of economic, political, and social change, carried out by Garvey and other leaders of the Black Radical Tradition, including A. Phillip Randolph, Chandler Owen, Cyril V. Briggs, and Richard B. Moore.

Another valuable source of Garvey's visionary leadership was Booker T. Washington. Garvey found inspiration in Washington's Tuskegee Institute, which provided a model for Black-owned businesses. It prepared part of the Black leadership with the industrial skills necessary for racial advancement. What appealed most to Garvey were Washington's "economic self-help initiatives" (Verney, 2001, p. 120) and the illustration, through Tuskegee, of "practical self-help for Black Africans [and] successful independent Black endeavor" (Verney, p. 123). Garvey understood, as did his predecessor, that "the most important area for the exercise of independent effort was economic" (Martin, 1976, p. 33). For Garvey, no progress could be made in political and social arenas without first advancing economic initiatives and engendering a commitment and loyalty to Black business ventures. Economics became central to the Black political movement and served as a guiding philosophy of education for Blacks. Although Garvey remained a staunch supporter of Washington, and his work served as a continuation of his predecessor's, he was critical of the obvious contradiction in Tuskegee's reliance on White philanthropy, and consequently, sought to establish "a genuinely autonomous Black business and ultimately an independent Black African state" (Speech by Marcus Garvey, 1921; cited in Verney, p. 124).

Consistent with his belief in the need for independent Black enterprises, Garvey was critical of existing educational systems and believed it was necessary to establish a system of education that was designed *for* and *by* Black people. Garvey continued to set his sights on establishing an institution of higher education in Jamaica modeled after the Tuskegee Institute, but with greater emphasis on race-consciousness and Black Nationalism. The establishment of Booker T. Washington University and Smallwood-Corey Industrial Institute (renamed Liberty University), in 1923 and 1926 respectively, were Garvey's attempts to fulfill this goal. Although short lived, the mission of Booker T. Washington University was to prepare future leaders of the UNIA. It offered training in agriculture and commerce, and the opportunity to send an informed constituency throughout the Diaspora to educate "our people in the art and science of fruit raising, agriculture, and business administration and efficiency" (Convention Reports, 1922; cited in Verney, 2001, p. 114). In 1937, Garvey made another attempt at establishing an economically independent and sustainable Black educational institution. He started the School of African Philosophy in Toronto for the purpose of preparing Blacks for leadership in the UNIA. The curriculum in African philosophy included "a range of over forty-two subjects" and a course in racial leadership (Garvey 1938; cited in Hill & Bair, 1987, p. xlix). Based on principles of self-improvement and self-education, the School of African Philosophy sought mental emancipation and prepared Blacks for the great effort toward liberation. Pointing to Africa as both a symbolic and physical space of emancipation, and establishing race as a point of analysis, Garvey instituted an educational program that was truly in the Pan-African and Black-nationalist spirit.

A close look at the UNIA and Garvey's philosophies reveals a strong and unceasing commitment to education as a revolutionary force for Black liberation. Garvey wanted the UNIA "to unite the African race through an educational program that focused on race pride and unity, economic development, and the redemption of Africa" (Colin, 1996, p. 49). The policy statement of the UNIA, "The Declaration of the Rights of the Negro Peoples of the World" (1920; cited in Van Deburg, 1967), listed criticisms against the existing provisions of education for Blacks and articulated demands for a more emancipatory education:

> Article 30. We demand the right of unlimited and unprejudiced education for ourselves and our posterity forever (p. 28). *Article 31.* We declare that the teaching in any school by alien teachers to our boys and girls, that the alien race is superior to the Negro race, is an insult to the Negro people of the world (p. 28). *Article 49.* We demand that

instructions given Negro children in schools include the subject of "Negro History," to their benefit. (p. 31)

The Garvey movement was also characterized by a model of popular education, with the use of public forums, mass meetings, and street oration as forms of racial education (Hill & Bair, 1987). Garvey even purchased Edelweis Park in Kingston, Jamaica, for use as a meeting space, which he envisioned as a "great educational center" and a "center of people of intellect" (Garvey, 1932; cited in Hill & Bair, p. xlv). As James (1998) concedes, "Garvey saw himself first and foremost as a teacher and Liberty Hall a center of learning" (p. 79). Garvey was dedicated to self-education, and believed that learning should be a lifelong endeavor. According to Garvey, life was to be understood through experience, but also through the literary works of great men and women. Since it is not possible for all knowledge to be obtained within the span of a single lifetime, he believed that it was important to learn from noble individuals by reading a variety of works. He professed that knowledge is out there in the world, only to be discovered through our search for the truth. This quest should be guided with the intent of discovering knowledge that would benefit the Black race.

Another primary goal of education for Garveyites was to change consciousness and uproot racist myths of inferiority. As Campbell (1991) notes, "the rise of Garveyism was concerned with the fundamental principle of correcting the falsification of the place of Africa" (p. 168) and the redemption "of the African motherland" (p. 173). Through his Pan-Africanist sentiment, Garvey sought to rediscover and recover the identity and heritage of the Black race and to fight for African liberation from colonialism and racism. Through the activities of the UNIA, Garvey helped to restore Black people's cultural identity by glorifying the African past.

Garvey's philosophy of "African Fundamentalism" set forth a racial plan to encourage pride and unity, and a sense of agency for Blacks to think and act for themselves and become emancipated from hegemonic ideology. According to Garvey (1930), "Any race that accepts the thoughts of another race, automatical[l]y, becomes the slave race of that other race" (cited in Hill & Bair, 1987, p. 7). Garvey believed that Blacks must regain "a proud sense of selfhood" by rediscovering the achievements of Africans in the past (Hill & Bair, p. xxxvii). As Garvey (1925) proclaimed:

The time has come for the Negro to forget and cast behind him his hero worship and adoration of other races, and to start out immediately to create and emulate heroes of his own. We must canonize our own saints, create our own martyrs, and elevate to positions of fame and honor Black men and women who have made their distinct contributions to our racial history. (Also cited in A.J. Garvey, 1986, "African Fundamentalism")

Central to Garvey's program of education was an understanding that liberation of Africa and its peoples necessitated a "revisioning" of a liberated African identity. Consequently, he emphasized the importance of rewriting history to uproot myths of racial inferiority. To this end, Garvey viewed history and education as potential tools for liberation, and pointed to Africa as a source of racial pride. Black freedom could not be achieved until the rich history and cultures of Africa were restored. Furthermore, he recognized that true emancipation could only be achieved through racial and political consciousness, and an understanding of the systematic processes of domination and the nexus of power relations that operate within society.

Seeking true emancipation for Black people worldwide, Garvey's philosophy and the established aims of the UNIA were premised on an internationalist perspective that emphasized global connections. Like Garvey, Julius Nyerere drew on international-socialist, nationalist, and Pan-Africanist thought to counter neocolonialism in the era of African political independence in the 1960s.

Nyerere and Tanzania's Education for Liberation Movements

Man can only liberate himself or develop himself. He cannot be liberated or developed by another. For Man makes himself. . . . Education has to increase men's physical and mental freedom to increase their control over themselves, their own lives, and the environment in which they live. The ideas imparted by education, or released in the mind through education, should therefore be liberating ideas; the skills acquired by education should be liberating skills. Nothing else can properly be called education. Teaching which induces a slave mentality or a sense of impotence is not education at all—it is an attack on the minds of men. (Nyerere, 1978; cited in Hall & Kidd, 1978, pp. 27–28)

Julius Kambarage Nyerere was an unusual politician; he was a man of high principle, exceptional intelligence, and one of Africa's most revered independence leaders. Throughout most of his political life he was known as *Mwalimu*, or teacher, because he had a vision of education that was dynamic and innovative. Nyerere was born in 1922 on the eastern shore of Lake Victoria in Northwest Tanganyika, not far from the town of Musoma, where he first attended school. He later transferred to the Catholic-run Tabora Government Secondary School, where he excelled in his studies. Ultimately, he received a teaching degree at Makerere University in Kampala (Uganda). Nyerere taught for several years before entering the University of Edinburgh on a government scholarship to study history and political economy (Assensoh, 1998). While at

University, Nyerere came into contact with many students from the African Diaspora and Europe who influenced him with the ideas of African and Caribbean nationalism and Fabian socialism (Ishumi & Maliyamkono, 1995). In particular, Nyerere began to develop his distinct vision of combining socialism with African concepts of family, communal living, and progress (Nyerere, 1967a; Nyerere, 1967b; Nyerere, 1967c; Nyerere, 1967d).

After his studies in the United Kingdom, Nyerere returned home to Tanganyika, where his political activities soon put him at odds with local colonial authorities. Indeed, the absence of meaningful change in the lives of indigenous peoples of colonial Tanganyika only served to increase his African nationalist sentiments, the desire for self-rule, and the impetus for a liberation movement. In post–World War II Tanzania, Julius Nyerere proved to be an ideal leader to mobilize the people of Tanganyika. He and other leaders worked tirelessly to meld several nationalist factions into one organization, finally succeeding in 1954 with the formation of the Tanganyika African National Union (Ishumi & Maliyamkono, 1995).

In December 1961, the British granted independence to colonial Tanganyika, and Nyerere was elected the first president in 1962—a post he held until he stepped down in 1977. In the wake of the 1964 coup in Zanzibar, and an attempted coup in mainland Tanganyika itself, Nyerere convinced the new Zanzibari leaders to join together and form a united government, the Republic of Tanzania. However, this union of former colonies was not without contradictions.

The early years of independence started with somewhat romantic notions about modernization and development—what Ake (1996, p. 8) terms the "Development Paradigm"—but were soon displaced with a grim reality. With the end of British political rule in 1961, Tanzania was granted "flag independence" but economic control remained external. While the political power and bureaucratic structure was Africanized, the Tanzanian economy still rested in the colonial mode of production and exploitation. At independence Tanzania was one of the world's poorest countries; and like many other emerging African nation states, it suffered from the ravages of neocolonialism: foreign indebtedness, declining "foreign aid," and no price controls over its major agricultural exports. (Shivji, 1976)

To comprehend the importance of Nyerere in Tanzanian political economy, and education reform policies in particular, it is necessary to understand the basic tension that existed between the competing policies of building "peripheral capitalism" and coordinating a "socialist transition in Tanzania." (Samoff, 1990, p. 219) In this process there were three major political trajectories or paths of the new state: (1) a peripheral capitalist state; (2) a state in transition; and (3) a nascent socialist state. Over the last forty years, each trajectory represented a period of continuing struggle for "control of state power" and resulted in educational policy inconsistencies (Samoff, p. 220).

In the face of uncertainties and contradictions, Nyerere proclaimed the "Arusha Declaration," which, in the interests of the people and government, laid the foundation for the system of *Ujamaa*, or Tanzanian socialism and communal life. The objectives of the Arusha Declaration were to ensure that all members of Tanzanian society would have equal rights and opportunities, and be protected against systematic injustice and exploitation. Furthermore, he believed all citizens should have an opportunity to improve their economic and material circumstances and obtain a standard of living consistent with the most basic necessities of life, "before any individual lives in luxury" (Nyerere, 1967b, p. 340). His solution was a unique blend of African socialism, which included agricultural collectivization (or *Ujamaa* "villagization") and large-scale nationalization of local industries.

To get a better understanding of the importance of this measure, it is essential to understand the nature of Tanganyikan colonialism in the formation of these societies. Many historians (e.g., Shivji, 1976; Iliffe, 1979) argue that both the German and British colonial powers constructed the colonial state and colonial economy to serve as an extension of European imperialism. And likewise, in the case of formal African education, this same colonial system was an extension of imperialism and an essential aspect of control through the "ideological structure of the colonial state" (Mbilinyi, 1979, p. 236).

The colonial education system in Tanganyika, or what British colonial officials referred to as "Education for Adaptation," was geared to training "natives" to be good workers and to keep them contented with their lot in the colonial system (Buchert, 1994; p. 17). Thus, colonial assertions aside, the real purpose of education in the colonial period was not to prepare Africans for self-rule; on the contrary, it functioned as an arm of the colonial state, whose primary function was to indoctrinate and control. The educational basis of colonialism had important ramifications for the postcolonial period, and particularly regarding Nyerere's transition policies from "education for adaptation" to "education for modernization" (Buchert, pp. 68–69).

Three different school classifications evolved under the British scheme, based on a strict racial and class hierarchy: European, Asian, and African. Additionally, within each racial category there were specific class subdivisions of education for "leaders" (petite bourgeoisies) and the African "masses" (working class and peasantry). The primary function of such formal education in the colonial context included: (1) to produce a small group of *skilled, literate African workers and clerks* to work for White settlers, mission stations, and colonial government departments; (2) to create a group of educated elites or *internal aliens,* who, after receiving formal schooling in the colonial system, became "native informants"; (3) later, especially in the 1950s, the system produced a stratum of *literate progressive farmers* who were highly productive cash-crop producers and supporters of the "ideological tendencies" of colonial capitalism. Yet, ironically, the colonial state and colonial economy were dependent on the labor of an illiterate, unschooled (in the Western context) peasantry (Mbilinyi, 1979, p. 248; Buchert 1994). Not surprisingly, one of the first major policies of the newly independent Tanzanian government was to integrate the school system, doing away with race-based schools.

Thus, the period between 1946 and 1961 witnessed an evolving pyramid educational structure, as well as a racially segregated curriculum for European, Asian, and African—the opportunities being much greater for the first two groups:

> By the end of the colonial period, the pyramid education structure of today was firm-
> ly implanted, and its specific relationship to the hierarchical occupational structure
> cemented . . . there was a severe shortage of highly trained Africans to take over the
> future independent government, a result of deliberate colonial policies. . . . These poli-
> cies reflected the objective place Africans were allocated in the colonial economy;
> unskilled and semi-skilled labourers. (Mbilinyi, 1979, pp. 269–270)

In the immediate post-independence period, Nyerere preached with a somewhat romanticized optimism about modernization and development in Tanzania. His writings urged Tanzanians to become more aggressive and "catch up with the West" (Ake, 1996, p. 8). But within a few years this original optimism was shaken by a series of political and economic crises, which necessitated a further shift in policy. The end of the 1960s witnessed the transition to a new developmental strategy and educational policy, symbolized by the phrase "education for self-reliance" (Samoff, 1990).

One of the precipitating crises that pointed to the failure of the liberal modernist hope was the 1966 university-student uprising. In October of that year, more than 400 Tanzanian students protested against their forced enlistment in a two-year national service; the demonstrators saw the financial hardships of salary reduction as unfair treatment (Rodney, 1968). In the wake of the protest, Nyerere sent the students home, ostensibly to think about the implication of their protest and the elitism that it reflected. This protest had a direct impact on his ideological pronouncements that were soon to follow (Peter & Mvungi, 1985). In 1967, Nyerere announced the "Arusha Declaration" and the establishment of Tanzanian socialism (*Ujamaa*), which formed the basis of his subsequent speech on "Education for Self-Reliance" (Nyerere, 1967b). The main thrust of the new policy was to indict the old developmental-education ideal in Tanzania while simultaneously lessening dependence on the capitalist world. In addition, Nyerere became progressively more concerned with what he perceived as increased social and class divisions.

Congruent with these principles, Nyerere's (1967b) educational philosophy was based on notions of cooperative effort and "the common good" (p. 273). Viewing the educational system as an agent in the process of developing a society where individuals were committed to the total community, Nyerere (1967b) called for schools to encourage and prepare young people to take responsibility for developing a society where "all members share fairly in the good and bad fortune of the group, and in which progress is measured in terms of human well-being" (p. 273). According to Nyerere, "Schools must, in fact, become communities—and communities which practice the precept of self-reliance" (p. 282). He believed that schools in Tanzania needed to become "economic communities" in addition to being "social and educational communities" (p. 9). Recognizing the importance of transforming the neocolonial economic conditions in Tanzania, Nyerere (1971) argued that

> Although it is a critically important aspect, educational transformation alone will never lead to the total liberation of the society. Indeed it is dialectically impossible for profound changes to take place in the old educational system without antecedent and concomitant transformations of all aspects of the political economy. (p. 99)

Another guiding principle of Nyerere's (1967b) pedagogical philosophy was his belief in education's relevance to society. He believed that it must serve the needs and purposes of Tanzania and stress values and knowledge that are appropriate to its citizens. Consequently, he admonished uncritical acceptance of a colonial system of education that was "motivated by a desire to inculcate the values of the colonial society and to train the individuals for the service of the colonial state," that emphasized "subservient attitudes," and "induced attitudes of human inequality" (Nyerere, 1967b, p. 269). According to Nyerere, a spirit of elitism and a separation of the individual from society characterized colonial education. Furthermore, colonial systems of education adhered to a belief that all knowledge is acquired from books and that the "educated" individual is one who has received formal schooling (Nyerere, 1967b, p. 277). In challenging the notion of an "educated" individual, Nyerere points out that precolonial Africa did not have "schools" per se (Nyerere, 1967b, p. 268); instead, children learned by living and doing, and the adults around them were the teachers. In fact, all adults were teachers in the sense that they transmitted important wisdom and knowledge from one generation to the next, and prepared the youth for active participation in society. This process of education was held in high regard, and the adult teachers were revered in their role. Despite the lack of formality of this educational process, it had direct relevance to the society. Overall, in his philosophy and policies, Nyerere (1967b) sought to counter the colonialist legacy of education in both assumptions and practices.

Nyerere's policies were also directed toward adult education, lifelong learning, and learning for liberation. In the "Declaration of Dar es Salaam," he made a strident call for adult education to be directed at helping people to help themselves, and for it to be approached as part of life: "integrated with life and inseparable from it" (Nyerere, 1968, p. 29). For him, adult education stretched far beyond the classroom. It includes "motivation" and "political mobilization and the awakening of critical awareness of their environment." (Kassam, 1979a, p. 153) Also, for Nyerere—borrowing from Paulo Freire (1970)—adult education was a continuing process throughout an individual's life (Kassam, 1978; Kassam, 1979a). "We must accept that education and working are both parts of living and should continue from birth until we die" (Nyerere, 1973: pp. 300–301). As he himself tried to embody, Nyerere believed that a teacher (and thus a leader) of adults should be "a guide along a path which all will travel together" (p. 34).

Thus, by the beginning of the 1970s, Tanzanian social and educational policies began to transition again, this time from self-reliance to a better-articulated form of Tanzanian socialism. Again Nyerere led the way as he repeatedly stressed that Tanzania's socialist development could not focus solely on children—adults must also receive attention. In more practical terms this approach proved successful. Mass literacy campaigns were initiated and were quite successful—between 1967 and 1983 illiteracy fell from 67 to 15 percent, and by 1986 it was at 9.6 percent (Samoff, 1990, p. 231). Various health and agricultural programs were mounted—for example the *Mtu ni Afya* (Man Is Health) campaign in 1973, and *Chakula ni Uhai* (Food Is Life) in 1975 (Hinzen & Hunsdörfer, 1979, p. 156). In addition, other adult-education initiatives like Folk Development Colleges (FDCs) and village libraries made significant contributions to mobilizing people for development (Hinzen & Hunsdörfer, ch. 5–6; Kassam, 1979b).

While Nyerere's policy of free primary education gave Tanzania one of the highest school enrollment and literacy rates in Africa, this changed under Nyerere's successors with the imposition of IMF structural adjustment programs in the mid 1980s. These "liberalization" policies, which Samoff (1990) calls "the consolidation of peripheral capitalism" (p. 219), signal the reemergence of the development paradigm, and the marginalization of socialist transition—particularly in education. Thereafter, enrollment and literacy declined as tuition became a financial burden for parents. In 1996, the government reinstated free primary education, enabled by reductions in Tanzania's international-debt load.

To what degree were Nyerere's principles, outlined in his speeches and policies, successful in reformulating the Tanzanian educational system? There has been no consensus on this issue over the years. One of the earliest commentators on the subject was the historian/activist Walter Rodney, an advocate of socialist construction in Tanzania and a participant in the process as a University of Dar es Salaam faculty member. Rodney took a sympathetic but critical look at this topic in his 1968 article "Education and Tanzania Socialism." As he envisioned the situation, Nyerere's duel concerns were for building socialism and developing self-reliance as a way of coping with neocolonialism. But the difficulty was that "the changes took place within the same inherited capitalist milieu, and for this reason the revamped educational system failed to serve the best interests of the workers and peasants of Tanzania" (Rodney, 1968, p. 74).

In the early 1980s—when the Arusha Declaration, *Ujamaa* villages, and Tanzanian socialism were not talked about much—Marjorie Mbilinyi (1979) commented that "[e]fforts to alter the educational system in line with the 'Education for Self-Reliance' policy have not modified the basic capitalist and class nature of the educational system which was established under colonial rule" (p. 271). Others who believe that the education system has not changed fundamentally with the abandonment of socialist construction, mandated by IMF and World Bank structural adjustment policies (SAPs), have echoed her frank evaluation.

More recent analyses of the topic have taken only a slightly different view. As Yusuf Kassam (1995) has argued, Nyerere's educational philosophy and his interest in self-reliance shares a great deal with Gandhi's approach, in seeking to counteract the colonialist assumptions and practices of the dominant, formal means of education. Employing Braudel's model of multi layered time perspective, Buchert (1994) believes that Tanzanian education has seen more continuity than change. "Both British administration and the independent Tanzanian government designed specific educational policies to fulfill goals for the economic and political development of the country" (p. 167). What is very obvious today is that Tanzania, and thus Tanzanian education, is still very much antinomic.

Joel Samoff has acknowledged that the educational reforms met with some success and some failures. He goes on to note that the language of the bureaucratic bourgeoisie has changed from education being "to liberate" oneself, to providing skills and attitudes: "from the proudly political to the aggressively apolitical, from self-consciously socialist to dispassionately neutral, from education as social transformation to education as the transmission of skills and attitudes" (p. 268). He ends by saying "[t]he Tanzanian experience points to the powerful obstacles, and perhaps the limits, of a nonrevolutionary transition.

Where the workers and peasants have yet to seize power, where the political revolution has yet to be completed, schools cannot be primarily a vehicle for constructing a new order" (p. 268).

Whatever the extent to which Nyerere was successful in reformulating the Tanzanian educational system, he was above all else a visionary who dreamed of a nation and a world without exploitation or racial and ethnic strife. He was also a Pan-Africanist, a revolutionary, and a dreamer—but more than anything he was a teacher in the Black Radical Tradition who believed in "the revolutionary potential of education," and its corollary, "the educational potential of revolution."

At the same time Nyerere was seeking freedom and *Ujamaa* for the people of Tanzania, a voice was resounding across the Atlantic in a Radical Black Feminist Movement that was emerging in the United States. That voice belonged to Audre Lorde, whose work as a poet, activist, and educator created a new space and vision for Black women who had been silenced in the Women's Movement and the male-dominated Black Liberation Movement.

Audre Lorde: "Warrior" Poet, Educator, and Activist in the Black Radical Tradition

. . . and when we speak we are afraid
our words will not be heard
nor welcomed
but when we are silent
we are still afraid
So it is better to speak
remembering
we were never meant to survive.

(Audre Lorde, "A Litany for Survival," in *The Black Unicorn*, 1978b)

In a recent book entitled *Freedom Dreams: The Black Radical Imagination*, Robin Kelley (2002), discusses his life experiences as a Black radical in the U.S. Like many other Black radicals—whether educators, artists, or cultural workers—his ultimate goal was to change the society in which he lived and create "alternative visions and dreams that inspire new generations to continue to struggle for change" (p. ix). The point that Kelley drives home is that this "Black radical imagination . . . [was] a collective imagination engaged in an actual movement for liberation. It [was] fundamentally a product of struggle" (Kelley, 2002, p.150). But he believes that many of the struggles for these "visions and dreams" have failed because power relations have remained relatively unchanged. He believes that it is necessary to reexamine these relationships "to recover ideas—visions fashioned mainly by those marginalized Black activists who proposed a different way out of our contradictions" (Kelley, p. xii). Foremost in this group of marginalized activists were Black women who were forced to construct their own way out. Kelley goes on to say,

> Social movements generate new knowledge, new theories, new questions. The most radical ideas often grow out of a concrete intellectual engagement with the *problems of aggrieved populations confronting systems of oppression* . . . gender analysis was brought to us by the feminist movement, not simply by the individual genius of the Grimke sisters or Anna Julia Cooper, Simone de Beauvoir, or Audre Lorde. Thinking on gender and the possibilities of transformation evolved largely in relationship to social struggle. (Kelley, 2002, p. 9)

For Black women, the problem was essentially that they were invisible in these radical freedom dreams. Even for the American left, Black women fell through the cracks, between "The Negro Question and the Woman Question" (Kelley, p. 136). According to Kelley this was largely due to the way Black people and their struggle for liberation were seen as "undifferentiated" and "gender neutral" (Kelley, p. 137). However, it was not until the 1960s and 1970s that a rigid and thoroughgoing critique of these conceptions of Black liberation emerged. During this time, radical Black feminism emerged, which began a "revolutionary conversation about how all of us might envision and remake the world" (Kelley, p. 137).

One of the most notable women in this revolutionary effort was Audre Lorde, whose greatest contribution to the Black Radical Tradition was, perhaps, her radical imagination and clear vision expressed through poetry as both an aesthetic and political expression—as a means of protest and weapon of social justice. However, Lorde was more than simply a writer and activist; she was an educator who served as a catalyst for change and inspired a critical analysis of social and political consciousness.

In 1983, writer Claudia Tate published *Black Women Writers at Work,* which contained an interview with Audre Lorde. Among the many issues the two discussed was the paramount relationship between teaching, pedagogy, and survival. In response to Claudia Tate's question "Is writing a way of growing, understanding?" Lorde replied,

> Yes. I think writing and teaching . . . all of the things I do are very much a part of my work. They flow in and out of each other, help to nourish each other. That's what the whole question of survival and teaching means. That we keep our experience afloat long enough, that we share what we know, so that other people can build upon our experience. There are many ways of doing that in all aspects of our lives. So teaching for me is in many respects identical to writing. Both become ways of exploring what I need for survival. They are survival techniques. Because I write, as I teach, I am answering those questions that are primary for my own survival, and I am exploring the response

to these questions with other people; this is what teaching is. I think that this is the only way that real learning occurs. Learning does not happen in some detached way of dealing with a text alone, but from becoming so involved in the process that you can share that illumination. (Tate, p. 105)

Teaching and learning were therefore critical elements of her life of activism, which spanned across social movements within the Black Radical Tradition, including the Black Arts Movement, Civil Rights Movement, and Black Feminist Movement.

Public recognition of Lorde's work came at a critical time of racial unrest in the 1960s and became part of a new expression of Black radical protest, one that celebrated the power of language as a tool of resistance and demonstrated the inextricable connection between language, social consciousness, and political action. She became a significant voice in the Black Arts Movement, a literary movement that originated in 1965 following the assassination of Malcolm X. Unlike Civil Rights literature that urged "protest and petition," the poetry and prose of the Black Arts Movement was predicated on the notion of "Black Power" and emerged within a more militant ideology (Salaam, 1997, p. 70).

As a significant voice in the Black Arts Movement, Lorde was committed to "social engagement" and believed that, "the question of social protest and art is inseparable" (Tate 1983, p 108). Lorde (1984c) also believed that poetry "lays the foundation for a future of change" (p. 38). In addition to its political power, Lorde (1984c) believed that poetry and language were pedagogical tools that were essential to survival: allowing for the avowal of those things we feel deeply; to get in touch with the things we find not "intolerable or incomprehensible and frightening"; to tap into those "hidden sources of power from where true knowledge, and therefore, lasting action comes"; and to speak and act against injustices and the struggles that exist across differences (p. 37). With an appreciation for the slow, painful, and imitable death that occurs through silence, Lorde found a powerful voice in poetry and used it as a pedagogical means to break silence and speak out and act against injustice. In her own words, Lorde (1984e) exclaims, "I have come to believe over and over again that what is most important to me must be spoken, made verbal and shared, even at the risk of having it bruised or misunderstood" (p. 40). These words would become a mantra for Black women's survival under the silencing effects of a White patriarchal system.

Through her poetry and activism, Lorde helped to champion the Black Feminist Movement, which grew out of, and in response to, the Black Liberation Movement and the Women's Movement. In the 1970s, Black women found themselves racially marginalized in the Women's Movement and sexually oppressed in the male-dominated Black Liberation Movement. Not surprisingly, activists and other politically conscious and militant Black women like Lorde began to organize the Black Feminist Movement. They believed that Black men and White women needed to be educated about the effects of sexism and racism on Black women's lives, and that education was the key— although it was not solely the responsibility of Black women to do so. As Audre Lorde (1984b) noted:

> Women of today are still being called upon to stretch across the gap of male ignorance and to educate men as to our existence and our needs. This is an old and primary tool of all oppressors to keep the oppressed occupied with the master's concerns. Now we hear it is the task of women of Color to educate white women—in the face of tremendous resistance—as to our existence, our differences, our relative roles in our joint survival. This is a diversion of energies and a tragic repetition of racist patriarchal thought. In light of these facts, the women decided to forge their own movement, the Black Feminist Movement. (p. 113)

In her commitment to women's political organizing and worldwide liberation, Lorde called for global communion and demonstrated the importance of preserving and respecting differences along racial, class, gender, national, and geographic lines. Lorde believed that men and women alike must struggle to find ways of speaking across differences, with the understanding that liberation of all oppressed people necessitates the destruction of interlocking systems of oppression (i.e., capitalism, imperialism, and patriarchy). Much of Lorde's work in the Black Feminist Tradition addressed the need to deal with differences and delegitimate the myth of a monolithic Black or feminist experience. Through her work, Lorde (1984b) highlights the importance of celebrating differences and the need to build unity and strength in diversity

> Difference must be not merely tolerated, but seen as a fund of necessary polarities between which our creativity can spark like a dialectic. Only then does the necessity for interdependency become unthreatening. Only within that interdependency of different strengths, acknowledged and equal, can the power to seek new ways of being in the world generate, as well as the courage and sustenance to act where there are no characters. (p. 111)

In 1981, Lorde, along with fellow writer-activist-critics Barbara Smith and Gloria Hull, founded Kitchen Table: Women of Color Press "as a literary/cultural and political activist organization . . . devoted to publishing writings by women of color of all racial/cultural heritages, nationalities, classes, and sexual orientations" (Lockett, 1997, p. 423). The founding of Kitchen Table was a significant turn in women's political activism, and allowed, for the first time, for the words of women of color to be heard collectively. Kitchen Table provided a space for the voices, perspectives, and concerns of women, which were previously ignored by mainstream publishing companies. Furthermore, it demonstrated women's collective agency in working against interlocking systems of domination. According to Lockett (1997),

> As one of the few significant means of communication in the world to be controlled by women of color, Kitchen Table's goal is to be a revolutionary tool for empowering society's most dispossessed members. It is a vehicle for shaping ideology that serves as a foundation for making practical social and political change. (p. 423)

Out of the Black Feminist Movement emerged a broader visibility of lesbians of color in the later 1970s, and especially into the 1980s, notably with the work of Audre Lorde, and such authors as Barbara Smith and Cherríe Moraga, among others, and after the peak of lesbian feminist-separatist movements. The best example of this occurred in 1977 with the Combahee River Collective's "Black Feminist Statement," which was an extremely complex, radical position paper on the intersectional aspect of "racial, sexual, heterosexual, and class oppression" (p. 362). Lorde's insistence on recognizing, not denying, differences and the essential place of the "erotic" in the politics of life has had wide influence as well. By bringing the issue of sexuality—which is usually considered part of the private domain—into political life, Lorde challenged the world to see that the private is always political. In bringing the issue of sexuality to the center of the liberation struggle, along with issues of race, class, and gender, Lorde also helped to revolutionize prevailing notions of what constitutes feminist and Black political activism.

These views are explored in one of her most pedagogically powerful books, *Sister Outsider: Essays and Speeches* (1984d), which has become a classic work taught in Black Studies, Women's Studies, and Queer Studies courses throughout the United States and the world. In this collection of speeches and articles, Lorde (1984a) teaches us not only to confront those things that lie deep within each of us—the anger, fear, hatred, and silence, those things that come out of our individual experiences and collective histories—but also to engage the "other," the "sister outsider" whose knowledge and customs are too "alien to comprehend" (p. 117).

Another aspect of Lorde's pedagogical impact derives from her position as a staunch internationalist; she has connected women across the United States, the Caribbean, Europe, South Africa, Australia, and New Zealand. Lorde was keenly aware that the struggle of Black people in general, and Black women in particular, is connected to a global struggle. According to Lorde,

> The battles we fight in this country as Black Americans, as African Americans, these battles against racism, police brutality, unemployment and miseducation—the battles against the destruction of our children, the destruction of our history, of our earth, of

our planet, these battles must not blind us to the fact that they are not our battles alone, that we are as members of an international community of people of color, connected to these battles all over the world. (Griffin and Parkerson, 1996)

Lorde also delineates the connectedness of the African Diaspora. Her Pan-African sentiments are best articulated in the following excerpt from the film *A Litany for Survival*:

> The first time I was there [St. Croix], I was transported suddenly to another place, another time. A synthesis. Standing there as an African Caribbean American woman, I could feel flowing through me Africa—the horrors of the middle passage; those father and mothers of mine who survived that; who came to these shores, here; who came to Granada, Barbados. The connection there with the indigenous people of the island and who I am as I sit in this place; it felt as if there was a total consciousness for one moment of all of these threads. (Griffin and Parkerson, 1996)

Lorde's work has also contributed to the development of a Black Feminist pedagogy that draws on African mythology to explore themes of woman-hood, motherhood, spirituality, and racial pride. In her book of poetry *The Black Unicorn* (1978a), she examines the Black Diaspora and "opens up the myths of Africa to American readers and calls upon the female African gods to grant her wisdom, strength, and endurance" (Kulii, 1997, p. 462). In *The Black Unicorn*, we see Lorde's envisioning of a Black Transatlantic tradition and dual heritage originating in Africa, as she evokes the names of Yemanja, Seboulisa, King Toffah, Dahomey, along with 125th Street in Harlem, and Abomey. According to Lorde,

> African tradition deals with life as an experience to be lived. It's not turning away from pain, error, but seeing these things as part of living, and learning from them. This characteristic is particularly African, and it is transposed into the best of Afro-American literature. In addition, we have the legends of our struggle and survival in the New World. (cited in Tate, 1983, p. 112)

For Lorde, understanding the African past is critical to dispelling myths about what it means to be Black, a woman, a lesbian, and to open possibilities for women to define themselves, for themselves.

Lorde's influence reached global proportions, as she lectured throughout the United States, Europe, and Africa, and was instrumental in the establishment of women's coalitions worldwide. For example, she taught several courses at the Free University in West Berlin, where she met Black German women. Her presence sparked a process of growing awareness that led to the 1986 book *Showing Our Colors: Afro-German Women Speak Out* (*Farbe Bekennen: Afro-deutsche Frauen Auf Den Spuren Ihrer Geschichte*) by May Opitz, Katharina Oguntoye, and Dagmar Schultz. For the first time, a group of Afro-German women wrote about the history of Blacks in Germany and interviewed Black German women of different ages and backgrounds. Indeed, Lorde and the book's authors, replacing words like "Mulatto" and "Mischling," or half-breed, coined the phrase Afro-German. In the same year, a group of Afro-Germans founded the Initiative Schwarze Deutsche (Black German Initiative, or I.S.D.), a group dedicated to breaking through the isolation in which Black Germans had been living, providing a supportive environment in which to explore their identity, and disseminating information about Blacks in Germany.

Lorde's dedication reached around the world in other ways as well. For instance, she became an unceasing fighter in the Anti-Apartheid movement and was a founding member of Sisters in Support of Sisters in South Africa. In 1986 she and Merle Woo coauthored the book *Apartheid U. S. A. & Our Common Enemy, Our Common Cause: Freedom Organizing in the Eighties*. In the wake of Hurricane Hugo (1989), she helped organize disaster relief efforts for the Caribbean Island of St. Croix. Lorde also established the St. Croix Women's Coalition and was living in St. Croix at the time of her death.

Defining her work as "teaching and survival" (cited in Tate, 1983, p. 108), Lorde's significant educational influence was not in the realm of policy or curriculum, but rather in the area of ideas, critiques, and dreams. For that reason Lorde and her pedagogy have to be viewed along with other pioneering Black feminists like Barbara Smith, Angela Davis, June Jordan, Barbara Omolade, Flo Kennedy, bell hooks, and Michelle Wallace. As Kelley (2002) has explained,

> These women's collective wisdom has provided the richest insights into American radicalism's most fundamental questions: How can we build a multiracial movement? Who are the working class and what do they desire? How do we resolve the Negro Question and the Woman Question? What is freedom? (p. 156)

To that must be added the question, how can we use the ideas and dreams of people like Audre Lorde to educate others and ourselves to the importance of unity in struggle? Truly Lorde's greatest legacy to education was showing us how to create "alternative visions and dreams that inspire new generations to continue to struggle for change" (Kelley, 2002, p.156).

Conclusion

This work shares the lessons of Garvey, Nyerere, and Lorde as revolutionaries, critical social theorists, and educators. While these individuals are most often remembered for their activism and for the power of their words, which will live in perpetuity, they must also be acknowledged for the ways in which their work helped to the formulate the ideological and philosophical underpinnings of Black Liberation Movements. The "alternate visions and dreams" of these leaders have contributed to emergent educational discourse and emancipatory pedagogy. Furthermore, their writing—whether in policy, prose, or poetry—creates a significant body of literature that serves as educative text.

Admittedly, this is just a beginning and much work remains to be done in the effort to unearth a Black Radical Tradition in education. Yet studying the various pedagogical philosophies that have emerged within Black Liberation Movements over time, space, and modality is important for several reasons. First, it points to the long tradition of "scholarly" activity in Black communities throughout the Diaspora, which sought to create an alternative to Eurocentric perspectives and colonial systems. Furthermore, it reveals a tradition rooted in a spirit of survival and African heritage (Robinson, 2000), which valued education as part of our spiritual and cultural existence. If we are to change existing practices and attain the goal of liberating education, we must look to this tradition. As noted historian and educator Asa Hilliard (1997) points out, "We cannot wait for a more humane pedagogy to evolve. We must produce and assert it. We must draw from the wellspring of our traditions, and from all successful traditions. We must change the world" (p. 122).

Second, there are some important implications for community when we look at education through revolutionary action rather than limiting our analysis to the context of schools. In doing so, we find that the aims and purposes of education are not always constructed within the limits of highly bureaucratized institutions, or by individuals who are defined as "teachers" in the traditional sense. Through this perspective we are able to broaden our understanding of "education" and move from elitist colonial notions, which equate education to formal systems of schooling and tend to ignore the sources of knowledge that emerge from, and exist within, our own communities and have the potential to serve political, as well as educational purposes. For the most part, education as defined by leaders of Black Liberation Movements is not a distinct function separate from community but instead is integrated with the collective needs and struggles of community. Furthermore, it is part of a holistic response to the larger struggle for self-determination and self-definition. Education defined within liberation movements *is* relevant education and is connected to the African experience and daily life. This must always be our understanding of education.

Finally, in looking to the Black Radical Tradition in education, we are reminded that education as revolution can awaken consciousness and empower people to act. Through this realization, we are at once able to embrace the words of Lorde who, in an interview with Charles H. Rowell (2000), proclaims,

> I want my poems—I want all of my work—to engage, and to empower people to speak, to strengthen themselves into who they most want to be and then to act, to do what needs being done. . . . As we move toward empowerment, we face the other insepa-rable question, what are we empowering ourselves for? In other words, how do we use this power we are reaching for? We can't separate those two. June Jordan once said something which is wonderful. I'm paraphrasing her—that her function as a poet was to make revolution irresistible. Well, o.k., that is the function of all of us, as creative artists, to make the truth, as we see it, irresistible. (p. 62)

These are the lessons Garvey, Nyerere, and Lorde would have wanted us to carry into the future of Black Liberation Movements, into the educational realm of the Black Radical Tradition.

References

Ake, C. (1996). *Democracy and Development in Africa*. Washington, DC: The Brookings Institution.

Assensoh, A.B. (1998). *African Political Leadership: Jomo Kenyatta, Kwame Nkrumah, and Julius K. Nyerere*. Malabar, FL: Krieger Publishing.

Buchert, L. (1994). *Education in the Development of Tanzania 1919–90*. London: James Currey.

Campbell, H. (1991). "Garveyism, Pan-Africanism and African Liberation in the Twentieth Century." In *Garvey: His Work and Impact*, R. Lewis & P. Bryan, eds. pp. 167–188. Trenton, NJ: Africa World Press, Inc.

Colin, S.A.J., III. (1996). Marcus Garvey: Africentric Adult Education for Self-Ethnic Reliance. In *Freedom Road: Adult Education of African Americans*, E.A. Peterson, ed. Malabar, FL: Krieger Publishing.

Combahee River Collective, The (1977). "A Black Feminist Statement." In *Capitalist Patriarchy and the Case for Socialist Feminism*, Z.R. Eisenstein, ed., pp. 362–372. New York: Monthly Review Press.

Freire, Paulo, (1970). *Pedagogy of the Oppressed*. New York. Herder and Herder Publishing.

Garvey, A.J., comp. (1986). *The Philosophy & Opinions of Marcus Garvey: Or, Africa for the Africans*. Dover, MA: The Majority Press.

Garvey, M.M. (1923). "Man Know Thyself." In *The Philosophy & Opinions of Marcus Garvey: Or, Africa for the Africans*, A.J. Garvey, comp. pp. 38–39. Dover, MA: The Majority Press, 1986.

Garvey, M.M. (n.d.). "Aims and Objects of the U.N.I.A." In *Marcus Garvey: Life and Lessons*, R.A. Hill & B. Bair, eds. pp. 206–214. Berkeley and Los Angeles: University of California Press, 1987.

Garvey, M.M. (1925). *African Fundamentalism*. In *Marcus Garvey: Life and Lessons*, R.A. Hill & B. Bair eds. pp. 3–6. Berkeley and Los Angeles: University of California Press. (Reprinted from Negro World, June 6, 1925).

Garvey, M.M. (1930). African Fundamentalism: Fount of Inspiration (Speeches by Marcus Garvey). In *Marcus Garvey: Life and Lessons,* R.A. Hill & B. Bair eds. pp. 7–25. Berkeley and Los Angeles: University of California Press. (Reprinted from the Blackman, 1930).

Griffin, A.G. & Parkerson, M., producers (1996). *A Litany for Survival: The Life and Work of Audre Lorde* [Television broadcast]. New York: Third World Newsreel.

Harrison, H.H. (1914). "On a Certain Conservatism in Negroes." In *A Hubert Harrison Reader,* J.B. Perry, ed., pp. 42–46. Middletown, CT: Wesleyan University Press, 2001.

Harrison, H.H. (1920). "Race First Versus Class First." In *A Hubert Harrison Reader,* J.B. Perry, ed., pp. 107–109. Middletown, CT: Wesleyan University Press, 2001.

Hill, R.A. & Bair, B., eds. (1987). *Marcus Garvey: Life and Lessons.* Berkeley and Los Angeles: University of California Press.

Hilliard, A.G. III (1997). *SBA: The Reawakening of the African Mind.* Gainesville, FL: Makare Publishing Company.

Hinzen, H. & Hundsdörfer, V.H., eds. (1979). *The Tanzanian Experience: Education for Liberation and Development.* Hamburg: UNESCO Institute for Education.

Iliffe, J. (1979). *A History of Tanganyika.* New York: Cambridge University Press.

Ishumi, A.G. & Maliyamkono, T.L. (1995). In *Mwalimu: TheInfluence of Nyerere,* C. Legum & G. Mmari, eds., pp. 46–60. Trenton, NJ: Africa World Press.

James, W. (1998). *Holding Aloft the Banner of Ethiopia: Caribbean Radicalism in Early Twentieth-Century America.* New York: Verso.

Kassam, Y.O. (1978). *The Adult Education Revolution in Tanzania.* Nairobi: Shungwaya Publishers.

Kassam, Y.O. (1979a). "Literacy and Development: What Is Missing in the Jigsaw Puzzle?" In *The Tanzanian Experience: Education for Liberation and Development,* H. Hinzen & V.H. Hundsdörfer, eds. Hamburg: UNESCO Institute for Education.

Kassam, Y.O. (1979b). *The Voices of New Literates in Tanzania.* Dar es Salaam: Tanzania Publishing.

Kassam, Y.O. (1995). "Julius Nyerere." In *Thinkers on Education,* Z. Morsy, ed. Paris: UNESCO Publishing.

Kelley, R.D.G. (2002). *Freedom Dreams: The Black Radical Imagination.* Boston, MA: Beacon Press.

Kulii, B.T. (1997). "Audre Lorde." In *The Oxford Companion to African American Literature,* W.L. Andrews, F.S. Foster, & T. Harris, eds., pp. 461–463). New York: Oxford University Press.

Lockett A.M. (1997). "Kitchen Table: Women of Color Press." In *The Oxford Companion to African American Literature,* p. 423. New York: Oxford University Press.

Lorde, A. (1978a). *The Black Unicorn: Poems.* New York: W.W. Norton & Co., Inc.

Lorde, A. (1978b). "A Litany for Survival." In *The Black Unicorn: Poems.* New York: W.W. Norton & Company, Inc.

Lorde, A. (1984a). "Age, Race, Class, and Sex." In *Sister Outsider: Essays and Speeches,* pp. 114–123. Freedom, CA: The Crossing Press.

Lorde, A. (1984b). "The Master's Tools Will Never Dismantle the Master's House." In *Sister Outsider: Essays and Speeches,* pp. 110–113. Freedom, CA: The Crossing Press.

Lorde, A. (1984c). "Poetry Is Not a Luxury." In *Sister Outsider: Essays and Speeches*, pp. 36–39. Freedom, CA: The Crossing Press.

Lorde, A. (1984d). *Sister Outsider: Essays and Speeches.* Freedom, CA: The Crossing Press.

Lorde, A. (1984e). "The Transformation of Silence into Language and Action." In *Sister Outsider: Essays and Speeches*, pp. 40–44. Freedom, CA: The Crossing Press.

Mackie, R., ed. (1981). *Literacy and Revolution: The Pedagogy of Paulo Freire.* New York: Continuum.

Mahai, B.A.P. & Joachim, A.K. (1979). "'Chakula ni Uhai': A Radio Study Group Campaign in Mass Adult Education." In *The Tanzanian Experience: Education for Liberation and Development*, H. Hinzen & V.H. Hundsdörfer, eds. Hamburg: UNESCO Institute for Education.

Martin, T. (1976). *Race First: The Ideological and Organizational Struggles of Marcus Garvey and the Universal Negro Improvement Association.* Dover, MA: The Majority Press.

Mbilinyi, M. (1979). "African Education during the British Colonial Period 1919–61." In *Tanzania under Colonial Rule*, M.H.Y. Kaniki, ed., pp. 236–275. London: Longman Group.

McLaren, P. (2000). *Che Guevara, Paulo Freire, and the Pedagogy of Revolution.* Lanham, MD: Rowman & Littlefield Publishers.

Nyerere, J.K. (1967a). "The Arusha Declaration: Socialism and Self-Reliance." In *Freedom and Socialism: A Selection from Writings & Speeches, 1965–1967*, J.K. Nyerere, pp. 231–250. Dar es Salaam: Oxford University Press, 1968.

Nyerere, J.K. (1967b). "Education for Self-Reliance." *In Freedom and Socialism: A Selection from Writings & Speeches, 1965–1967*, J.K. Nyerere, pp. 267–290. Dar es Salaam: Oxford University Press, 1968.

Nyerere, J.K. (1967c). "The Purpose Is Man." *In Freedom and Socialism: A Selection from Writings & Speeches, 1965–1967*, J.K. Nyerere, pp. 315–326. Dar es Salaam: Oxford University Press, 1968.

Nyerere, J.K. (1967d). "Socialism and Rural Development." In *Freedom and Socialism: A Selection from Writings & Speeches, 1965–1967*, J.K. Nyerere, pp. 337–366. Dar es Salaam: Oxford University Press, 1968.

Nyerere, J.K. (1968). *Freedom and Socialism: A Selection from Writings & Speeches, 1965–1967.* Dar es Salaam: Oxford University Press.

Nyerere, J.K. (1971). "Education." In *Education and Black Struggle: Notes from a Colonized World*, The Institute of the Black World, ed., pp.100–105. Cambridge, MA: Harvard Educational Review, 1974.

Nyerere, J.K. (1973). *Freedom and Development.* Oxford: Oxford University Press.

Nyerere, J.K. (1978). "Development Is for Man, by Man, and of Man: The Declaration of Dar es Salaam." In *Adult Learning: A Design for Action*, B.L. Hall & J.R. Kidd, eds., Oxford: Pergamon, 1978.

Oguntoye, K., Opitz, M. & Schultz, D., eds. (1992). *Showing Our Colors: Afro-German Women Speak Out.* Amherst: University of Massachusetts Press.

Peter, C. & Mvungi, S. (1985). "State and the Student Struggles." In *State and the Working People in Tanzania*, I.G. Shivji, ed., pp. 157–198. Dakar, Senegal: Codesria Book Series.

Perry, J.B. (2001). *A Hubert Harrison Reader.* Middletown, CT: Wesleyan University Press.

Robinson, C.J. (2000). *Black Marxism: The Making of the Black Radical Tradition*. Chapel Hill: University of North Carolina Press

Rodney, W. (1968). "Education and Tanzanian Socialism." In *Tanzania: Revolution by Education*, I.N. Resnick, ed., pp. 71–84. Arusha, Tanzania: Longman Group.

Rowell, C.H. (2000). "Above the Wind: An Interview with Audre Lorde." In *Callaloo*, 23(1), pp. 52–63.

Salaam, K. (1997). "Black Arts Movement." In *The Oxford Companion to African American Literature*, pp. 70–74. New York: Oxford University Press.

Samoff, J. (1990). "'Modernizing' Socialist Vision: Education in Tanzania." In *Education and Social Transition in the Third World*, M. Carnoy & J. Samoff, eds., pp. 209–273. Princeton, NJ: Princeton University Press.

Shivji, I.G. (1976). *Class Struggles in Tanzania*. New York: Monthly Review Press.

Tate, C. (1983). *Black Women Writers at Work*. New York: Continuum Publishing Co.

Turner, R.B. (1997). *Islam in the African-American Experience*. Bloomington: Indiana University Press.

Van Deburg, W.L. (1967). "Declaration of Rights of the Negro Peoples of the World." In *Modern Black Nationalism: From Garvey to Louis Farrakhan*, W.L. Van Deburg ed., pp. 23–31. New York: New York University Press.

Verney, K. (2001). *The Art of the Possible: Booker T. Washington and Black Leadership in the United States, 1881–1925*. New York: Routledge.

Walker, J. (1981). "The End of Dialogue: Paulo Freire on Politics and Education." In *Literacy and Revolution: The Pedagogy of Paulo Freire*, R. Mackie ed., pp. 120–150. New York: Continuum Publishing Co.

Chapter Two

DANIEL PERLSTEIN

Minds Stayed on Freedom

POLITICS AND PEDAGOGY IN THE AFRICAN AMERICAN FREEDOM STRUGGLE*

To examine how analyses and visions of American society shape the appeal of progressive pedagogy, this article focuses on the evolution of political and educational ideas among African-American civil rights activists who created alternative schools for Black children in the 1960s and 1970s. Activists developed, abandoned, recreated, and again abandoned open-ended, progressive approaches to the study of social and political life. The curricular shifts mirrored sea changes in the broader African-American freedom struggle. Rarely have Americans demanded with such insistence that education serve democratic purposes. The article concludes that support for progressive pedagogy depends on the expectation that students will be able to participate fully in the promise of civic life. The history of the freedom and liberation schools developed by Black activists suggests that no curricular project can fundamentally transform knowledge and its distribution if it is not part of a process of transforming social relations as well.

Calls for schools to build on children's interests, promote active problem solving, and connect learning to life are commonplace in American discussions of education. Contemporary constructivism[1] is but the most recent incarnation of a discourse that has echoed through American educational reform since the days of the common school movement and that achieved its quintessential expression in the Progressive Era a century ago.[2]

The enduring appeal of this pedagogy owes much to the way that it resonates with widely held American political values. "The basic thesis of democracy," as W.E.B. DuBois put it, "[is] that the best and only ultimate authority on an individual's hurt and desire is that individual himself" and that "life, as any man has lived it, is part of that great reservoir of knowledge without which no government can do justice."[3] Shared by constructivist and progressive theorists, the ideal of self-actualizing learners defining their environment mirrors the liberal democratic political synthesis of individual autonomy and collective self-determination.[4]

John Dewey captured the confluence of liberal political and pedagogical ideals in his claim that by providing students with "the instruments of effective self-direction" while saturating them with a "spirit of service," schools could "sustain and extend greater individualization on one hand, and broader community of interest on the other" and thus would constitute "the deepest and best guaranty of a larger society which is worthy, lovely, and harmonious."[5] Like progressives of yesteryear, constructivists today frequently assert that student-centered learning foreshadows democratic living. Education, in the words of psychologist Jerome Bruner, should "be conceived as aiding young humans in learning to use the tools of meaning making and reality construction, to better adapt to the world in which they find themselves and to help in the process of changing it as required."[6] Indeed, educators today who claim that constructivist methods constitute ideal preparation for democratic citizenship frequently, and aptly, call themselves progressives.[7]

If, however, progressive pedagogy resonates with liberal democratic ideals, it also presumes an environment that nurtures democratic aspirations. Critics have struggled to reconcile the democratic claims of progressivism with reservations about its appropriateness for poor and minority students. The liberal ideal of encouraging "children to become autonomous . . . in the classroom setting without having arbitrary, outside standards forced upon them," as Lisa Delpit has argued, may well serve the interests of privileged students. Children who have not already internalized "the culture of power," however, are often left to drift with little chance of academic success or social mobility.[8]

Delpit follows in a long line of African-American educators and intellectuals who have charged that in imagining meaning making as the relatively painless and unconstrained exploration of a relatively benign environment, progressive educators mistakenly generalize from White experience. Active inquiry into social life, as Horace Mann Bond argued in 1935, presupposes "an elastic, democratic social order in which there are no artificial barriers set against the social mobility of the individual. In such a society classes are assumed to be highly fluid, and there can be no such thing as caste."[9] "The Black[10] child," veteran educator and Civil Rights activist Septima Clark echoed, "is different from other children because he has problems that are the product of a social order not of his making or his forebears."[11] "Those streets, those houses, those dangers, those agonies" that surround the Black child, writer

James Baldwin reminded teachers, are "the result of a criminal conspiracy to destroy him." Unlike White children, Baldwin argued, African-American youth are faced with a paradox: "Precisely at the point when you begin to develop a conscience, you must find yourself at war with your society."[12]

Still, at times, Black intellectuals and activists have been persuaded that democratic elements in American life or in the Black community were overcoming the brutalizing impact of racial exclusion and oppression. At those moments, Black scholars and educators have gambled that the democratic potential of progressive pedagogy outweighed the special difficulties that Black children confronted as they experienced a racist environment organized to dehumanize them. Septima Clark's work was animated by such a hope, and she pioneered the application of progressive methods in teaching citizenship and literacy classes to disenfranchised Black adults.[13]

Black educational visions have mirrored the sea changes in the broader African-American freedom struggle, and the optimism that characterized Clark's pedagogy has ebbed and flowed in the shifting history of American race relations. To illuminate how assessments of the nature and direction of race relations have shaped support for progressive pedagogy for disenfranchised youth, this article examines the evolution of political and educational ideas in the African-American civil rights movement of the 1960s and 1970s, when activists developed, abandoned, recreated, and again abandoned open-ended, progressive pedagogical approaches to the study of social and political life.

The relationship of civil rights activists' pedagogical ideas to their political analysis is particularly evident in the history of the Student Nonviolent Coordinating Committee (SNCC) and the Black Panther Party. The activism of SNCC and the Black Panthers constitutes a single strand in the history of the African-American freedom struggle. Indeed, such SNCC leaders as James Foreman, H. Rap Brown, and, especially, Stokely Carmichael all joined the Black Panther Party, whose very name was created in a SNCC organizing project headed by Carmichael.[14] A commitment to the simultaneous fostering of personal and social transformation infused both groups with pedagogical concerns, leading both to devote considerable attention to the creation of alternative schools for Black children. Although other organizations, notably the NAACP, may have had a greater influence on educational policy, none embodied more fully than SNCC and the Panthers the evolving ideals of the African-American freedom struggle as it moved from integrationism to nationalism in the 1960s and the pedagogical implications of that evolution.

In focusing on SNCC and Black Panther activists, this article does not offer a full history of the impact of the civil rights movement on American education or even an evaluation of teaching and learning within movement schools.

Neither does it pretend to resolve empirical questions about the impact of progressive education on disenfranchised children. Rather, it seeks to illuminate how pedagogical choices are informed by political values and analysis.

SNCC and Progressive Pedagogy

A new politics, infused with pedagogy, emerged at the outset of the 1960s, a politics announced by lunch counter sit-ins and represented organizationally by the founding of the Student Nonviolent Coordinating Committee. Like the more established civil rights organizations, SNCC sought to achieve racial integration and to win equality for African Americans. In addition to protesting racial injustice, however, the young activists centered around SNCC sought to live their beliefs. The sit-ins derived their power from this ability of protesters to reconstitute the meaning of their own humanity, while they also demanded the abolition of unjust laws. In their own words, SNCC activists viewed the freedom struggle as "the closest thing in the United States to Paul Goodman's 'anti-college' where students learn because they want to learn, learn in order to do and to discover who they are."[15]

As activists worked to expand their protests into a mass movement for social justice, they engaged poor southern Blacks in the same project of self-discovery and social transformation to which they had committed themselves. No less than the activists themselves, SNCC's Charles Sherrod explained, the masses of southern Blacks were "searching for a meaning in life."[16] The "freedom" that the movement sought, as SNCC's Charlie Cobb explained, "is affirmative; [it] starts with deciding what you want to achieve and is reached by finding the ways and means of organizing toward that goal." Although SNCC activists "wanted to end segregation, discrimination, and white supremacy," Cobb made clear, "the core of our efforts was the belief that Black people had to make decisions about and take charge of the things controlling their lives. . . . Most of us organizing soon learned that our main challenge was getting Black people to challenge themselves. Stated another way, people would have to redefine themselves."[17] This commitment to a politics of self-discovery, self-expression, and self-determination imbued SNCC's work with pedagogical concerns.

Far from being alienated from American society, SNCC activists, as historian Clayborne Carson argues, wanted to solidify their entry into it.[18] The movement, in the words of activist Jimmy Garrett, was "for the Black people, a search for acknowledgment of presence and a desire for recognition."[19] Activism was sustained by a belief that Whites would respond to protesters' moral action and that therefore Blacks could become equal partners in an America that fully realized its democratic creed. Nonviolent protest thus drew on faith that America could live up to its integrationist ideals. "Through nonviolence," SNCC proclaimed in its 1960 statement of purpose, "mutual regard cancels enmity. Justice for all overthrows injustice. The redemptive community supersedes systems of gross social immorality. . . . Integration of human endeavor represents the crucial first step toward such a society."[20] Far from being a mere tactic for social change, activists' rhetoric of nonviolence articulated both the desire for a radical reformation of America and a belief in the capacity of America to transform itself.

By 1963, Mississippi had become the focal point of SNCC's work. Even among southern states, Mississippi was extreme in its resistance to justice for Blacks. In the decade following the Brown decision, no schools in Mississippi had been integrated. Organizations such as the Citizens Council and the Ku Klux Klan used a range of terrorist tactics, including murder, to disenfranchise Blacks, and the courts protected White racists while threatening with stiff penalties Black activists who demanded their rights.[21]

To crack the closed society of Mississippi, a coalition of activists under SNCC's leadership created the 1964 Freedom Summer. Organizers deployed hundreds of privileged White volunteers to act as a buffer between Blacks and local authorities, to make the federal government enforce the American creed, and to test and fortify activists' own commitment to interracial fellowship. Among the core programs of the Freedom Summer was the establishment of a network of "freedom schools."[22]

Charlie Cobb, who first proposed the creation of the Mississippi freedom schools, argued that by objective criteria Mississippi education was the worst in the United States and that Negro education was the worst in Mississippi. The "complete absence of academic freedom," he maintained, "squash[ed] intellectual curiosity" and thus produced "social paralysis" in both Whites and Blacks.[23] In imagining new schools for Mississippi, SNCC did not reject what it took to be the essence of American public schooling. Rather, a 1963 SNCC study called for the integrationist goal of bringing Mississippi up to national standards in schooling.

SNCC's faith in national educational norms drew on a belief in the possibility and power of racial integration. Mississippi had no compulsory schooling law, activists argued, because

> children out of school . . . can be used to perpetuate the poverty of the people in *Mississippi,* mostly Negro people. But white people as well. People who spend their working hours in the cotton fields and who are uneducated cannot ask such questions as *"WHY?"* They cannot question the system of oppression which keeps them . . . and their children in the fields . . . or on the plantations. . . . Negroes and whites aren't allowed to know each other. . . . *How* can a people who are separated from their fellow men live the truth?[24]

For activists, then, the act of questioning was not just a step in a process of intellectual growth but also a repudiation of subordination and an assertion of fellowship.

At the same time as SNCC activists believed that Black consciousness was distorted by segregation, they were convinced that Blacks were able to draw from their experience an understanding of the nature and promise of American society. Freedom schools, Charlie Cobb argued, could "fill an intellectual and creative vacuum in the lives of young Negro Mississippians, and to get them to articulate their own desires, demands and questions."[25] Organizers' faith in students' ability to make sense of their world-their faith that American society was not irretrievably alien to Black youth-inspired them to embrace a student-centered curriculum. "The value of the Freedom School," volunteer teachers were reminded, "will derive from what the teachers are able to elicit from the students in terms of comprehension and expression of their experiences."[26]

The commitment to giving students the opportunity to construct meaning from their experiences reflected the belief that African-American students could collectively reshape their world.[27] To "train people to be active agents in bringing about social change," teachers were instructed to begin by having students describe the schools that they attended. The freedom school curriculum included a dozen sample questions such as, "What is the school made of, wood or brick?" Students were then asked to compare Black schools with White ones. Similarly detailed questions focused on housing conditions, employment, and medical care. Later, students explored social differences among Whites and why poor Whites identified with the power structure. SNCC activists explained to freedom school volunteers,

> We have attempted to design a developmental curriculum that begins on the level of the students' everyday lives and those things in their environment that they have already experienced or can readily perceive, and builds up to a more realistic perception of American society, themselves, the conditions of their oppression, and alternatives offered by the Freedom Movement. It is not our purpose to impose a particular set of conclusions. Our purpose is to encourage the asking of questions, and the hope that society can be improved."[28]

The activists planning the freedom school curriculum declared that they were "not so interested in quantity of facts but concerned mainly with connections and associations which will be able to cross-cut the political, economic, and social elements of a given problem. We hope that the creativity of the class sessions will be mirrored by the creativity of the research as the students associate and pull incidents from their own experiences." Examination of topics "related to the experiences and life situation of the students in Mississippi," the planners believed, "demands very active participation," through which students would "develop a new way of thinking and be awakened to their powers of analytic reasoning." In all classes, the goal assigned to volunteer teachers was to "stimulate latent talents and interests that have been submerged too long . . . causing . . . youth in Mississippi to QUESTION."[29]

The politics and pedagogy of the freedom schools were embodied in a widely celebrated lesson taught by SNCC activist Stokely Carmichael. Carmichael began the class by writing four pairs of sentences on a blackboard. "I digs wine" was matched with "I enjoy drinking cocktails"; "The peoples wants freedom" with "The people want freedom"; and so on. "What do you think about these sentences?" Carmichael asked.

> "'Peoples'," Zelma answered, "isn't right."
> "Does it mean anything?" Carmichael persisted.
> "Peoples," Milton acknowledged, "means everybody." Conventionally incorrect usage, students affirmed in answer to Carmichael's continued questioning, was widely spoken and understood in their community.

At the end of the hour-long lesson, it was left to a student rather than to the teacher to draw the conclusion that rules of correct English are used to reproduce the social order. "If the majority speaks" nonstandard English but it has lower status than proper English, a student named Alma explained, "then a minority must rule society."[30]

For Carmichael, teaching consisted entirely of asking a series of questions. SNCC activist Jane Stembridge observed that Carmichael "trusted" students' understanding of political and social life and their ability to articulate that understanding. He "spoke to where they were" and relied on "the movement of the discussion" to deepen analysis.[31] Activists publicized his lesson because it epitomized SNCC's political analysis and ideals.

Freedom Summer, historian Vincent Harding suggests, represented the movement's view that "human beings are meant to be developmental beings; that we find our best identity and purpose when we are developing ourselves and helping to develop our surroundings."[32] The hope that Blacks could participate fully in American democratic life was a precondition for activists' pedagogy, as for their politics. The Freedom Schools, according to SNCC's Charlie Cobb, reflected "traditional liberal concepts and approaches to education." Although the schools did not "grapple with the deeper flaws in education and society," they contributed "to expanding the idea in Black Mississippi that Black people could shape and control at least some of the things that affected their lives."[33]

Political Shifts and Pedagogical Changes

In the years that followed the Mississippi Freedom Summer, the trust-in America and in students' understanding—that infused SNCC's activism and Stokely Carmichael's teaching began to dissipate. The displacement of integrationism by nationalism was embodied in the electrifying demand for "Black Power," which Carmichael popularized in 1966. Although SNCC launched the politics of Black Power in the rural South, the slogan also resonated among Blacks confined in northern ghettos, for whom the goals and strategies of the nonviolent, integrationist southern civil rights movement held little appeal. SNCC activists' growing belief that America was hopelessly racist and that efforts to reshape Black humanity could not rely on the decency of Whites mirrored the trajectory of the civil rights movement. This ideological shift precluded pedagogies growing out of students' American experience and led to increasingly didactic approaches to teaching.

In part, activists' declining faith in integration was ironic testimony to the movement's achievements. "Young Black people," activist Jimmy Garrett observed, "began to see that the inequalities placed upon them by American society were not individual inequities taking place at odd moments, but rather a group activity against a group of people regardless of their education or economic status. They began to see that there were continuous activities by the White community to shut them out of the major society."[34]

Although the freedom schools were part of a campaign that led to the dismantling of the most brutal structures of American segregation, activists' reliance on the presence of White volunteers to focus America's attention on conditions in Mississippi testified to the enduring power of American racism.[35] According to activist Dave Dennis, organizers had come "to Mississippi looking for the dissimilarities" between the South and the American mainstream. They saw federal intervention as the solution to the southern race problem. During and after the summer, however, the refusal of the federal government and the Democratic Party to match activists' democratic commitments, together with interracial tensions among activists in Mississippi, increasingly convinced organizers that "the only difference is that the political oppression and control in Mississippi is much more conspicuous, much more overt."[36]

Matters came to a head at the 1964 Democratic Party national convention in Atlantic City. Much of Freedom Summer had been dedicated to organizing the Mississippi Freedom Democratic Party (MFDP) among Blacks excluded from the segregated regular Democratic Party. MFDP representatives petitioned the Democratic Party, seeking to replace the all-White Mississippi delegation in Atlantic City. "If the Freedom Democratic Party is not seated,"

Mississippi activist Fannie Lou Hamer told the convention in a riveting speech, "I question America." "How could we not prevail?" SNCC activist John Lewis would still wonder decades later. "The law was on our side. Justice was on our side. The sentiments of the entire nation were with us." President Lyndon Johnson, however, was not with the delegates. Seeking to appease segregationists, the Democrats refused to seat the integrated and integrationist MFDP delegation. For Lewis and countless other activists,

> this was the turning point of the civil rights movement . . . Until then . . . the belief still prevailed that the system would work, the system would listen. . . . Now, for the first time, we had made our way to the very center of the system. We had played by the rules, done everything we were supposed to do. [We had] arrived at the doorstep and found the door slammed in our face.[37]

As activists confronted racism on a national scale, they were forced to conclude that southern segregation laws were only the most visible form of American racism. The successes that the movement had achieved in dismantling Jim Crow offered little guidance in challenging the deeply rooted racial and economic oppression exemplified by conditions in northern ghettos. There, the right to vote and the absence of segregation laws appeared incapable of preventing racial inequality in schooling, the legal system, housing, or employment. Rather, government agencies, business groups, and labor unions combined to promote the growing comfort of White citizens and the growing isolation of Blacks in deindustrializing cities. Meanwhile, the northern school integration movement foundered in the face of opposition from White parents, real estate interests, and educators.

The belief that America itself was hopelessly racist precluded political mobilization through a language of shared American values. Gradually, as the notion that one could live the truth while living in America receded, so too did the belief that the open-ended questioning of students' experiences could lead to understanding and to the perception of a universally shared sense of freedom. A focus on self-discovery and self-expression among the voiceless was replaced by a desire to articulate a critique of society to the oppressed. Ironically, then, more radical critiques of American racism led to more traditional banking approaches to teaching, by means of which predetermined "correct" answers were transmitted to students.

The years following the Freedom Summer saw SNCC retreat, step by step, from the pedagogy it had developed for Mississippi. In the summer of 1965, SNCC created a Residential Freedom School in Chicago for Black youth from around the United States. To the dismay of activists, the southern civil rights movement offered few lessons that applied to life in the ghetto. "We went into the southside talking about 'freedom,' which to the southern kid meant the vote, education, eating where you wanted to, etc.," noted activist Judy Richardson. "But 'freedom' to the southside kids meant getting out of the ghetto and they couldn't really see how this fit into what the southern kids were talking about." Amid the oppressive, seemingly intractable conditions of northern ghetto life, students' lives offered fewer insights than they had in Mississippi. In even the best lessons, teaching became abstract and removed from activism and experience. Meanwhile, declining faith in the possibility of creating a truly integrated society led organizers to bar Whites from teaching Negro history, a role they had played in 1964.[38]

The 1966 efforts of SNCC's Atlanta Project represented a further erosion of the integrationist ideal. Atlanta leader Bill Ware noted that had Freedom Summer had "presupposed that Mississippi schools were so far below the national norm that freedom schools were needed to help bring Mississippi Negroes up to some kind of national norm." Rather, Ware claimed,

> our experience in this country has taught us something about this country: it lies. . . . The lies that little Black children learn about themselves leave a crippling scar. . . . which results in their feeling that they are worthless and that they cannot approve of themselves. . . . The country has taught them that they are intrinsically inferior.

Whereas the 1964 Freedom Schools drafted White volunteer teachers from across the United States, the Atlanta group recruited from Atlanta's Black colleges; whereas in 1964 organizers delegated much of the curriculum planning to a wide range of Black and White activists, the 1966 group opted not to delegate such work. Abandoning national ambitions, the Atlanta effort represented an increasingly isolated form of activism.[39]

Declining trust in the White activists was matched by a declining interest in the study of American society and a declining sense that pedagogy should flow from students' experiences. When SNCC activists in Washington, D.C, planned a 1968 "liberation school," three of the four courses covered African history and culture. The transmission of information had become more important than students' exploration of their own experiences.[40]

SNCC veteran Jimmy Garrett embodied both the evolution and the continuities of SNCC's politics and of the educational ideas it generated. Through the mid-1960s, Garrett had ardently embraced SNCC's integrationist vision as a vehicle for the empowerment of African Americans. A freedom school, he argued in a 1965 proposal to expand SNCC's educational work from Mississippi to Los Angeles, was "an area, atmosphere, situation-any place where young people, whether Black or White, rich or poor, come to deal with real questions as they relate to their lives," a place that lets "young people challenge not only the authority which stifles them, but also . . . challenge themselves."[41] Then, in 1965, came the Watts "riot," a six-day rebellion in which thousands of Blacks participated and to which authorities responded with massive military force.[42] Although Garrett continued to believe in the democratic ideal of people's articulating and enacting their desires, his faith in the possibility of winning Black rights in the United States and his commitment to integration began to wane.

In 1966, Garrett left SNCC's Los Angeles office and headed to San Francisco State College. "The reason I came to the campus," Garrett would later tell the National Commission on the Causes and Prevention of Violence, was "to do some organizing. I wasn't interested in going to school for any other reason than to organize students." Garrett's campus organizing drew on SNCC's founding theory, which deemed efforts to build the movement more important than efforts to build SNCC as an organization. Rather than working for the integration of Blacks into mainstream institutions, however, he now sought to enable Blacks to "build their own institutions."[43]

At San Francisco State, Garrett led efforts to create the first Black Students Union (BSU) in the United States, and under his leadership, the BSU pioneered efforts to bring militant demands for Black Power and community involvement to northern campuses. Garrett and the San Francisco State BSU, together with a group of students at nearby Merritt College that included Black Panthers Huey Newton and Bobby Seale, led the fight to establish the first Black studies programs at American universities. Although Garrett drew on the Mississippi freedom school curriculum in imagining Black studies, the new program abandoned SNCC's trust in students to decide what was of value in their culture.[44] Rather, the goal of Black studies, argued SNCC veteran Mike Thelwell, was "the rehabilitation of . . . a culture and a heritage they have been taught to despise."[45]

The BSU quickly became the preeminent voice of Black students, and when the group initiated San Francisco State's Third World Liberation Front, the college became one of the principal centers of campus activism in the United States. Still, as Garrett became skeptical of the possibility of integration into the American mainstream, he became skeptical also about the power of grassroots organizing. Convinced that "an organized minority controls the world," Garrett, like many activists in the late 1960s, became increasingly convinced that an organized minority could catalyze the radical transformation of American society.[46]

James Garrett's growing skepticism about integrating Blacks into American society shaped his educational efforts. BSU programs, he declared, sought to "build Black consciousness" by teaching Black elementary, secondary, and college students "their history and values as a People."[47] No longer did he see Black and White students as united by common yearnings. "Black people are not western," he argued in 1969. "They are westernized. In much the same way as one might get simonized. We are painted over with whiteness." Criticizing the assimilationist politics of the Brown decision and the civil rights movement ideals that it embodied, Garrett argued that Black children failed in school "because the information that Black children receive is alien to them, dealing almost completely with white culture. . . . There is little in any curriculum that starts with Black people as a specifically cultured people."[41]

In the late 1960s, activists maintained the commitment to self-determination for Blacks that had always shaped SNCC's work, but they no longer believed that the creation of an integrated American society would allow them to achieve their goal. As activists concluded that racism was a permanent feature of American society, they became convinced that Black students could not draw from their American experience an understanding of their real needs, desires, or identity. A progressive pedagogy that trusted students to discover the truth gave way to one in which students were informed about politics and culture. Whatever term one uses to describe the alternative to progressive pedagogy—*teacher-centered, traditional, banking,* and *direct instruction*[49] *are popular terms*—its essential characteristic is that a predetermined body of information or skills that students lack is delivered to them. Such an approach won increasing support from Black activists.

Black Power, Revolution, and Direct Instruction

The San Francisco State BSU worked closely with the Black Panther Party. Garrett's grim drama of racial conflict, *And We Own the Night,* was first performed at a 1967 Panther rally.[50] Fellow SNCC veteran Stokely Carmichael was among the featured speakers at the play's premiere,[51] and like Garrett, Carmichael had abandoned the open-ended pedagogy and optimistic integrationism of SNCC's early years. The changes in Black activists' analysis of American society and the pedagogical lessons they drew from it are epitomized in Carmichael's evolving thought.

Carmichael no longer believed it possible to create a community that would unite Blacks with the majority of Americans. "When you have nothing to say about a force inside our community," he argued at an August 1968 Black Panther rally protesting racist murders by Los Angeles police, "then it's an occupying force." Whereas poor Whites were merely exploited in America, Blacks were "a colonized people." No longer viewing Blacks and Whites as potential allies, Carmichael contrasted the militant "who just found out he's a Black man and now he's getting mad so he can sit by the white man" with the Black nationalist who "works to overturn, root out, and destroy the racial oppressor."[52]

Whereas Carmichael's Mississippi teaching had suggested that African-American vernacular resembled the forms of English used by the White majority of Americans, in 1968 he saw Black vernacular as a repudiation of American life:

> We are an African people, we have always maintained our own value system. Our people have resisted for 413 years in this wilderness. We resisted in every way you can point to. Take the English language. There are cats who come here from Italy, from Germany, from Poland, from France-in two generations they speak English perfectly. We have *never* spoken English perfectly. And that is because our people consciously resisted a language that did not belong to us. Never did, never will, anyhow they try to run it down our throat, we ain't gonna have it.[53]

Carmichael's new understanding transformed his educational project. SNCC activists had once engaged in nonviolent protests aimed at recovering the personhood of disenfranchised Blacks through integration into the American mainstream. Nationalists, on the other hand, believed that participation in American life precluded such a transformation. Instead, they sought to create an education capable of fostering what Malcolm X had called a "psychic conversion," through which Blacks could reject "captivity to white supremacist ideology and practice."[54] Abandoning failed campaigns to integrate American schools and society, they worked to transmit to students a Black humanity that was not dependent on the dominant White American culture.

"The honky," Carmichael maintained, "has channeled our love for one another into love for his country-*his* country." Meanwhile, the victims of colonization "have been so dehumanized, we're like a dog that the master can throw out of the house, that the master can spit on, and whenever he calls, the dog comes running back."[55] No longer did Carmichael trust students to draw from their experience a sufficient political understanding. "The first stage" of the liberation struggle, he argued, "is waking up our people. We have to wake them up to the impending danger. So we yell, Gun! Shoot! Burn! Kill! Destroy! They're committing genocide! until the masses of our people are awake. Once they are awake, it is the job of the revolutionary intelligentsia to give them the correct political ideology."[56]

Garrett and Carmichael, together with countless other Black activists, found a model of revolutionary activism in the Black Panther Party. No group embodied the repudiation of assimilation and nonviolence or captured and transformed the imagination of African America more fully than the Panthers. Founded in 1966, the Panthers first gained fame through public displays of weaponry and militant confrontations with the police. Advocating a synthesis of Marxism and nationalism, the Panthers proclaimed the need to replace rather than reform American institutions. They were, SNCC activist Julian Bond told ABC news correspondent Edward P. Morgan in 1970, the "standard of militance, of just forcefulness, the sort of standard we haven't had in the past."[57] "More than any other group of the 1960s," echoes historian Clayborne Carson, "the Black Panther Party inspired discontented urban African Americans to liberate themselves from oppressive conditions."[58]

A commitment to transmitting their revolutionary analysis led the Panthers to use a banking language in their educational proposals. The group's 1966 program demanded "education for our people that exposes the true nature of this decadent American society."[59] The main purpose of "the vanguard party," Panther founder Huey P. Newton explained, was to "awaken . . . the sleeping masses" and "bombard" them "with the correct approach to the struggle."[60] "Exploited and oppressed people," argued Panther leader Eldridge Cleaver, needed to be "educating ourselves and our children on the nature of the struggle and . . . transferring to them the means for waging the struggle."[61]

George Murray, a San Francisco State instructor and Panther Minister of Education, led efforts in the summer of 1968 to develop the Panthers' political education program for members, modeled on Mao's efforts to educate Red Army troops in 1929.[62] Political education classes became a central Party activity, recalled Panther Chief of Staff David Hilliard, through which Party leaders and theoreticians could "disseminate" their ideas to the cadre.[63]

In addition to classes for the cadre, the Panthers promoted political education in the community through lectures about Panther ideology.[64] "Imagine people living in a cave," Huey Newton explained:

> They've been there all their lives. At the end of the cave shines a light. Now one person among them knows the light is the sun. The rest are afraid of the light. They've lived in darkness and think that the light is some kind of evil. Now let's say the person who knows about the light tells them it's not evil and tries to lead them out of the cave. They'll fight and probably overpower and maybe even kill him. Because all they know is darkness, and so quite logically they would be fearful of the light. So instead he has to gradually lead them toward the light. Well, it's the same with knowledge. Gradually you have to lead people toward an understanding of what's happening. . . . One never drops a flowerpot on the head of the masses.[65]

Like progressive education, the transmission of political theory required consideration of the intellectual steps through which students could move from what they knew to a fuller understanding. Still, the Panthers did not believe they could rely on Blacks living in darkness to discover the path to liberation. It was up to their teachers to light the way.

No less than SNCC's earlier commitment to eliciting students' own questions, this Panther commitment to teacher-centered inculcation activated rather than dulled the Black community. "I had been taught only to revere White people," former Panther Regina Jennings would recall. "Panther teachers . . . taught us from an Afrocentric perspective, whereby the needs and interests of African people determined our perception of the world. The void I used to fill with drugs was now filled instead with a pure and noble love for my people."[66]

As the Panthers expanded their educational program, they began to teach children as well as adults. Here too their goal was to transmit Party ideology to Blacks living in an environment so oppressive that it precluded their discovering the truth. Among the most prominent of the Panther educational programs was a network of "liberation schools" through which the Panthers taught children "about the class struggle in terms of Black history."[67] First established in 1969, the Panther liberation schools were perhaps the closest counterpart in the late 1960s of the freedom schools of 1964. Both had an ephemeral existence, but both epitomized the political and pedagogical values of the most dynamic African American activism of their day. Together, the two programs therefore illuminate the evolving relationship of politics and pedagogy.

Whereas SNCC had once embraced a pedagogy of open-ended inquiry, the Panthers applauded explicit, direct instruction in revolutionary analysis. "Black people and other poor and oppressed people must begin to seek an education, a true education that will show them how those in power wage outright war against us," the Party argued. "Our eyes must be opened to the social brutality." To open Black eyes, the Panthers' school would "expose those people that are in power and who are waging a war against us."[68] At the high school level, Panther leader Bobby Seale elaborated:

> We will probably teach more about revolutionary principles. At the grammar school level we will . . . teach little Black kids about how to identify not only a white pig, but also a Black pig. . . . We're going to be talking about downing the class system, cultural nationalists and capitalists, both Black and white, who are the same: exploitative.[69]

The first liberation school opened in Berkeley, California, on June 25, 1969. There, elementary- and middle-school students were taught to "march to songs that tell of the pigs running amuck and Panthers fighting for the people." Employing a curriculum "designed to . . . guide [youth] in their search for revolutionary truths and principles," the Panthers taught the children "that they are not fighting a race struggle, but, in fact, a class struggle . . . because people of all colors are being exploited by the same pigs all over the world." The children learned to work for the "destruction of the ruling class that oppresses and exploits, . . . the avaricious businessman. . . . and the racist pigs that are running rampant in our communities."[70]

At the Panthers' San Francisco Liberation School, "everything the children do is political. . . . The children sing revolutionary songs and play revolutionary games." The entire curriculum contributed to students receiving a clear and explicit ideology. Teachers avoided lessons "about a jive president that was said to have freed the slaves, when it's as clear as water that we're still not free." Instead, students learned the origins and history of the Black Panther Party and could "explain racism, capitalism, fascism, cultural nationalism, and socialism. They can also explain the Black Panther Party Platform and Program and the ways to survive."[71]

In Chicago, a Panther free breakfast program offered an occasion to talk to children about community concerns. Akua Njeri and her fellow activists "explained to the children that we are not the people out there committing a crime. . . . The police are the ones who are committing the crime because they just snatch us up at whim, particularly African men, and beat us up. . . . It has nothing to do with whether a person has committed a crime or not because that was not what the pig's role in our community was. . . . We let the young brothers and sisters know what the real deal was."[72]

In the Panthers' eyes, the public schools of northern cities were no different from the Jim Crow schools that the movement had condemned in the segregated South. Across the United States, public schools were shaped by the realization that "those who can control the mind can control the body." "The power structure," the Panthers argued,

> allowed Black people to go to school but totally controlled . . . the amount and type of education. . . . The method and process of teaching are . . . all designed to fit the individual into the present oppressive system. The student is taught that obedience to school rules is primary, and knowledge secondary, or unnecessary.

To counter "the distorted reality put forth by the power structure," the Panthers created alternative schools that articulated "the reality of the situation which the Party has put forth."[73]

Black children went to school "and learned nothing," Panther Akua Njeri argued, "not because they're stupid, not because they're ignorant. . . . We would say, 'You came from a rich culture. You came from a place where you were kings and queens. You are brilliant children. But this government is fearful of you realizing who you are. This government has placed you in an educational situation that constantly tells you you're stupid and you can't learn and stifles you at every turn so that you can't learn."[74] In the Panthers' judgment, their own use of direct instruction was needed to counter the brutalizing impact of American schools and society.

In 1971, the Panthers built on the liberation school pedagogy with the establishment of an elementary school in Oakland for the children of Party members. Its evolution provides a window into activists' evolving political and pedagogical thought. In addition to providing academic classes, the Intercommunal Youth Institute (IYI) offered instruction in the ideology of the Party and engaged in fieldwork "distributing the *Black Panther* newspaper, talking to other youths in the community, attending court sessions for political prisoners and visiting prisons." The children also learned to march in the Panthers' military uniforms.[75] An IYI student reported to *Black Panther* readers that, unlike public school students, "at this school we don't have to salute the flag." Instead, "over here they teach us about what the pigs are doing to us" and about "philosophy, ideology, dialectical materialism, and stuff like that."[76]

Gendered concerns about the burden that racism placed on the Black man played a central role in the Panthers' politics and pedagogy. America, Huey Newton wrote in 1967, treats the Black man as "a thing, a beast, a nonentity." Refusing to "acknowledge him as a man," society reduced the Black man to "a constant state of rage, of shame, of doubt."[77] Armed self-defense and teacher-centered approaches to education reflected dominant American notions of masculine assertiveness even as they challenged racial subordination.[78]

Community Organizing and Progressive Pedagogy

Within a few years of the Party's founding, however, the Panthers' politics and approach to education began to shift. Abandoning revolutionary aspirations, activists gradually returned to community organizing and rediscovered progressive teaching methods. As historian Tracye Matthews notes, the Panthers' "militaristic style" diminished as women, many from relatively privileged backgrounds, played an increasingly prominent role in Party activity.[79] (The rise of women in the Party owed a good deal to the successful government campaign to jail or kill the male leadership. Prosecutors and judges joined with local and national police agencies in anti-Panther operations, which included hundreds of acts of bugging, forgery, and nearly constant harassment, along with assassinations. This brutal, illegal government attack both lent credence to the Panthers' rhetoric and exacerbated their often self-destructive tendencies.)[80]

During the government campaign to force the Panthers into a doomed shoot-out, the Party, as David Hilliard has put it, became "a split organization," its militant displays of Black manhood degrading into macho thuggery while its community service programs encouraged grassroots organizing, the "two halves operating in completely separate spheres."[81] The opposing tendencies in Panther activism—a declining capacity to articulate revolutionary demands and a growing capacity to foster grassroots activism—reshaped the Panthers' educational ideas. As grassroots organizing gained strength, the commitment to progressive pedagogy returned to activists' educational work. "All you have to do is guide [children] in the right direction," explained Berkeley liberation schoolteacher Val Douglas. "The curriculum is based on true experiences of revolutionaries and everyday people they can relate to. . . . The most important thing is to get the children to work with each other."[82]

Although the Panthers argued that public school brainwashing precluded students' autonomy, they increasingly considered the inculcation of Panther ideology compatible with student-centered learning. Activists contrasted the Intercommunal Youth Institute, where students were "regarded as people whose ideas and opinions are respected," with public schools, where children who questioned the dominant ideology were "labeled troublemakers." The liberation school encouraged students to "openly criticize all areas of school activity" and allowed them to "make most of the decisions in reference to activities that take place. . . . The purpose for this is to give each one the opportunity to make decisions, to do things for themselves, and to put things into practice." Power, Panther leader Huey Newton reminded Blacks, "is the ability to define a phenomenon and make it act in a desired manner." In language echoing Deweyan pragmatism and the Mississippi freedom schools, the Panthers justified the teaching of "the basic skills—reading, writing, math, science"-by arguing that such study enabled students to "begin to define the phenomena around us and make all phenomena act in a desired manner."[83]

For a few years, historian Craig Peck notes, the IYI mixed "vestiges of prior Panther ideological training" with "progressive educational modes."[84] At the same time that students learned liquid and dry measures by baking brownies, they learned English by writing to political prisoners.[85] The Panthers' mix of progressive and transmissive pedagogies mirrored the ambiguity of their politics. As they swayed between revolution and reform, the Panthers were undecided as to whether the Black community had the capacity to articulate its own demands or whether it had to depend on a vanguard to reveal the truth about its situation: "We know that because the People, and only the People, are the makers of world history, we alone have the ability to struggle and provide the things we need to make us free. And we must . . . pass this on to all those who will survive."[86]

Whatever the merits of the IYI curriculum, the Panthers' political evolution precluded their maintaining the institute's delicate educational balance. As Craig Peck argues, the very opening of the IYI school reflected a profound shift away from revolutionary aspirations toward reformist electoral politics.[87] By 1973, the Panthers acquired a new, larger home for the Oakland school and assigned to it a central role in the Party's new focus on local electoral campaigns. In its decade-long existence, the institute's mission shifted from the training of future Panthers to the establishment of a "progressive" school[88] that could serve as a model of a "humane and rewarding educational program" for poor urban youth.[89]

IYI pedagogy shifted increasingly away from the inculcation of revolutionary political theory toward open-ended lessons reminiscent of the earlier freedom schools. "The goal of the Intercommunal Youth Institute," the Party explained, was to "teach Black children basic skills necessary to survive in a technological society and to teach children to think in an analytical fashion in order to develop creative solutions to the problems we are faced with."[90] IYI students, *The Black Panther* now told readers, received "the greater portion of their education through direct experience." The school used field trips, including ones to the zoo, an apple orchard, Mount Diablo, and the trial of the San Quentin Six, to "teach the children about the world by exposing them to numerous learning experiences."[91] Claimed IYI director Brenda Bay, "the world is [the students'] classroom." Through "individualized instruction," the institute offered children "equipment to analyze and interpret their experiences."[92] "We're not here to teach our children WHAT to think," Panther leader Bobby Seale announced at a 1973 school ceremony. "We're here to teach our children HOW to think!"[93]

In 1974, the IYI was renamed the Oakland Community School (OCS), further distancing it from its revolutionary Panther roots. In the words of Erika Huggins, who replaced Brenda Bay as the school's director, the OCS offered poor Oakland youth "individual attention in reading, mathematics, writing, and really, an understanding of themselves and the world." The public school system, Huggins told educator Herb Kohl in a January 1974 KPFA radio interview, "does not allow for the individual mind or personality." OCS, on the other hand, was "very concerned about children relating to their environment and to this world as it really is." To do so, the school relied on

> practical experience as a basis of our learning experience. That is, if we want to know what makes trees grow, then we won't go to a book about trees or have a science demonstration and just talk about trees. We might have the children go outside to see a tree or trees of various sizes or trees in various stages of development. We would see what makes them grow and what keeps them from growing and thereby try to understand what would be the best way to help a tree grow.[94]

Students built their vocabularies through "words we use around town" and "at home": library, physician, china, chair. They learned mathematics by going to

the store and getting change. "We consider [children] people who have personalities of their own and experiences of their own," the Panthers maintained. "The difference between them and us is the lack of experience on their
part." OCS educators argued, in words echoing classic American progressivism,
that through the use of concrete objects to teach math, "thought and action
become one."[95]

In the new OCS, the educator served "primarily as a demonstrator and a
reference" so that students could "draw their own conclusions."[96] Teachers, the
OCS Instructor Handbook stressed, "do not give opinions in passing on information; instead, facts are shared and information discussed. . . . Conclusions
are reached by the children themselves."[97] "In contrast to public school instruction, which consists mainly of memorization and drilling," *The Black Panther*
now maintained, the OCS "encourages the children to express themselves
freely, to explore, and to question the assumptions of what they are learning,
as children are naturally inclined to do." And again, "Unlike traditional public schools where 'discipline' means a set of rules, punishments and rewards that
are imposed by teachers and authority figures, the Institute emphasizes *internal* discipline. The children progress at their own rate, and it is not uncommon
for a seven-year-old student to learn math with 10-year-olds and reading with
five-year-olds."[98]

Like the Panther's earlier liberation schools, the OCS reflected activists'
egalitarian project of transforming the education and lives of poor Black youth.
However, the political analysis underlying the school's pedagogy had shifted.
Returning to the goal of SNCC's freedom schools, the OCS hoped to integrate
poor Blacks into liberal American society and educational practice. The
Panthers' flagship school and its educational ideals continued to reflect a political mission, but that mission was now framed as the incorporation of poor
Black youth into the mainstream of American life rather than the abolition of
an oppressive social order.

The Abandonment of Activism and the Eclipse of Progressivism

The Panthers' local organizing led to some influence in Oakland's local politics, but those limited successes could not compensate for the atrophied aspirations they embodied. Activists' embrace of mainstream progressivism
therefore proved to be as tenuous as their earlier effort to construct a revolutionary curriculum. By 1974, the Panthers criticized not only the repressive-
ness of public schooling but also its failure "to adequately teach English or
grammar." At OCS, in contrast, students "recite[d] consonant blends" and
studied word endings, diacritical marks, and alphabetization.[99] By 1976,

Panther leader Elaine Brown repudiated the OCS's ideological roots. "This is not a Black Panther school, per se," she told *Jet* magazine. "It's not a 'freedom school' or a 'liberation school' in the sense that we teach the children rhetoric." *Jet* supplemented Brown's views with descriptions of younger students learning "basic English—not 'Black English' or 'Ghetto English'"—and of older students reading such mainstream works as *Animal Farm* and *Jonathan Livingston Seagull*.[100]

By the end of the 1970s, Craig Peck notes, OCS "instructor handbooks reveal[ed] a minimal attention to Black and ethnic studies and, importantly, contain[ed] no references to the Black Panthers." Moreover, rote education in basic skills continued to supplant progressive methods of instruction. Whereas IYI language arts classes had once focused on the works of Black authors, teachers were now directed to stress "phonics. . . . handwriting. . . . and language mechanics." "In this country," the handbook argued, "the ability to speak and read Standard English is essential." The OCS justified its focus on "Standard English" with the observation that "language barriers have systematically been used to oppress Black and other poor people in the country."[101] Although perhaps true, earlier Panthers would have observed that this claim confused the means through which oppression is reproduced with the forces that reproduce it. Gone were hopes of even modest social change and with those hopes went much of OCS's progressivism.

A social sciences unit on California's government suggests how much the Panthers' hopes for political transformation had narrowed. The unit-plan objectives called for students to state who "the current governor of California is and what his job entails." Whereas in an earlier era the Panthers would have articulated the state's role in policing the oppressed, the OCS instructor now evaluated students' ability to state, "The governor's job is to carry out the laws of the state and make life better for people living in the state."[102]

The conventionalism of the OCS curriculum reflected the Panthers' diminished sense of the capacity of Blacks to determine their individual or collective destinies. Instead of "trying to build a model school, provide a *real* education to Black kids," Panther chief Elaine Brown lamented,

> [R]ight now, I think, we're mostly saving a bunch of lives. I mean, we've got a six-year-old girl whose entire right leg is marred by third degree burns. She said her "uncle" had dropped a pan of hot grease onto her leg-her whole leg? There's a nine-year-old boy who's been shooting heroin into his mother's veins before school every morning. Three kids from one family came to us with no shoes. . . . One of my own student's back was imprinted with permanent welts from being beaten so much. . . . [Keeping them away from] the snake pits of their neighborhoods . . . and keeping anybody from doing any more damage than has already been done . . . seems to clear the way to teach them . . . skills.[103]

The OCS never fully abandoned its critique of racial and economic oppression or its progressive practices. "I love freedom, power, and community" one elementary student wrote on a drawing displayed on an OCS bulletin board.[104] Similarly, the 1975 OCS Christmas pageant featured skits of "the upper middle-class and wealthy wallowing in their greed" and "Rudolf the Black Nose Liberator."[105] Educators employed peer tutoring, individualized instruction, and other progressive techniques. Moreover, the school served a community-building function in Oakland no matter what its pedagogy. Still, as the radical hopes of the late 1960s faded, the school abandoned the idea that students could either make meaning of their world or be instructed so as to understand their oppression.

Conclusion

Pedagogy is shaped not only by one's understanding of cognition but also by one's understanding of political and social relations. The SNCC freedom schools and Black Panther liberation schools emerged from one of the most dynamic moments of democratic thought and activism in American history. The civil rights movement not only gave birth to the schools; it also shaped teaching and learning within them. This dual role of the African-American freedom struggle both justifies interest in the movement schools and precludes their offering a model of education directly applicable to public school classrooms. Rather, the evolving goals and pedagogy of the movement illuminate the relationship of political analysis and vision to pedagogical values.

American interest in progressive pedagogy has peaked at moments when the expanding reach of the market economy has heightened tensions between individual autonomy and social bonds, moments that have exposed both the democratic possibilities of modern life and its pernicious inequalities. At times of such uncertainty, movements for social change have flourished, and progressive educators have tested the possibilities and limits of educational reform.[106] In the decades following World War II, when the mechanization of agriculture was undermining the profitability of the South's racial caste system and deindustrialization was transforming American cities, the classic dilemmas of liberal democracy reemerged and placed Blacks at the center of struggles to determine the direction of American life. In the civil rights movement, as in the common school movement of the 1840s and the Progressive Era, social reformers and political activists were drawn to progressive pedagogy in the ever-fragile project of enhancing freedom and equality in American life.

As in the earlier eras, elements of activists' educational program were absorbed at least partially by the public school system. A number of public schools inspired by freedom schools have demonstrated that progressive approaches to education can structure classrooms in which disenfranchised students are encouraged to do serious work.[107] The expanded, multicultural history and literature curricula commonly found in schools today are directly traceable to civil rights movement lessons about the role of Blacks in the forming of American society.[108] The movement also encouraged the development of cooperative learning and other progressive techniques as tools in promoting equality in schooling.[109]

And yet the ideas, ideals, and activities of the African-American freedom struggle signal that meaningful change in education is not reducible to any new policy, program, or technique. The movement and its schools serve as a reminder that no curricular project can fundamentally transform knowledge and its distribution if it is not part of a process of transforming social relations as well.[110] Movement schooling thus stands as a repudiation of any approach to schooling that reduces method to decontextualized technique.[111] If, as constructivists argue, learning is the product of interaction with an environment, teaching methods must address the specific social and historical circumstances in which children find themselves.[112] Celebrations of active meaning-making constitute an empty promise for students who, in James Baldwin's phrase, find themselves at war with their society.[113]

Black activists' support for progressive approaches to the education of Black children required the utopian hope-reflected in and sustained by the African-American freedom struggle- that the United States would fulfill its democratic promise so that Blacks too would be in a position, individually and collectively, to define and shape their situation. When White America made that hope implausible, pedagogical aspirations shifted along with political ones.

Thus the evolution of movement schooling demonstrates that no single pedagogical approach inherently serves the cause of social justice. The Black Panthers' most significant achievement in transforming the consciousness of African America, that is, their most significant achievement as an educational agency, occurred in the years when their work was least informed by progressive techniques. Despite their crucial differences, both the SNCC schools and the Panther schools offered students an alternative to the ideologies of racial supremacy and economic oppression that surrounded them. Both exposed students to the culture of power but also initiated a critique of it. Both conveyed a transcendent sense of possibility, appropriate to their times. What distinguishes the movement schools from most of public education is not primarily the techniques they employed. Rather, at issue was whether curriculum and pedagogy would perpetuate racism and other forms of social inequality or would foster change. Any discussion of educational methods for disenfranchised students that omits the centrality of social change-or opposition to it-omits an essential element of the educational process.[114]

Educational ideals inevitably reflect not only an analysis of what is but also a vision of what might be. The liberatory curricula of the African American freedom movement did not primarily grow out of students' lives or culture but arose, rather, from their struggles. "The average Negro is very authoritative," a local Mississippi activist commented during the Freedom Summer. "All my life white people have told me what to do. My daddy's been bossed all his life by some white man, so he bossed the children, bossed his wife. The Negro school teacher's bossy. . . . It's not because of race, but it is because of training and education, and largely, it has to do with economics." This man embraced the optimistic, open-ended pedagogy of the freedom schools not because it was congruent with his culture but because it was congruent with his dreams.[115]

The hopes that gave rise to the movement schools have faded. Unlike the claims of progressive educators in the past, which received validation from broad movements for social and political justice (of which educational reform was a part), contemporary interest in constructivism is accompanied by few powerful movements for democratic social change. Even more than in the past, the efforts of today's progressive educators to foster democracy in American schools and society face uncertain prospects, and the claims of constructivism stand as an empty promise for many dispossessed children. The history of the African-American freedom struggle thus proves neither that progressive pedagogy is inherently applicable to the needs of disenfranchised students nor that American society will extend full citizenship to all. Although the flowering of contemporary constructivist research in literacy, science, mathematics, and other subjects appears to owe little to the African-American freedom struggle, the ability of progressive approaches to serve all children depends still on the realization of the political ideals that animated the movements' schools.

Notes

*   Reprinted with permission from the *American Educational Research Journal*, Summer 2002, Vol. 39, No. 2, pp. 249–277.

1.   Within education, constructivism generally refers to a set of theories that hold that knowledge is not a body of facts, skills, and interpretations to be transmitted to students but rather is actively constructed by learners as they interact with their environment. D.C. Phillips, "The Good, the Bad, and the Ugly: The Many Faces of Constructivism," *Educational Researcher* 24 (Oct. 1995): 5.

2.   Although child-centered, process-oriented methods are often contrasted with "traditional" ones, "progressive" approaches have been an enduring tradition in American education since

the invention of public schooling. The teacher's job, common-school movement reformer Horace Mann argued, was to build upon "the life, the zest, the eagerness with which all children . . . seek for real objects." Anticipating whole-language theorists, Mann claimed that literacy instruction should rely on the interest and self-discipline of students engaged in reading meaningful texts, a claim that led to one of the most celebrated battles of the common school movement. The "abcderian approach" of "conservative" schoolmasters who scolded or whipped students into sounding out "ba be bi bo bu" and hundreds of other "senseless particles," Mann charged, "banished" children "from this world into the realms of vacuity." Philosopher John Dewey anticipated constructivism even more fully. The child, he maintained, is "intensely active" and learns through engagement with the environment. By "taking hold of [the child's] activities" and "giving them direction," Dewey argued, teachers could foster "at every stage an added capacity of growth." He disputed both those who viewed learning as the unfolding of students' latent powers and those who imagined it as students' "passive absorption" of information which the teacher "pour[ed] in." Horace Mann, *Reply to the "Remarks" of Thirty-one Boston Schoolmasters on the Seventh Annual Report of the Secretary of the Massachusetts Board of Education* (Boston: W.B. Fowle and N. Capen, 1844), 100–107; John Dewey, *The School and Society* (Chicago: University of Chicago Press, 1990), 36, 56; John Dewey, *Democracy and Education* (New York: Free Press, 1966), 38, 54. See also Jim Garrison, "Deweyan Pragmatism and the Epistemology of Contemporary Social Constructivism," *American Educational Research Journal* 32 (1995): 716–40; Patrick Shannon, *The Struggle to Continue: Progressive Reading Instruction in the United States* (Portsmouth, N.H.: Heinemann, 1990), 1–3; and Diane Ravitch, *Left Back: A Century of Failed School Reforms* (New York: Simon & Schuster 2000), 441–448.

3. W.E.B. DuBois, "The Revelation of Saint Ogrne the Damned" (1938), in W.E.B. DuBois, *The Education of Black People: Ten Critiques, 1906–1960* (New York: Monthly Review, 1973), 119.

4. Thomas Popkowitz, "Dewey, Vygotsky, and the Social Administration of the individual: Constructivist Pedagogy as Systems of Ideas in Historical Spaces," *American Educational Research Journal* 35 (1998): 559; and; Eamorm Callan, Creating Citizens: Political Education and Liberal Democracy (Oxford: Clarendon Press, 1997), 10.

5. Dewey, *School and Society*, 29, 36; Dewey, *Democracy and Education*, 87.

6. Jerome Bruner, 7 *The Culture of Education* (Cambridge, Mass.: Harvard University Press, 1996), 19–20. See also Shirley Engle and Anna Ochoa, *Education for Democratic Citizenship* (New York: Teachers College Press, 1988).

7. Lisa Delpit, "Skills and Other Dilemmas of a Progressive Black Educator," *American Educator* 20 (Fall 1996): 10–11; bell hooks, Teaching to Transgress: Education as the Practice of Freedom (New York: Routledge, 1994), 157; and Kathe Jervis and Carol Montag, *Progressive Education for the 1990s*: Transforming Practice (New York: Teachers College Press, 1991). Like constructivism, progressivism has encompassed a broad range of theories and activities. Any use of either term or comparison of the two is therefore inevitably problematic. Moreover, contemporary constructivists are more likely to focus on the specific content of individuals' understandings than was Deweyan progressivism, which highlighted the social creation of knowledge and the improvement of society. Still, the theoretical and practical similarities of constructivists and progressives have frequently led scholars to use the terms interchangeably. See, for instance, Kenneth Howe and Jason Berv, Constructing Constructivism, Epistemological and Pedagogical," in D. C. Phillips, ed.,

58 | *Black Protest Thought and Education*

Constructivism in Education: Opinions and Second Opinions on Controversial Issues: Yearbook of the National Society of the Study of Education, 99th, pt.1 (Chicago: National Society for the Study of Education, 2000), 37. On the varying definitions of progressive education, see Herbert Kliebard, *The Struggle for the American Curriculum* (New York: Routledge, 1995), 231–241. On the Piagetian roots of the constructivist interest in the cognition of individuals, see Catherine Twomey Fosnot, "Constructivism: A Psychological Theory of Learning," in Catherine Twomey Fosnot, ed., Constructivism: Theory, Perspectives, and Practice (New York: Teachers College Press, 1996), 11, 18.

8. Lisa Delpit, "The Silenced Dialogue: Power and Pedagogy in Educating Other People's Children," *Harvard Educational Review* 58 (1988): 285. Whereas Delpit suggests that social mobility is limited by the failure of educators to teach explicitly the dominant social codes, sociologist Basil Bernstein argues that self-regulation in situations where standards of work and behavior are implicit constitutes the code of professional and managerial class occupations, a disposition that advantaged parents pass on to their children and which progressive education accentuates. Anticipating Bernstein's charge of class bias, sociologist George Counts argued in the 1930s that progressive celebrations of individual autonomy justified social inequality and offered little guidance to those seeking a more equitable society. Basil Bernstein, *Class, Codes and Control*, Vol. 3: *Towards a Theory of Educational Transmissions* (London: Routledge & Kegan Paul, 1980), 116–156; George Counts, "Dare Progressive Education Be Progressive?" *Progressive Education* 9 (1932): 258–260. See also Daniel Perlstein, "There Is No Escape . . . from the Ogre of Indoctrination": George Counts and the Civic Dilemmas of Democratic Educators," in Larry Cuban and Dorothy Shipps, eds., *Reconstructing the Common Good in Education*: Coping with Intractable American Dilemmas (Stanford, CA: Stanford University Press, 2000), 51–67.

9. Horace Mann Bond, "The Curriculum and the Negro Child, "*Journal of Negro Education* 4 (1935): 167.

10. Some African Americans capitalize "Black"; others do not. For the sake of consistency, Black is capitalized throughout this article, and White is capitalized as well.

11. Tomiko Brown-Nagin, "The Transformation of a Social Movement into Law? The SCLC and NAACP's Campaigns for Civil Rights Reconsidered in Light of the Educational Activism of Septima Clark," *Women's History Review* 8 (1999): 89.

12. James Baldwin, "A Talk to Teachers," in William Ayers and Patricia Ford, eds., *City Kids, City Teachers: Reports from the Front Row* (New York: New Press, 1996), 226.

13. Clark had studied at Teachers College in 1930, when the influence of progressive educators was at its height, and it was there, she maintained, that she "found out how to use the expressions of the children to teach them the words that they used every day." Septima Clark, with Cynthia Stokes Brown, *Ready from Within: Septima Clark and the Civil Rights Movement* (Navarro, Calif.: Wild Trees Press, 1986), 115. Philosopher of education Alain Locke shared Clark's optimism about the direction of race relations and also about the benefits of progressive pedagogy for Black youth. "The general formula of progressive education," Locke reasoned, advanced the belief that all children could and should work together in cooperative problem solving, a belief that challenged segregated schooling. Daniel Perlstein, "American Dilemmas: Education, Social Science, and the Limits of Liberalism," in Pinar Batur-VaderLippe and Joe Feagin, eds., *The Global Color Line: Racial and Ethnic Inequality and Struggle from a Global Perspective* (Stamford, Conn.: JAI Press, 1999), 355–377.

14. Hugh Pearson, *The Shadow of the Panther: Huey Newton and the Price of Black Power in America* (Reading, Mass.: Addison-Wesley, 1994), 85, 162–63. On the preeminent place of SNCC in the evolution of the integrationist Civil Rights Movement, see Julian Bond, "1964 Mississippi Freedom Summer," in Susie Erenrich, ed., *Freedom Is a Constant Struggle: An Anthology of the Mississippi Civil Rights Movement* (Montgomery, Ala.: Black Belt Press, 1999), 78. On the preeminence of the Panthers in the Black Power movement, see Earl Anthony Henderson, "Shadow of a Clue," in Kathleen Cleaver and George Katsiaficas, eds., *Liberation, Imagination, and the Black Panther Party: A New Look at the Panthers and Their Legacy* (New York: Routledge, 2001), 197.

15. "Fifth Annual Spring Conference of the Student Nonviolent Coordinating Committee," (1964), 1, in *Student Nonviolent Coordinating Committee Papers, 1959–1972* (Sanford, NC: Microfilming Corporation of America, 1981), Reel 18, 0929.

16. CIayborne Carson, *In Struggle: SNCC and the Black Awakening of the 1960s* (Cambridge: Harvard University Press, 1981), 57–58.

17. Charlie Cobb, "Organizing Freedom Schools," in Erenrich, *Freedom Is a Constant Struggle*, 134.

18. Carson, *In Struggle*, 13.

19. James Garrett, "Black Power and Black Education," *Washington Free Press*, 16 April 1969, 8.

20. Mary Aickin Rothschild, *A Case of Black and White: Northern Volunteers and the Southern Freedom Summers, 1964–1965* (Westport, Conn.: Greenwood Press, 1982), 7–8.

21. Viola Brooks, "Freedom Schools," 12–13, SNCC Papers, A=VIII=122, 0068.

22. Staff Meeting Minutes, June 9–11, 1964, 30, SNCC Papers, A=111= 1, 0990. For a fuller account of the Freedom Summer, see Daniel Perlstein, "Teaching Freedom: SNCC and the Creation of the Mississippi Freedom Schools," History of Education *Quarterly* 30 (1990): 297–324.

23. Charles Cobb, "A Summer Freedom School in Mississippi," 14 January 1964, 1. SNCC Papers, A=VIII=122, 0131.

24. Untitled, incomplete report, 2, 6, SNCC Papers, A=VIII=122, 0001, 0003.

25. Cobb, "A Summer Freedom School in Mississippi," 1.

26. Part 1: Academic Curriculum," reprinted in *Radical Teacher* 40 (Fall 1991): 7.

27. In addition to relying on their own analysis and experience, Freedom School organizers drew on existing movement adult political education programs. The Highlander Folk School, which had been educating southern activists since the 1930s, played a vital role in the training of Mississippi activists. At Highlander workshops, participants analyzed their shared experiences to discover possible solutions to their problems. This reliance on learners' experiences and problems was directly influenced by John Dewey, with whom Highlander founder Myles Horton corresponded for many years. "If ideas, meaning, conceptions, notions, theories, systems are instrumental to an active reorganization of the given environment," Horton would say, quoting Dewey, "they are reliable, sound, valid, good, true." In addition to the Highlander workshops, the Citizenship School program that Septima Clark created in the decade before the Freedom Summer, first under Highlander's aegis and then under that of the Southern Christian Leadership Conference, offered a model of progressive pedagogy in the service of activism for social justice. Citizenship schools began with and were guided by student interests. In the schools, thousands of southern Black activists discussed the prob-

lems they encountered in daily life, analyzed the political forces that contributed to them, and learned skills necessary to address them. Perlstein, "Teaching Freedom," 306–308; Brown-Nagin, "The Transformation of a Social Movement," 93.

28. "Part II: Citizenship Curriculum," reprinted in *Radical Teacher* 40 (Fall 1991): 9.

29. Report of a subgroup of the Leadership Development and Current Issues Committee at the Mississippi Summer Project Curriculum Conference," March 21–22, 1–2, SNCC Papers, A=XV=164, 1257.

30. Jane Stembridge, *Freedom School Notes* (Boston: New England Free Press, n.d.), 1–2.

31. Stembridge, *Freedom School Notes*, 3. The White college students who staffed the Freedom Schools made consistent use of the pedagogy developed by SNCC activists. The experience of future feminist theorist Florence Howe was typical. The Freedom School teacher Howe wrote, "is not to be an omnipotent, aristocratic dictator, a substitute for the domineering parent or the paternalistic state. He is not to stand before rows of students, simply pouring pre-digested, pre-censored information into their brains." Instead, "in your 'class,' your teacher sat with you in a circle, and soon you got the idea that you could say what you thought and that no one, least of all the teacher, would laugh at you or strike you." Florence Howe, "Mississippi's Freedom Schools," (1964), in Florence Howe, *Myths of Coeducation* (Bloomington: Indiana University Press, 1984), 3. On implementation of the Freedom School pedagogy by the White volunteer teachers, see Perlstein, "Teaching Freedom," and George Chilcoat and Jerry Ligon, "Developing Democratic Citizens: The Mississippi Freedom Schools," *Theory and Research in Social Education* 22 (1994): 128–175. On the impact of SNCC's pedagogical ideas on the women's movement and the New Left, see Doug McAdam, *Freedom Summer* (New York: Oxford University Press, 1988).

32. Rachel E. Harding, "Biography, Democracy and Spirit: An Interview with Vincent Harding," *Callaloo* 1998): 685. Harding argues, "the conventional term 'civil rights is too narrow to capture the essence of the Black-led freedom struggle, which asserted that democracy involves "participating in the creation of something new and better, something more whole than what had existed previously." Harding's notion of democracy mirrors that of John Dewey, who also maintained that "democracy is more than a form of government; it is primarily a mode of associated living, of conjoint experience." Harding, "Biography," 685; Vincent Harding, *Hope and History: Why We Must Share the Story of the Movement* (Maryknoll, N.Y.: Orbis, 1990), 6; Dewey, *Democracy and Education*, 87.

33. Cobb, "Organizing Freedom Schools," 137.

34. Garrett, "Black Power and Black Education," 8.

35. Doug McAdam, "'Let It Shine, Let It Shine, Let It Shine,'" in Erenrich, *Freedom Is a Constant Struggle*, 488.

36. Perlstein, "Teaching Freedom," 322.

37. John Lewis, *Walking with the Wind: A Memoir of the Movement* (New York: Simon & Schuster, 1998), 286–88, 291. Even the development of significant federal War on Poverty programs failed to dissuade activists from the growing conviction that racial oppression was a fundamental element of American society and not a deviation from American norms of freedom and equal opportunity. Unlike freedom schools, activist John O'Neal argued, programs like Head Start "stopped being programs about making demands and started being about giving services." John O'Neal, Interview, Palo Alto, Calif., 12 February 1988.

38. Judy Richardson, Memo to SNCC Executive Committee RE: Residential Freedom School, 6 September 1964, SNCC Papers, A=11=4, 0367; Judy Richardson, "Residential Freedom School Report," August 1965, 3, 6, 12, 13, SNCC Papers, reel 20, 0101.

39. Bill Ware, "Freedom Schools: The Reason Why," 1966, SNCC Papers, A=X=8, 0084; Minutes, "Freedom School Meeting on April 25, 1966," SNCC Papers, A=X=8.

40. SNCC Papers, C=1=74, 0009, 0040, 0171, 0173.

41. Jimmy Garrett, "The Why of Freedom Schools," no date, 1, SNCC Papers, C=1=74, 0168. See also Mary King, in Cheryl Lynn Greenberg, *A Circle, Of Trust: Remembering SNCC* (New Brunswick, N.J.: Rutgers University Press, 1998), 131.

42. Gerald Horne, *Fire This Time. The Watts Uprising and the 1960s* (Charlottesville: University Press of Virginia, 1995).

43. William Orrick, Jr., *Shut It Down! A College in Crisis, San Francisco State College*, October 1968–April 1969 (Washington: National Commission on the Causes and Prevention of Violence, 1969), 78, 80, 124.

44. John C. Waugh, "Angry Young Black Changed All That," *Christian Science Monitor*, 6 May 1969, 6; Darlene Clark Hine, "The Black Studies Movement: Afrocentric-Traditionalist-Feminist Paradigms for the Next Stage," *Black Scholar* 23 (1992): 12; Reginald Major, *A Panther Is a Black Cat* (New York: William Morrow, 1971), 82; Robert Smith, Richard Axen, and DeVere Pentony, *By Any Means Necessary: The Revolutionary Struggle at San Francisco State* (San Francisco: Jossey-Bass, 1970), 131; James Garrett, "Black/ Africana/Pan African Studies: From Radical to Reactionary to Reform," *Journal of Pan African Studies* 1 (1998–1999): 161.

45. Michael Thelwell, "Black Studies: A Political Perspective," *Massachusetts Review* (Autumn 1969): 704, 712.

46. Orrick, *Shut It Down*, 81, 100.

47. Orrick, *Shut It Down*, 80, 87.

48. Garrett, "Black Power and Black Education," 8.

49. Unlike constructivism, direct instruction assumes the existence of a truth that is independent of the knower. A preset curriculum breaks this knowledge into components, and examples are presented to children at a high rate in teacher-centered lessons. Errors are corrected immediately. Direct instruction is particularly popular in remedial programs and those aimed at poor students. Although Panther practices resembled direct instruction, there is no reason to believe that they were influenced by the work of educational researchers. See Carl Bereiter and Siegfried Engelmann, *Teaching Disadvantaged Children in the Preschool* (Englewood Cliffs, N.J.: Prentice-Hall, 1966), 51 .

50. Jimmy Garrett, "And We Own the Night: A Play of Blackness," *Drama Review* 12 (Summer 1968): 69; "Black Theater Groups: A Directory," *Drama Review* 12 (Summer 1968): 173; "An Angry Benefit for S.F. Black Panthers," *San Francisco Chronicle*, 26 May 1967, 2.

51. Garrett, "And We Own the Night," 69.

52. Fred Hoffman, "Stokely Teaches in Watts," *Los Angeles Free Press*, 30 August 1968, 8, 18.

53. Stokely Carmichael, "Free Huey" (17 February 1968), in *Stokely Speaks* (New York: Random House, 1971), 113–114.

54. Cornel West, *Race Matters*, (Boston: Beacon, 1993), 100.

55. Carmichael, "Free Huey," 113–114, 120–121.

56. Stokely Carmichael, "Pan-Africanism" (April 1970), in *Stokely Speaks*, 185, 190. 'Just like it took time for Brother Malcolm to wake some of us up," Carmichael argued in 1968, "it's gonna take time for those of us who are awake now to wake the others up." Stokely Carmichael, "A New World to Build" (9 December 1968), in *Stokely Speaks*, 151.

57. Julian Bond, Preface, in Philip Foner, ed., *The Black Panthers Speak* (New York: Da Capo, 1995), xix.

58. Clayborne Carson, Foreword, in Foner, *The Black Panthers Speak*, ix.

59. Huey Newton, *War against the Panthers: A Study of Repression in America* (New York: Harlem River Press, 1996), 121.

60. Huey P. Newton, "The Correct Handling of a Revolution," in Huey P. Newton, *To Die for the People: The Writings of Huey P. Newton* (New York: Vintage, 1972), 15–16.

61. Eldridge Cleaver, *Education and Revolution* (Washington: Center for Educational Reform, 1970), 1, 6, in Joy Ann Williamson, "Educate to Liberate! SNCC, Panthers, and Emancipatory Education." Paper presented at the annual meeting of the American Educational Research Association, April 2000, 6, 13, 9–10.

62. G. Louis Heath, *Off the Pigs!: The History and Literature of the Black Panther Party* Metuchen, N.J.: Scarecrow Press, 1976), 149.

63. David Hilliard and Lewis Cole, This Side of Glory: *The Autobiography of David Hilliard and the Story of the Black Panther Party* (Boston: Little, Brown, 1993), 143, 161.

64. JoNina Abron, "'Serving the People': The Survival Programs of the Black Panther Party," in Charles E. Jones, ed., *The Black Panther Party Reconsidered* (Baltimore: Black Classic Press, 1998), 185.

65. Hilliard, *This Side of Glory*, 121.

66. Regina Jennings, "Why I Joined the Party: An Africana Womanist Reflection," in Jones, *Black Panther Party Reconsidered*, 259–60.

67. Chairman's Press Conference at Safeway Boycott," *Black Panther*, 21 June 1969, 14.

68. Joe Davis, "The Liberation School," *Black Panther*, 2 August 1969, 14.

69. Peck, "From Guns to Grammar," 5. See also Charlayne Hunter, "Panthers Indoctrinate the Young," *New York Times*, 18 August 1969, reprinted as "Panthers Educate the Young," *Black Panther*, 6 September 1969.

70. Val Douglas, 'The Youth Make the Revolution," *Black Panther*, 2 August 1969. See also "The Young People Are the Most Active and Vital Force in Society; They Are the Most Eager to Learn and the Least Conservative in Their Thinking," *Black Panther*, 2 August 1969, 12-13; "Liberation Means Freedom," *Black Panther*, 25 June 1969.

71. "San Francisco Liberation School," *Black Panther*, 2 August 1969, 14; "Liberation Means Freedom."

72. Akua Njeri, *My Life With the Black Panther Party* (Oakland: Burning Spear Publications, 1991), 15.

73. "Educate to Liberate," *The Black Panther*, 27 March 1971, 1. The Panthers' critique of public schooling was based in part on firsthand experience with racist teachers and schools. Hilliard, *This Side of Glory*, 75–6, 199–200; Huey P. Newton, *Revolutionary Suicide* (New York: Writers and Readers, 1995), 45.

74. Njeri, *My Life With the Black Panther Party*, 15–16.

75. "Educate to Liberate."

76. "A Talk with the Students of the Huey P. Newton Intercommunal Youth Institute," *Black Panther*, II November 1971.

77. Huey Newton, *To Die for the People*, 80–81.

78. Despite her "exasperation with chauvinism of Black Panther men," Panther leader Elaine Brown remained convinced that "sexism was a secondary problem. Capitalism and racism were primary." Elaine Brown, *A Taste of Power: A Black Woman's Story* (New York: Pantheon, 1992), 357, 367.

79. Tracye Matthews, "'No One Ever Asks What a Man's Place in the Revolution Is'; Gender and the Politics of the Black Panther Party 1966–1971," in Jones, *Black Panther Party Reconsidered*, 277–78. See also Madalynn Rucker and JoNina Abron, "'Comrade Sisters': Two Women of the Black Panther Party," in Gwendolyn Etter-Lewis and Michele Foster, eds., *Unrelated Kin: Race and Gender in Women's Personal Narratives* (New York: Routledge, 1996), 155.

80. Manning Marable, *The Crisis of Color and Democracy* (Monroe, Maine: Common Courage, 1992), 204. See also Hilliard, *This Side of Glory*, 220; Newton, *War against the Panthers*, 11; Charles Jones, "The Political Repression of the Black Panther Party, 1966–1971: The Case of the Oakland Bay Area," *Journal of Black Studies* 18 (1988): 415–421; Major, *A Panther Is a Black Cat*, 134; United States Congress, House Committee on Internal Security, "Black Panther Party Hearings, Ninety-first Congress, Second Session (Washington: U.S. Government Printing Office, 1970–71).

81. Hilliard, *This Side of Glory*, 363. See also Brown, *A Taste of Power*, 444.

82. Douglas, "Youth Make the Revolution."

83. "Educate to Liberate."

84. Craig Peck, "From Guns to Grammar: Education and Change in the Black Panther Party" (paper presented at the annual meeting of the History of Education Society, 2000), 19.

85. "'Love Freedom, I Love Community,'" *Black Panther*, 20 April 1974, 9,

86. "Educate to Liberate."

87. Peck, "From Guns to Grammar," 11.

88. "Oakland Community School: A History of Serving the Youth, Body and Soul," *Black Panther*, 16 October 1976, 4. See also Abron, "'Serving the People,'" 186.

89. "Group 7: Method Is Very important," *Black Panther*, 4 May 1974, 4.

90. "Youth Institute Opens," *Black Panther*, 15 September 1973, 4.

91. "Youth Institute's Environmental Studies Project an Educational Experience," *Black Panther*, 5 January 1974, 5.

92. "The World Is Their Classroom," *Black Panther*, 3 November 1973, 4.

93. "Bobby Seale Dedicates New Youth Institute and Son of Man Temple to Community, " *Black Panther*, 27 October 1973, 3.

94. "Youth Institute Succeeding Where Public Schools Failed: Interview with School's Director Erika Huggins," *Black Panther*, 2 February 1974, 4. *Black Panther* now referred to the OCS as a "progressive" school. "Youth Institute Teachers Have 'Great Love and Understanding': Interview with Erika Huggins, Director of Model School" *Black Panther*, 9 February 1974, 4.

95. "Group 4: Language Arts with Novelty," *Black Panther* 13 April 1974, 4; "Group 7: Method Is Very Important," *Black Panther*, 4 May 1974, 4.

96. "Group 7."

97. Williamson, "Educate to Liberate!" 11–12.

98. Jim Hoffman, "Reading, Writing and Fighting in the Oakland Ghetto," *Black Belt*, August 1975, reprinted in *Black Panther*, 30 June 1975.

99. "Group 4."

100. Bob Lucas, "East Oakland Ghetto Blooms with Growth of Black Panther School," *Jet*, 5 February 1976.

101. "Peck, "Guns to Grammar," 28.

102. "Peck, "Guns to Grammar," 25.

103. Brown, *A Taste of Power*, 392–94.

104. "'I Love Freedom, I Love Community,'" 4.

105. "'Mighty Panthers' Drill Team Highlights O.C.S. 'December Festival,'" *Black Panther*, 27 December 1975, 4.

106. David Hogan, "'To Better Our Condition': Educational Credentialing and the 'Silent Compulsion of Economic Relations' in the United States, 1830 to the Present," *History of Education Quarterly* 36 (1996): 245–46. In the half century preceding the common school movement, wage earning came to occupy a central place in the American economy, a process that Horace Mann witnessed firsthand when his family, like others in his hometown, began to manufacture straw braid for market. A commitment to fostering liberal capitalist reform shaped not only Mann's school reform efforts but also his work as an abolitionist and as a promoter of railroads. Jonathan Masserli, *Horace Mann: A Biography* (New York: Knopf, 1972), 16–17, 104–107, 484–522.

107. See especially Robert Moses, *Radical Equations: Math Literacy and Civil Rights* (Boston: Beacon Press, 2001).

108. James Banks, "African American Scholarship and the Evolution of Multicultural Education," *Journal of Negro Education* 61 (Summer 1992): 273–86.

109. Elizabeth G. Cohen, Rachel A. Lotan, eds., *Working for Equity in Heterogeneous Classrooms: Sociological Theory in Practice* (New York: Teachers College Press, 1997). White students have of course been as much the beneficiaries of these trends as Blacks.

110. See Richard Cloward et al., "Educating the Children of the Welfare Poor: A RECORD Symposium," *Teachers College Record* 69 (1968): 305.

111. See Lilia Bartolome, "Beyond the Methods Fetish: Toward a Humanizing Pedagogy, " *Harvard Educational Review* 64 (Summer 1994): 173–194.

112. For an early critique of narrow notions of method, see Dewey, *Democracy and Education*, 179.

113. Baldwin, "A Talk to Teachers," 226.

114. The point applies to public schools no less than to movement ones. "Social conditions," John Dewey observed, "are running in different, often opposed directions. Because of this fact the educator . . . is constantly compelled to make a choice. With what phase and direction of social forces will he throw in his energies?" John Dewey, "Can Education Share in Social Reconstruction?" *The Social Frontier* 1 (October 1934), 12.

115. Anonymous Oral History, Box 7, folder 179, 0337, 15–16, Project South Collection, Department of Special Collections, Stanford University, Stanford, Calif. Paulo Freire also highlighted the capacity of oppressed students to interrogate and alter their world. Paulo Freire, *Literacy: Reading the Word and the World* (South Hadley, Mass.: Bergin & Garvey, 1987); see also John Rachel, "We'll Never Turn Back: Adult Education and the Struggle for Citizenship in Mississippi's Freedom Summer," *American Educational Research Journal* 35 (1998): 167–98.

Chapter Three

HAROON KHAREM
AND EILEEN M. HAYES

Separation or Integration

EARLY BLACK NATIONALISM AND THE EDUCATION CRITIQUE

Introduction

The purpose of this paper is to examine the emergence of black nationalist thought in the context of the Abolitionist Movement and to outline the critique of its leading proponents about the effect of the U.S. education system on black people. By and large, these early proto black nationalists regarded the educational system as a vehicle for the assimilation of Blacks into the dominant white society. Focusing on the period of 1776–1884, this essay addresses stances posed by activists representing different schools of thought regarding tactics for black racial progress. While one group of activists advocated for the assimilation of blacks into mainstream society via formal education, another argued that black self-determination could be effected through the so-called separation of the races. Often, the latter group advocated for the creation of separate black schools. The historical debate outlined in these pages foreshadows salient issues of concern to those engaged in black education today.

Early Black Achievements in Education

The achievements of Blacks in formal education encompass a history that can be traced to the continent of Africa and to the societies established in early Egypt and Nubia (Hilliard, 1994). This history, however, is frequently omitted in standard history curricula. Egyptians, for example, studied the sciences, architecture, and other various disciplines, and recorded what they accomplished. Scholars have documented the ways that the empire-states of

---

* Lower case "b" is used when black is an adjective; upper case "B" is used to describe the race of people.

Ghana, Mali, Songhai, and the Moors, who controlled the Iberian Peninsula of Spain and Portugal, functioned as important centers of learning in West Africa (Bennett, 1987; DeGraft-Johnson, 1954; Jackson, 1970; Carew, 1992; Pimienta-Bey; 1992; Scobie, 1992). By the 15th century, Islamic and European scholars were coming to study at the University of Sankore in Timbuktu (DeGraft-Johnson, 1954; Bennett, 1987). Basil Davidson, for example, states that by that time, literacy had existed for several hundred years in Western Sudan, noting that there was a "big demand for books" in Timbuktu (1987, p. 92–93).

In contrast to these examples, the typical curriculum today suggests either by omission or commission that Blacks discovered literacy and learning only upon coming into contact with Whites after being enslaved. The standard curriculum makes no room to teach black children that Blacks have had a major role in creating a critical voice against racism in America. Many black children today have never heard the critical Black Nationalist voices of David Walker, Maria W. Stewart, Denmark Vesey, Nat Turner, Ella Baker, Malcolm X, Huey Newton and the Black Panthers, Marcus Garvey, and others who criticized the United States about its creed that "all men are equal."

Responding to views of this type, Nathan Huggins in *Black Odyssey: The African American Ordeal in Slavery* (1990, p. xvii), maintains that "American history . . . was written as if Blacks did not exist and their experience was of no consequence." Since the Colonial period, Blacks have expressed the desire to educate their children and to overcome racism through self-help and self-determination. From the Virginia laws in 1661 that forbade Blacks to be educated, to the warehousing of black children in the dilapidated urban schools of the Reagan–Bush eras, black children have had to overcome obstacles at every turn. The persistence and endurance of this struggle—not only by black parents, but also by the children who attended school despite institutional racism—attests to the determination of a people who have the utmost respect for education (Anderson, 1988; Kozol, 1991; Macedo, 1994; Feagin, Vera, & Imani, 1996; Spring, 2001). Unfortunately, the history of Blacks' advocacy on behalf of themselves in regard to education has been systematically overlooked in many scholarly accounts.

The Continuum of Black Nationalist Thought

As Black people waged an uphill battle against white supremacist ideology dating from the colonial period, they created an epistemological, critical-theoretical framework, years before critical pedagogy became a familiar discourse in the mid 20th century. Strategies invoked by Blacks in the struggle for social advancement included integration, assimilation, or separation. Regardless of the strategies employed by black intellectuals and activists, the views they expounded were characterized by what scholars have described as a nascent black nationalistic philosophy. Sterling Stuckey, for example, suggests that the Middle Passage forced the various groups of Africans into "becoming a single people" (Stuckey 1987). He describes the Middle Passage as the "incubator" of Black Nationalism, and that the Africans on those slave ships put into practice the whole idea of their "natural rights" long before the colonists even thought about it (p. 3). Stuckey argues that the traditional African "community settings" allowed the various ethnic African groups to come together on the slave ships and begin to forge a common African nationality as they resisted Whites who used every means to eradicate from them all of their African cultural norms. The slave ships forced Yorubans, Akans, Ibos, Angolans, and other ethnic groups to become one people under one cause to struggle against White domination.

Though often characterized as the militant ethos of black separatists, Black nationalism is more clearly viewed as a philosophical outlook that has over the centuries been adopted by thinkers of African descent throughout the Diaspora. Blacks living during the colonial and antebellum periods had an awareness of themselves as beings of African descent. They used their conceptualizations of their Africanness to promote a black nationalist ideology as a direct response to the racism and white supremacist beliefs that White Americans practiced as they enslaved, discriminated against, and refused to acknowledge Black humanity (Horton, 1993; Stuckey, 1987). White colonists assumed that the New World land mass they occupied was reserved for them. The supremacist ideology they perpetuated supported their belief in an Anglo-Protestant manifest destiny, that is, that God reserved the Americas for them, that an inherent African inferiority made Blacks unsuitable to participate in white society, that Blacks were well-suited to perpetual enslavement, and that Blacks were even unfit for freedom even in their own native lands. In support of this assertion, most Whites believed that Blacks were better off enslaved than being free and controlling their own destiny in Africa, where they were supposedly degenerate savage beings. Some Christian theology even taught that God cursed Black people to labor for the benefit of White people (Jordan, 1968; Friedman, 1975; Horseman, 1981; Wood, 1990).

The Colonial Period

Black resistance during the colonial period took various forms. Prior to the English colonies' rebellion against the British Crown, there were many attempts by enslaved Blacks to liberate themselves. Some petitioned against their slave owners for the freedom they regarded as their inalienable right, and to be sent back to Africa. Maroon communities throughout the South presented major problems for Whites because of their locations deep in the swamps and mountains. These societies engaged in guerrilla warfare until the end of the Civil War (Mullin, 1972; Wood, 1974; Genovese, 1979; Aptheker, 1991).

Others resisted in various ways. In 1773 Peter Bestes, Sambo Freeman, Felix Holbrook, and Chester Joie petitioned the Thompson town representatives to ask the Massachusetts Legislature to allow them to work until they could buy their freedom and return to Africa (Aptheker, 1951; Porter, 1971). Blacks such as Prince Hall, Benjamin Banneker, Absolom Jones, Richard Allen, and others brought forth strong denunciations against the newly formed Republic. As Vincent Harding comments in *There Is a River: The Black Struggle in America for Freedom* (1981, p. 43), Blacks "took the ideology of the white revolutionaries more seriously than did the whites themselves." Blacks embodied the revolutionary zeal for freedom from oppression, and sought means of obtaining liberation for themselves, some joining the rebel colonists and many others joining the British.

Antebellum Period

White abolitionists neither believed in nor supported the enslavement of Black people. Many, however, agreed with proslavery propagandists who argued in books, newspapers, periodicals, Sunday-morning sermons, and public lectures; mainly, that Blacks had failed to develop any viable civilization and that they were a danger to the United States and therefore should be deported. White abolitionists believed that slavery was sin. Others argued against slavery on economic grounds. White workers in the North refused to compete with free black labor, while Whites in the midwest feared that slave labor would put them out of work (Berwanger, 1967; Roediger, 1991). Additional claims of white abolitionists included the proposition that Africans and African Americans were childlike and tranquil. These arguments claimed that Blacks' effeminate meekness and loyalty exemplified the highest Christian virtues and that therefore, racial enslavement was a sin (Fredrickson, 1971 & 1988; Wood, 1990).

While white abolitionists quoted biblical passages as further justification for removing Blacks from American society, proslavery supporters used the bible to support the practice of racial enslavement. The proposed basis for racial segregation and exclusion was that Blacks would engage in widespread miscegenation and precipitate the degeneration of the White race (Bodo, 1954; Berwanger, 1967 & 1972; Tice, 1987; Wood, 1990). Proponents of the emerging scientific racism argued that the physiological and anatomical make-up of Africans and their descendants was inferior to Whites.

While Whites perpetuated a discourse about black inferiority, some Blacks emerged to become leaders in their northern communities. The antebellum period saw the emergence of organized activism by African Americans. Individuals and groups protested against slavery and racial discrimination, and participated in numerous public rallies, meetings, and conventions advocating for rights. Black leaders developed into the foremost rhetoricians of their day.

Leading activists emerging from this period included Sojourner Truth, Maria W. Stewart, and a host of others. Stewart, a pioneering black abolitionist, champion of women's rights, and public orator, taught in the African Free Schools in New York City and later became matron of the Freedmen's Hospital, now Howard University Hospital. Known to a lesser extent is Mary Ann Shadd, an abolitionist, teacher, and writer, who admonished Blacks to stop waiting for Whites to fight and speak for them. After the passage of the Fugitive Slave Law of 1850, Shadd emigrated to Canada to teach fugitive slave children. Early black abolitionist and black nationalist, David Walker, born in Wilmington, North Carolina, in the late 1780s, left the South due to the extreme racial codes restricting free Blacks. He moved to New York City where he met Samuel Cornish, editor of *Freedom's Journal* in the late 1820s and became an agent of *Freedom's Journal*, the first Black newspaper. After moving to Boston, Walker became one of the most recognized Blacks in that city. He published *David Walker's Appeal* in 1829, one of the most provocative documents of the 19th century opposing slavery and racism (Stuckey, 1987). Richard Allen, an influential Black activist in the early 1800s, founded Philadelphia's AME Bethel Church, which was dedicated on April 6, 1799 (Raboteau, 1988). Samuel Cornish, founder of *Freedom's Journal* (1827), and *Colored American* (1837) was another influential activist and leader of the early 1800s (Ripley, 1991). Edited by Cornish and John B. Russwurm in New York City, *Freedom's Journal* preceded the emergence of William Lloyd Garrison's *Liberator* by four years. In the first issue of *Freedom's Journal*, March 16, 1827, the editors stated: "We wish to plead our own cause. Too long have others spoken for us. Too long has the public been deceived by misrepresentation, in things which concern us dearly" (Gross, 1932; Aptheker, 1951, pp, 82–83).

Alexander Crummell, to whom Du Bois devotes a chapter in *The Souls of Black Folk* (1903), was one of the most important black intellectuals and activists to emerge in the antebellum and postbellum periods. Crummell grew up in New York City during the early 1820s and attended the African Free School on Mulberry Street in lower Manhattan. He graduated from Queens

College in New York with a bachelor's degree and later lobbied in political circles for Black suffrage. He also supported the establishment of Black newspapers and a college. For twenty years, Crummell served as pastor of Trinity Church in Monrovia, Liberia, returning after the Civil War to serve as pastor at St. Luke's Episcopal Church in Washington, D.C. While there, he was one of the founders of the American Negro Academy (Ripley, 1991; Moses, 1989 & 1992; Moss, 1988).

Other black leaders during this time included Martin Delany, author and emigrationist; Charles B. Ray and John H. Rock, respectively a lawyer and physician from Boston; and Charles Lenox Remond, whose parents, free Blacks from Curacao, immigrated to Salem, Massachusetts, in 1798. Remond's father, a merchant and abolitionist leader, led the battle to desegregate Salem's public schools. As one of the founding members of the American Antislavery Society, Remond lectured at numerous antislavery conventions throughout New England and Europe. In 1840 the American Anti-Slavery Society experienced a split as the radical faction called for a more militant approach aligned with the sentiments of William Lloyd Garrison, a leading white abolitionist influenced by the writings of David Walker. Following the Dred Scot decision, Remond, a Garrisonian, who had initially embraced moral persuasion, now advocated for slaves to arm themselves and fight for their freedom (Ripley, 1991, Vol. III, pp. 318–319). Additional black leaders included Samuel Ringgold Ward, abolitionist and orator; John Mercer Langston, activist; and the respected abolitionist Frederick Douglass. James McCune Smith, another influential activist, became the first Black man to become a doctor, graduating with a medical degree, from the University of Glasgow, Scotland. After completing an internship in Paris, he opened a business on Broadway in New York. J.M. Smith published numerous scientific papers that refuted scientific notions of Black inferiority. Henry Highland Garnet was a very influential person who dedicated his life to not only abolitionist work, but also served as a teacher and foreign minister. Garnet was the first Black to give a sermon in the United States Congress, and one of the early pioneers of the emigration to Africa movement (Morias, 1967; Harding, 1981; Ripley, 1991; Pasternak, 1995).

The roster of important black activists included fugitive slaves Lunsford Lane and Jermain Loguen. Loguen, born a slave in Tennessee, received his degree from the Oneida Institute, in Whitesboro, New York, and worked extensively on the Underground Railroad (Hunter, 1993). Loguen also became known as one of the great orators of his time (Foner, 1983, Vol II). J.W.C. Pennington, a fugitive slave from Maryland, moved to Hartford, Connecticut, and pastored the Talcott Street Church. Pennington taught himself to read and studied at Yale and later went on to study at the University of Heidelberg in

Germany. He lectured throughout Europe and New England and in 1843 founded an abolitionist newspaper called the *Clarksonian*. These black men and many others lectured in the North and led black people in the fight against racial slavery, discrimination, and disfranchisement, and formulated the foundations of a Black Nationalist ideology (Miller, 1975).

During the 1820s, two streams of protest within the black community emerged to challenge white supremacist ideologies; the first, characterized by militancy, the second, by moderation. David Walker and like-minded advocates called for independent, forceful action. Confrontational and aggressive, they believed that slavery and racism should be challenged by separate all-Black organizations. Walker and fellow advocates did not rule out the use of violence, if necessary, for use in self-defense during the ongoing struggle to free their enslaved brethren. Others, hopeful that change in the racial attitudes of Whites would be achieved through more conciliatory methods, continued to work with and supported the moral persuasion espoused by White abolitionists. Some Black leaders were encouraged by the growing numbers of emancipated Blacks and the abolition of slavery in the North, and called for moral reform, which soon became identified with Garrisonian Abolitionism. As Black people joined the white antislavery movement in the 1830s, they muted the militancy advocated by David Walker, and emphasized a more mollifying tone of reform until the later part of that decade.

During the 1830s and 1840s, Black leaders disagreed on how to abolish slavery and achieve racial equality. Some wanted to work with their White allies and integrate into the dominant White society, while others followed David Walker's thesis of aggressive action, and urged a more radical separate movement from White abolitionists. A few within the latter group advocated that Black people should emigrate to Africa, or another venue where a separate Black nation could be established. The ideological differences within the northern black community inspired two opposing factions to emerge in the 1840s. One faction was led by Martin Delany, newspaper publisher Mary Ann Shadd, and Henry Highland Garnet. They called for activism separate from white abolitionists and argued that both enslaved and free Blacks arm themselves and fight. Delany, Shadd, Garnet and some others called for a "Black nationality" (Miller, 1975) that included emigration from the United States. The opposing faction, identified as integrationists, were led by Frederick Douglass, William Wells Brown, and Dr. James McCune Smith. These activists advocated a Black nationality, while rejecting a separatist Black ideology. Although the latter group supported self-defense measures, they refused to embrace an armed struggle and rejected emigration of free Blacks from the United States (Dick, 1974; Pease & Pease, 1974; Schor, 1977).

Several historians have studied the Black Abolitionist Movement and the factors that figured prominently in its emergence. They have long emphasized that black people were the original force behind the antislavery movement and that Blacks were the staunchest and most clear-sighted members of the crusade against slavery. Other scholars have debated the degree of racism among the white abolitionists. While many white abolitionists supported the antislavery cause, they were unwilling to partake in the radical struggle for equality until John Brown pushed the envelope at Harper's Ferry, and put into action a plan to arm Blacks to fight against slavery. White abolitionists did not speak up against the racism and discriminatory practices of northern Whites who supported the subjection of black people to northern Jim Crow laws. Examples of the subjugation of northern blacks under Jim Crow included laws that demanded Blacks use only the "Black Pews" in churches. White abolitionists were criticized by black activists for making antislavery speeches yet ignoring the larger social and economic plight of black people. Black abolitionists confronted white abolitionists openly and publicly about their racist beliefs and their reluctance to accept Blacks as their equals (Foner, 1983, pp. 385–389; Ripley, 1991, pp. 189, 200–203, 274–275, 295–297).

During the antebellum period, free Blacks were forced to send their children to mostly segregated black schools and use the same curricula as the white schools. As segregated black schools spread throughout the North, the African Free Schools in New York City became a place from which many notable black abolitionists graduated in the 1820s and 1830s. As young people, Henry Highland Garnet, James McCune Smith, Charles L. Reason, the mathematician; Samuel Ringgold Ward; Ira Aldridge, the noted actor; and many others attended the No. 2 African Free School on Mulberry Street in New York City, which at first employed only white teachers and later on hired a few Black teachers. In 1830, the parents of the children of the African Free School No. 2 raised the question of whether Whites were suitable to teach black children, and began to send their children to private black schools to be taught by black teachers. The decline in the number of black children at the African Free School was the result of the changing attitudes of the black community concerning education. One of the main instigators for the change of attitude was James Andrews, a popular white teacher in the No. 2 School, who began to favor the idea of Blacks returning to Africa as colonizers. While Andrews expressed dislike of the racism against Blacks in New York City, the black community was repelled by Andrews's colonization views. The black community supported the No. 2 School on Mulberry Street, providing clothing and wood for heat, which helped boost the attendance to over 500 in 1832 (Kharem, 2000). Clearly, the debate within education concerning whether White teachers can teach Black children has precedents early in the 19th century.

Educated and literate Blacks of the early 19-century participated in gatherings of socially concerned citizens dedicated to racial progress. A number of such conventions were held across the United States during this period. Referred to as "conventions," these gatherings became important sites for discussions about black racial progress and the challenges that African Americans faced at the time. Philip Foner in *History of Black Americans Volume 2: From the Emergence of the Cotton Kingdom to the Eve of the Compromise of 1850* (1983), provides a concise narrative of the convention meetings. Foner concludes that the failure of moral reform of the 1830s was due to the emergence of a new generation of Black activists such as Henry Highland Garnet, Dr. James McCune Smith, Samuel Ringgold Ward, Jermain Loguen, and later Frederick Douglass, who became the spokesmen of the northern Black community. According to Foner, "these young men challenged the assumption that cooperation with Whites was the best route to Black achievement" (Foner 1983, p. 315).

In *Key Issues in the Afro-American Experience, Volume I* (1971), William and Jane Pease examine the Convention Movement and conclude that they developed "a more cohesive and distinctively black nationalist program" (Pease & Pease 1971:193). Jane and William Pease maintain that the black nationalist ideological program, formulated during the Negro Convention Movement, was a response to the lack of attention and concern by white abolitionists to the problems of exclusion that Blacks faced on a daily basis in the North. By the 1840s, Black activists were more adamant that Blacks should "rise up" against racial discrimination and "assert their rights" as Americans (p. 200). Garnet delivered his famous speech, "An Address to the Slaves of the United States of America," in which he advised all enslaved Blacks to revolt against their enslavement (Ofari 1972: 144–153).

Several important books expand our understanding of the Negro Conventions during the 1850s. In *A Survey of the Negro Convention Movement* (1969), Howard Bell credits numerous Blacks with being ready to emigrate from the United States, and points out that the first national convention supported emigration. During the 1850s, many free northern Blacks began to consider leaving the United States as a result of the Fugitive Slave Law of 1850. In his November 27, 1851, edition of the *Frederick Douglass Newspaper* (p. 2), Douglass wrote that many Black leaders left, including Jermain W. Loguen, William Wells Brown, Henry Highland Garnet, Alexander Crummell, Samuel Ward, and Henry Bibb. Disagreeing with Garnet and other Blacks over the emigration issue, Dr. J.M. Smith, like Douglass, believed that the United States was the home for Blacks, and that it was too late for the separation of the races (Bell, 1959, 1962; Litwack, 1961b, pp. 176–177).

Bell's (1969) findings demonstrate the overwhelming concern of James McCune Smith and other black activists regarding the advancement of northern black society that had been discussed and planned for during the conventions. Black leaders realized calculated tactics were necessary to put pressure on northern racism and southern slavery. They advocated for political, economic, and social elevation. In spite of the emigration of some Blacks to Africa, the majority of the northern black population was left to survive in utter poverty as they were excluded from any real participation within U.S. society.

In an effort to improve the economic and social conditions of Blacks in the United States, some black leaders were convinced that black people should relocate from urban centers into the countryside. While economics was an important issue, black leaders were also concerned that urban areas tended to lower the moral values of Blacks and that agrarian life was more virtuous and honorable. Although the idea ultimately failed, antislavery leader and philanthropist Gerrit Smith was encouraged by the idea of black people relocating to upstate New York and offered some of his land to Blacks (Litwack, 1961b, pp. 176–177), with the hope that they eventually would be eligible to vote under New York state laws. While James McCune Smith believed in integration, he supported separate black schools that advocated a curriculum that reflected a black perspective. Having been educated in the African Free Schools in New York City, James McCune Smith believed that black teachers had more success than white teachers with black children (Ripley, 1990, Vol. III p. 350–351). James McCune Smith also presented numerous suffrage petitions to New York's state legislature and told white abolitionists that they were not suited to fight the black man's battles, nor could they grasp his concern. In 1855, James McCune Smith joined his boyhood friend, Henry Highland Garnet, and presented suffrage petitions before the state. He participated in the Liberty Party (founded in 1839) convention and was elected chairman, an unprecedented act by Whites in electing a Black man, even among abolitionists (Pease & Pease, 1974, pp. 93, 119, 184; Foner, 1983, Vol. III, pp. 208–209, 210)

Foner concludes that the 1853 Rochester convention was the most important of its kind because it set forth the basic demands of black people and tried to organize Blacks on a state level (Foner, 1983, Vol. II, pp. 315, 317). Interestingly, he also discusses the Black State Conventions Movement. Emphasizing the importance of the documentation left by meeting participants, he writes, "For a keen analysis of the issues outlined and for breadth of research and argument, these addresses are among the outstanding political documents of the period" (Foner, 1983, p. 322).

Like Foner, William H. and Jane H. Pease attribute the 1853 Rochester Convention with rejecting "assimilation in which the black man would blend indistinguishably into the white mass, achieving theoretical equality but losing his identity" (Pease & Pease, 1971, p. 201). Black activists clearly understood that equality in the United States was only a theory, and that they would have to develop their own political and educational institutions. "Thus," write the Peases, "emerged a militancy born of racial slavery, prejudice, discrimination and frustration" (Pease & Pease, 1971, p. 201).

Foner credits the conventions with doing "more than any other instrument to refute the widespread theory of Black inferiority"(Foner, 1983, 323). He credits black leaders with improving the conditions of northern Blacks, constructing a Black Nationalist agenda, and counteracting, to some degree, the effect of racist propaganda on black people. In spite of these successes, the movement failed to remain viable because of divided leadership, conflicting agendas, interpersonal jealousies, the lack of finances, and factional disputes between those who wanted to separate from white involvement and emigrate, and those who wanted to continue working with white abolitionists and integrate into white Anglo-Protestant society (Foner 1983, 322–323).

The historiography of the black abolitionist period demonstrates scholars' varied assessments of the efforts and ideologies of black leaders during the antebellum period. Benjamin Quarles, in his work *Black Abolitionists* (1969), credits Black leaders for dissuading many white abolitionists from those who favored the idea of colonizing free black people somewhere outside the borders of the United States. The conversion of William Lloyd Garrison, for example, proved to be of enormous importance in the shift from advocating colonization and gradual emancipation to immediate emancipation (1969, 17–21). Quarles notes that on the other hand, some white abolitionists inspired many black leaders to modify their beliefs that all whites were their enemies. These black leaders continued to work with white allies in spite of the racism and discrimination they experienced. While white activists focused upon the abolition of slavery, black abolitionists also included in their crusade the work of racial uplift (Quarles 1969). Quarles follows historians like Carter G. Woodson, Henrietta Buckmaster, Herbert Aptheker, and others, in demonstrating that Blacks devoted their energies to organizing their own temperance, mutual aid programs, literary and cultural societies, and educational agenda. Woodson's *Education of the Negro Prior to 1861* (1915), *Negro Orators and Their Orations* (1925), and *The Negro in Our History* (1928); Henrietta Buckmaster's *Let My People Go: The Story of the Underground Railroad* (1941);

and Herbert Aptheker's *One Continual Cry: David Walker's Appeal to the Colored Citizens of the World, 1829–1830, Its Setting & Its Meaning* (1965), *The Negro in the Abolitionist Movement* (1941), and *Anti-Racism in U.S.: History the First Two Hundred Years* (1992), argue that Blacks pioneered abolition and were focused upon different goals than their white allies. White abolitionists advocated for the end of slavery but were unwilling to change the racialized social order. Blacks, on the other hand, fought to end slavery, end racial discrimination, achieve full equality under the law, and educate their children.

Not everyone, however, shares Quarles' conclusions on the efficacy of the joint efforts of Black activists and White abolitionists. Quarles suggests that as Blacks worked to establish their own social institutions they continued to work together with White abolitionists in spite of their racism. White abolitionists were not willing to eradicate the Black Codes that existed in the North, nor were they willing to integrate with Blacks for fear of miscegenation. William and Jane Pease in *They Who Would Be Free: Black's Search for Freedom, 1830–1861,* depict black activists as failures, maintaining "On all counts, black abolitionism fell short. Black pride and separatism competed with assimilation and Americanization . . . and racism made white men unalterably opposed to the goals for which black men struggled." They continue stating, "whites not only constituted the greater part of the population, especially in the North, but controlled the nation's economy and politics. In one word, then, black America was powerless" (pp. 297–298). According to William and Jane Pease, Blacks held no political or economic power to make any real changes in the conditions they were forced to live in by White Americans.

William and Jane Pease state that their objective was to analyze "the perceptions, attitudes, values, goals, and means of . . . Northern Negroes who struggled within and outside the Abolitionist crusade" (pp. v, 297–298). The Peases recognized a difference of opinion between the black abolitionists in their purposes and goals; some may have been due to personalities, yet the split that transpired between the black and white abolitionists seemed to go even deeper. According to the Peases, "a far deeper conceptual chasm" separated Black from White and generated a distinct black abolitionism. According to the Peases and other historians, white abolitionists saw freedom and slavery as mutually exclusive issues. Black leaders, however, regarded the experiences of northern free Blacks and southern slavery as on a "continuous spectrum" because of the imposition of laws that curtailed the civil rights of Blacks in the North (Bell, 1960; Berwanger, 1972; Kerber, 1967; Litwack, 1961b; Pease & Pease, 1965). The experience of freedom in the north offered Blacks little relief from racial discrimination; Blacks were not allowed to participate in society as citizens. Employment for free Blacks was limited to nonskilled manual labor.

Along with many other Black Codes under which they lived, Blacks were not allowed to ride on public transportation, attend public schools, or testify in court (Pease & Pease 1974, pp. 3–4). On the other hand, Frederick Douglass' life under slavery demonstrated the degrees of freedom even in bondage, especially when we see how Douglass moved from the plantation system in rural Virginia to the semiautonomous living of Baltimore, when his owner hired him out to work as a caulker in the shipyards.

According to Quarles, the emphasis of northern free Blacks was on self-help measures, while the white community's commitment to black equality was not a part of their argument. Whites were not interested in giving Blacks social equality in any form. Jane and William Pease observe that the commitment of the white abolitionists to black equality diminished during the 1840s. They suggest that this was because of the adverse reaction of the white community to what many may have perceived as a threat to their civil liberties. Many Whites also feared miscegenation and integration. This rupture led to increasing misunderstanding between white and black activists as the majority of northern free Blacks believed that white antislavery issues became ever more theoretical and remote. White abolitionists perceived that black activism was based on self-interest rather than on a dedication to antislavery principles. Many black activists questioned *whose* antislavery principles were being followed. Black activists felt that if the fight against northern racism were not included in the movement to eliminate slavery, then the status quo would be left unchallenged.

Many black leaders were discouraged by the lack of progress of the antislavery movement and of civil rights reform in the 1840s. Growing schisms between black activists and white abolitionists, the federal government's proslavery public policies, and the westward expansion of slavery suggested to Blacks a waning in the antislavery movement. In a letter dated December 28, 1846, Dr. James McCune Smith conveyed to Gerrit Smith the uncertainty of a political solution to slavery. James McCune Smith described the intractable quality of racial discrimination against Blacks in the North—"a hate deeper than I had imagined"—and concluded that any improvement in race relations was contingent upon the profound transformation of White attitudes (Ripley, 1991, Vol. III, p. 479). Smith's pessimistic evaluation of white people's racial attitudes toward Blacks served as the prelude to the development of a more radical black nationalist standpoint throughout the rest of the antebellum period. Thus, black nationalism became a direct response to the racial attitudes and beliefs of Whites, and their refusal to allow Blacks to participate within the American society (Pease & Pease, 1974, pp. vii, 5, 14–15).

Discussing the leadership of black activists, the Peases write that less than one-third of the black leaders were products of northern urban centers, had never been enslaved, and had complained about the shortage of consistent followers. Furthermore, the Peases claim that the two-thirds who had never been enslaved were from the Black middle class, and were better off than the masses of urban Black people (Pease, 1974, pp. 267–297). Finally, the Peases note that Black leaders too often suspected one another's motives, which undermined interpersonal cooperation. While many of the well-to-do black leaders were integrationists, many of the black separatist leaders were once enslaved or fugitive slaves and were not economically well off. Men like Henry Highland Garnet and Martin Delany did not achieve the elitist status of Frederick Douglass and Dr. James McCune Smith, who was considered the wealthiest Black in the country at the time (Pease, 1974, pp. 124–143; Foner, 1983, pp. 263–272).

Vincent Harding (1981, pp. xi–xii) disputes the proposition that the black abolitionists failed. Writing from an unabashed Afrocentric perspective, Harding presents a sweeping interpretation of African American history. He describes the history of Black people as a flowing river that is "powerful, tumultuous, and rolling with life . . . and running with blood." In the beginning of *There Is a River* (1981), Harding states that it is his "responsibility to write as a historian," his "commitment to the human liberation," and his "urgent determination to keep faith with that magnificent company of witnesses—my mothers and fathers—whose lives form the wellspring of the Black struggle for freedom in America."

Evoking picturesque metaphors, Harding presents the historical saga of African Americans as a great black river surging in opposition to the powerful currents of slavery and racism. He interprets the struggle in five phases: first, Blacks had to face their own immediate needs in the face of white violence; second, Blacks had to protest the destructive measures of segregation and discrimination; third, black institutions were imperative as a foundation against racism; fourth, more voices of protest were needed, like that of David Walker's; fifth, Blacks needed to actively assist fugitive slaves who found their way North (Harding, 1981, p.120). According to Harding, Garrison and other white abolitionists were deluded into thinking that once slavery ended, racism and discrimination would disappear quickly (Harding, p. 283). Harding concludes that at the end of the Civil War and Reconstruction, black people had finally begun (metaphorically speaking) to cross the Jordan River, and as they were crossing, Blacks remembered the past, moved forward, committed themselves to the unfinished struggles, and celebrated their victory over slavery. Harding defines black nationalism as the need for black people to rely primarily upon themselves in vital areas of life (economic, political, religious, and intellectual), in order to bring about their liberation. Harding attributes this attitude to West African traditions of group hegemony (Harding, 1981, p. 4–23).

Whether black leaders advocated assimilation or a separatist ideology during the antebellum period, they promoted change in the black community. Later on, black institutions provided a foundation from which a people emerged. Many of their ideas grew into more sophisticated articulations of black self-determination. The activities of black activists projected their expressions and beliefs into a national consciousness; they opened to black people the possibilities of power, and the vision of an egalitarian society free of the stigmas of racial enslavement, discrimination, and oppression.

Separate and/or Equal Debates in the 20th Century

The late 1960s and early 1970s saw the resurgence in black nationalist thought in education in the form of Black independent schools and a push toward an Afrocentric curriculum. In the first third of the century, Du Bois asked the question about the need for separate schools and institutions: Should Black students attend predominately white educational institutions of higher learning (Du Bois, 1935)? Du Bois maintained that separate educational institutions were tolerable as long as the educational facilities were equal to that of Whites (Du Bois, 1935). He believed that black teachers were not only "sympathetic" to black students, but also knowledgeable of the cultural setting, background, and history of black students, which brought about commitment to the children. Du Bois was not a separatist but understood that "race prejudice . . . is such that most Negroes cannot receive proper education in White institutions" (Du Bois, 1935, p. 328–9).

Horace Mann Bond (1935) criticized the public policy of separate schools as a problem for the black community. Bond argued that while Blacks advocated at times for separate schools as a result of racism, the schools never received equal funding, thus the quality of education was always inferior to the dominant white schools. He called the U.S. educational system a "long-sustained hypocrisy" that is carefully hidden to the unsuspecting mind (Bond, 1935). Both Du Bois and Bond clearly understood the damage of inferior separate schools, but were not against separation if the black schools received funding equal to the white schools. Although neither of them considered themselves black nationalists in the contemporary sense, the ideology espoused by proponents was along the same lines of thought as held by earlier generations of black activists. (Stuckey, 1987; Watkins, 1996).

Contemporary Theorizing and the Black Nationalist Legacy

At the root of the movement to create an African-centered curriculum that gave black children a knowledge of themselves, their history and culture, was the desire to address the schools' failure to meet the needs of black children. It was thought that this could be achieved through an African-centered pedagogical curriculum. Afrocentricity is an ideology that espouses the preeminence of the interests of the black community. Afrocentric forms of knowledge seek to bring attention to the political and economic concerns of Blacks. It seeks to revitalize the glory of an African past that began in Egypt. Afrocentric modes of analysis critique Western epistemologies as they are judged detrimental to Blacks (Asante, 2003). Those who espoused a black nationalist ideology in the early 1970s, for example, The Council of Independent Black Institutions (Institute for Independent Education, 1991; Kifano, 1996), criticized the dominant Eurocentric philosophy in education as a failure to educate black children in a positive light. While some argue that Afrocentric pedagogy is a feel-good theory, this begs the question: What is wrong with black children learning who they are? What is wrong with black children learning about their history and cultural norms? American schoolbooks are full of historical events and cultural norms to make white children feel good about who they are and where they come from (Shujja, 1992; Ratteray, 1992; Lee 1994). Proponents argue that an Afrocentric/Black Nationalist curriculum necessitates the employing of culturally sensitive teachers who understand the social and economic problems black children face every day. It allows teachers to bring to the classroom an understanding of how black children express themselves in non-standard English. Thus, children can speak without the fear of being punished because they may not use standard English, and teachers can be sensitive to teach standard English without destroying the child's culture and a willingness to learn (Delpit, 1995; Foster, 1997).

While black nationalist ideas of separate institutions were debated and at times put into practice, no organization was quicker than the Nation of Islam in manifesting the concept on a large scale. In 1932, the Nation of Islam opened forty-one schools, the first of which was in Detroit. Although the schools taught elementary and secondary grades, they were referred to as the Muhammad University of Islam. Many were closed when Elijah Muhammad died in 1975 and were reopened under the name of Sister Clara Muhammad by his son Wallace Muhammad, with a revised universal Islamic curriculum that moved away from Elijah's early teachings. Many Blacks today are turning to private Islamic schools to help their children decide what parts of Eurocentric culture should be accepted and what parts should be rejected (Zehr, 1999; *Education Week*, 1999).

In 1968, the controversy over whether black students were getting a good education erupted in the Ocean Hill–Brownsville section of Brooklyn in New York City with the "IS 201" court decision. Blacks, not satisfied with the way their children were being educated, decided to create black-controlled school boards in what were called "neighborhood schools" that pitted black parents against the United Federation of Teachers. The UFT lobbied in Albany against community-controlled schools, and in the end the courts sided with the UFT (NYCLU, 1969; Alsworth & Woock, 1969). Thus Blacks across the country initiated a movement that established for children, outside the public-school system, black educational institutions. By 1989, the Institute for Independent Education reported that 284 independent schools had been established in predominately Black communities. While the schools may not have espoused black nationalist theory openly, supporters followed in the steps of Blacks who had previously invoked black nationalist ideas in critiquing the white school system's failure to educate black children (Foster, 1992; Hoover, 1992; Kifano, 1996).

Conclusion

Future studies might examine Black Nationalism not as a separatist or racist ideology, but as a direct response to the racism Blacks have experienced in the United States from the colonial period to the present. Black nationalism must be understood not as a vehicle for separation, but as a continuum of thought and political directives adopted by black activists to promote a sense of solidarity and collective action, and to give black people political control of their neighborhoods and social and cultural institutions, including schools.

Further studies are needed to provide clearer insights into the debates black activists had among themselves on the issues of separation and integration. It is clear that these activists believed that to abolish the perpetual enslavement of their brethren in the South, they first had to identify and galvanize the aspirations, self-perceptions, and values of the masses of Blacks in the North.

Research is also needed to show how, during the antebellum period, both camps of black activists (integrationists and separatists) utilized the churches, newspapers, conventions, organizations, and emigration. All four institutions experienced developmental stages from experimentation to adjustment, reaching maturity in the 1850s. While there were differences of opinions, the integrationists and separatists worked together to harness their power to achieve some incremental triumphs. The very act of objecting to their oppression was empowering, and led to the construction of a policy of change that would ultimately benefit them, as well as other U. S. citizens. By no means was this empowerment complete, but the black leaders discussed herein set in motion a growing political consciousness and network of social support that continue to inform black political activities into the present moment.

References

Alsworth, Phillip L. & Roger R. Woock (1969). "Ocean Hill–Brownsville: Urban Conflict and the Schools." *Urban Education*, Vol. 4, pp. 25–40.

Anderson, James D. (1988). *The Education of Blacks in the South, 1860–1935*. Chapel Hill: University of North Carolina.

Aptheker, Herbert (1941). *The Negro in the Abolitionist Movement*. New York: International Publishers.

Aptheker, Herbert (1951). *Documentary History of the Negro People in the United States: From the Colonial Times through the Civil War*, Vol. I. New York: Citadel Press.

Aptheker, Herbert (1965). *One Continual Cry: David Walker's Appeal to the Colored Citizens of the World, 1829–1830, Its Setting & Its Meaning, Together with the Full Text of the Third, and Last, Edition of the Appeal*. New York: Published for A.I.M.S., Humanities Press.

Aptheker, Herbert (1991). *To Be Free: A Volume of the Studies in Afro-American History Dealing with Pre–Civil War Times, the Civil War and Reconstruction*. New York: Citadel Press.

Aptheker, Herbert (1992). *Anti-Racism in U.S.: History the First Two Hundred Years*. Westport, CT: Greenwood Press.

Asante, M. (2003). *Afrocentricity: The Theory of Social Change*. Chicago: African American Images.

Bell, Howard H. (1959). "The Negro Emigration Movement, 1849–1854: A Phase of Negro Nationalism," *Phylon*, Vol. 20, Summer, pp. 132–142.

Bell, Howard H. (1960), "Expressions of Negro Militancy in the North, 1840–1860," *Journal of Negro History*, Vol. 45, January, pp. 11–20.

Bell, Howard H. (1962). "Negro Nationalism: A Factor in Emigration Projects, 1858–1860," *Journal of Negro History*, Vol. 47 January, pp. 42–53.

Bell, Howard H. (1969) *A Survey of the Negro Convention Movement*. Ann Arbor: University of Michigan.

Bennett, Lerone (1987). *Before the Mayflower: A History of Black America*. New York: Penguin Books.

Berwanger, Eugene (1967). *The Frontier Against Slavery: Western Anti-Negro Prejudice and the Slavery Extension Controversy*. Urbana: University of Illinois Press.

Berwanger, Eugene (1972). "Negrophobia in Northern Proslavery and Antislavery Thought," *Phylon*, Vol. 33, pp. 266–275.

Bodo, John R. (1954). *The Protestant Clergy and Public Issues 1812–1848*. Princeton, NJ:Princeton University Press.

Bond, Horace Mann (1935). "The Extent and Character of Separate Schools in the United States," *Journal of Negro History*, Vol. 4, pp. 321–327.

Buckmaster, Henrietta (1941). *Let My People Go: The Story of the Underground Railroad*. New York: Harper and Brothers.

Carew, Jan (1992). "Moorish Culture Bringers: Bearers of Enlightenment." In *Golden Age of the Moors*, ed. Ivan Van Sertima. New Brunswick, NJ: Transaction Publishers.

Davidson, Basil (1987). *The Lost Cities of Africa*, rev. ed. Boston: Little, Brown & Company.

DeGraft-Johnson, J.C. (1954). *African Glory: The Story of Vanished Negro Civilizations*. Baltimore: Black Classic Press.

Delpit, Lisa (1995). *Other People's Children: Cultural Conflict in the Classroom*. New York: The New Press.

Dick, Robert C. (1974). *Black Protest: Issues and Tactics*. Westport, CT: Greenwood Press.

Du Bois, W.E.B. (1935). "Does the Negro Need Separate Schools?" *Journal of Negro History*, Vol. 4, pp. 328–335.

Du Bois, W.E.B. (1903). *The Souls of Black Folk*. 1996 Reprint. New York, Penquin Books.

Education Week Editorial (1999). "Islam, African American Style," *Education Week*, Vol. 18, p. 20.

Feagin, Joe E., Hernán Vera, & Nikitah Imani (1996). *The Agony of Education: Black Students at White College and Universities*. New York: Routledge.

Foner, Philip S. (1983). *History of Black Americans Volume 2: From the Emergence of the Cotton Kingdom to the Eve of the Compromise of 1850; Volume 3: From the Compromise of 1850 to the End of the Civil War*. Westport, CT: Greenwood Press.

Foster, Gail (1992). "New York City's Wealth of Historically Black Independent Schools," *Journal of Negro Education*, Vol. 61, pp. 186–200.

Foster, Michelle (1997). *Black Teachers on Teaching*. New York: The New Press.

Fredrickson, George M. (1971). *The Black Image in the White Mind: The Debate on Afro-American Character and Destiny 1817–1914*. Hanover, CT: Wesleyan University Press.

Friedman, Lawrence J. (1975). *Inventors of the Promised Land*. New York: Alfred A. Knopf.

Genovese, Eugene D. (1979). *From Rebellion to Revolution: Afro-American Slave Revolts in the Making of the Modern World*. Baton Rouge: Louisiana State University Press.

Gross, Bela (1932). "Freedom's Journal and the Rights of All," *The Journal of Negro History*, Vol. 17, July, pp. 241–286.

Harding, Vincent (1981). *There Is a River: The Black Struggle for Freedom in America*. San Diego: Harcourt Brace & Company.

Hilliard, Asa G. (1994). "Kemetic Concepts of Education." In *Egypt: Children of Africa*, ed. Ivan Van Sertima. New Brunswick, NJ: Transaction Publishers, pp. 377–387.

Hoover, Mary Eleanor Rhodes (1992). "The Nairobi Day School: An Independent School, 1966–1984," *Journal of Negro Education*, Vol. 61, pp. 201–210.

Horseman, Reginald (1981). *Race and Manifest Destiny: The Origins of American Racial Anglo-Saxonism*. Cambridge: Harvard University Press.

Horton, James Oliver (1993). *Free People of Color: Inside the African American Community*. Washington, DC, Smithsonian Press.

Huggins, Nathan (1990). *Black Odyssey: The African American Ordeal in Slavery*. New York: Vintage Books.

Hunter, Carol M. (1993). *To Set the Captives Free: Reverend Jermain Wesley Loguen and the Struggle for Freedom in Central New York*. New York, Garland Press.

Institute for Independent Education (1991). *On the Road to Success: Students at Independent Neighborhood Schools.* Washington, DC Institute for Independent Education.

Jackson, John G. (1970). *Introduction to African Civilizations.* New York: Citadel Press.

Jordan, Winthrop D. (1968). *White over Black: American Attitudes toward the Negro, 1550–1812.* New York: W.W. Norton and Company.

Kerber, Linda (1967). "Abolitionists and Amalgamators: The New York City Riots of 1834," *New York History*, Vol. 48, January, pp.28–39.

Kharem, H (2000). "The African Free Schools: A Black Community's Struggle against Cultural Hegemony in New York City, 1820–1850." *Taboo: The Journal of Culture and Education*, Vol. IV, Spring–Summer, 2000, pp. 27–36.

Kifano, Subria (1996). "Afrocentric Education in Supplementary Schools: Paradigm and Practice at the Mary McLeod Bethune Institute," *Journal of Negro Education*, Vol. 65, pp. 209–218.

Kozol, Jonathan (1991). *Savage Inequalities: Children in American Schools.* New York: Harper Collins Publishers.

Lee, Carol D. (1994). "African-Centered Pedagogy: Complexities and Possibilities." In *Too Much Schooling, Too Little Education: A Paradox of Black Life in White Societies*, ed. Mwalimu J. Shujja. Trenton, NJ: Africa World Press, pp. 295–317.

Litwack, Leon F. (1961a). "The Abolitionist Dilemma: The Antislavery Movement and the Northern Negro," *New England Quarterly*, Vol. 34, pp. 50–73.

Litwack, Leon F. (1961b). *North of Slavery: The Negro in the Free States.* Chicago: University of Chicago Press.

Macedo, Donaldo (1994). *Literacies of Power: What Americans Are Not Allowed to Know.* Boulder, CO: Westview Press.

Miller. Floyd J. (1975). *The Search for a Black Nationality: Black Emigration and Colonization, 1787–1863.* Urbana: University of Illinois Press.

Morias, Herbert M. (1967). *History of the Negro in Medicine.* New York: Publishers Company, Inc.

Moses, Wilson Jeremiah (1989). *Alexander Crummell: A Study of Civilization and Discontent.* Amherst: University of Massachusetts Press.

Moses, Wilson Jeremiah (1992). *Destiny and Race: Selected Writings, 1840–1898.* Amherst: University of Massachusetts Press.

Moss, Alfred (1988). "Alexander Crummell: Black Nationalist and Apostle of Western Civilization." In *Black Leaders of the Nineteenth Century*, eds. Leon Litwack & August Meir. Urbana: University of Illinois Press.

Mullin, Gerald W. (1972). *Flight and Rebellion: Slave Resistance in Eighteenth-Century Virginia.* New York: Oxford University Press.

New York City Civil Liberties Union (1969). "The Burden of Blame: A Report on the Ocean Hill–Brownsville School Controversy," *Urban Education*, Vol. 4. pp. 7–24.

Ofari, Earl (1972). *Let Your Motto Be Resistance: The Life and Thought of Henry Highland Garnet.* Boston: Beacon Press.

Pasternak, Martin B. (1995). *Rise Now and Fly to Arms: the Life of Henry Highland Garnet.* New York: Garland Publishing.

Pease, William H., & Jane H. Pease (1965). "Antislavery Ambivalence: Immediatism, Expediency, Race," *American Quarterly*, Vol. 17, pp. 682–695.

Pease, William H., & Jane H. Pease (1971). "The Negro Convention Movement." In *Key Issues in the Afro-American Experience*, Vol. I, eds. Nathan L. Huggins, Martin Klein, & Daniel M. Fox. New York: Harcourt Brace and Jovanovich.

Pease, Jane H., & William H. Pease (1974). *They Who Would Be Free: Blacks Search for Freedom, 1830–1861.* New York: Atheneum.

Pimienta-Bey, Jose V. (1992). "Moorish Spain: Academic Source and Foundation for the Rise and Success of Western European Universities in the Middle Ages." In *Golden Age of the Moor,* ed. Ivan Van Sertima. New Brunswick, NJ: Transaction Publishers.

Porter, Dorothy (1971). *Early Negro Writing, 1760–1837.* Boston: Beacon Press.

Quarles, Benjamin (1969). *Black Abolitionists.* New York: Oxford University Press.

Raboteau, Albert J. (1988). "Richard Allen and the African Church Movement." In *Black Leaders of the Nineteenth Century,* eds. Leon Litwack & August Meir. Urbana: University of Illinois Press.

Ratteray, Joan Davis (1992). "Independent Neighborhood Schools: A Framework for the Education of African Americans," *Journal of Negro Education,* Vol. 61, pp. 138–147.

Ripley, C. Peter, ed. (1991), *The Black Abolitionist Papers,* Vol. III & Vol. IV. Chapel Hill: University of North Carolina Press.

Roediger, Favid R. (1991). *The Wages of Whiteness: Race and the Making of the American Working Class.* New York: Verso Press.

Schor, Joel (1977). *Henry Highland Garnet: A Voice of Black Radicalism in the Nineteenth Century.* Westport, CT: Greenwood Press.

Scobie, Edward (1992). "The Moors and Portugal's Global Exanpansion." In *Golden Age of the Moors,* ed. Ivan Van Sertima. New Brunswick, NJ: Transaction Publishers.

Shujja, Mwalimu J. (1992). "Afrocentric Transformation and Parental Choice in African American Independent Schools," *Journal of Negro Education,* Vol. 61, pp. 148–159.

Spring, Joel (2001). *Deculturalization and the Struggle for Equality: A Brief History of the Education of Dominated Cultures in the United States.* New York: McGraw-Hill.

Stuckey, Sterling (1987). *Slave Culture: Nationalist Theory and the Foundations of Black Nationalist Thought.* New York: Oxford University Press.

Tice, Larry E. (1987). *Proslavery: A History of the Defense of Slavery in America, 1701–1840.* Athens: University of Georgia Press.

Watkins, William H. (1996). "Reclaiming Historical Visions of Quality Schooling: The Legacy of Early Twentieth-Century Black Intellectuals." In *Beyond Desegregation: The Politics of Quality African American Schooling,* ed. Mwalimu J. Shujaa. Thousand Oaks, CA: Corwin Press, Inc.

Wood, Forrest G. (1990). *The Arrogance of Faith: Christianity and Race in America from the Colonial Era to the Twentieth Century.* New York: Alfred A. Knopf.

Wood, Peter H. (1974). *Black Majority: Negroes in Colonial South Carolina from 1670 through the Stono Rebellion.* New York: W.W. Norton & Company.

Woodson, Carter G. (1915). *Education of the Negro Prior to 1861.* Washington, DC: Associated Publishers, Inc.

Woodson, Carter G. (1925). *Negro Orators and Their Orations.* Washington, DC: Associated Publishers, Inc.

Woodson, Carter G. (1928). *The Negro in Our History*. Washington, DC: Associated Publishers, Inc.

Zehr, Mary Ann (1999). "Guardians of the Faith," *Education Week*, Vol. 18, January 20, pp. 26–31.

Chapter Four

ANNETTE HENRY

Black Feminist Pedagogy

CRITIQUES AND CONTRIBUTIONS

Almost two decades ago, David Lusted (1986), offered an ever-relevant critique, namely, that pedagogy—to be distinguished from teaching—remains an under-defined and under-theorized area in need of conceptual work. While the scope of this paper cannot adequately address this enduring issue in depth, I want to present a brief map of some central premises in Black feminist pedagogy. I shall begin with a cursory discussion of feminism and Black women's feminist identities. Then, I shall discuss Black feminist thought in order to understand the epistemological underpinnings of Black feminist pedagogy. I will conclude with suggestions for educational theorists. I hope to show that Black feminist pedagogy is an important and overlooked perspective for educational theorists, as it encompasses a critique of traditional education, its curricula, and pedagogical practices.

Feminism is concerned with social justice and social change. It is plural, and yet an umbrella term for a plethora of theories "in the making," open to reexamination and redefinition (Combahee River Collective, 1982; hooks 1984; James, 1999; Jordan & Weedon, 1995; Sanders, 1989). Feminisms not only address theory in a range of disciplines, they are grounded in women's daily lives and experiences (Collins, 1991; Mirza, 1995; Smith, 1987). They represent a range of epistemologies that fall under diverse, sometimes overlapping and problematic rubrics (e.g., Black, Chicana, Third World, Afrocentric, postmodern, liberal, Christian, ecological, Muslim, psychoanalytic, socialist, existentialist, radical, woman-centered, post-structural, and womanist, to name only a few). They differ in their conceptualization of the primacy of gender in explaining women's status and function in society (Hamer & Neville,

2001). Moreover, feminisms are increasingly difficult to categorize due to shifting conceptual categories (e.g., "woman," "feminism," "gender") and shifting discursive frameworks. Furthermore, at this historical moment, it is a difficult task to categorize ever-new and emergent cultural critiques by women of color.

As many feminists have pointed out over the past thirty years, White middle-class feminists have often disregarded or misrepresented the range of feminist practices, especially by women of color, working-class, poor women, and women in grassroots organizations (Lorde, 1984; James, 1999; Vogel, 2000). Indeed, many Black women intellectuals and activists carry out their work outside the ivory tower (e.g., community and grassroots organizations) and throughout the world. This may be one reason that White, privileged feminists tend to not characterize Black feminisms as diverse, emerging, and plural. For example, White academic feminists often acknowledge the same one or two Black-feminist authors without adhering to their differing epistemic positions and politics (e.g., Patricia Hill Collins and bell hooks). As Hazel Carby (1992) has written, these become used and abused icons. The problematic relationships between Black and White feminist realities along dimensions such as race, class, sexuality, nationality, and so forth, account for many theoretical and practical tensions. However, I view these tensions as emerging out of the necessarily diffuse and diverse work of advancing issues of concern to all humanity, from the perspectives and standpoints of women.

Black Feminist Thought: Diverse Perspectives

Black-feminist thought addresses, and is grounded in, Black women's collective knowledge, historical-subject positions, lived experiences, and the political economy, or "White supremacist capitalist patriarchy" (hooks, 1992).[1] Black feminism "encompasses theoretical interpretations of Black women's reality by those who live in it," writes Collins (1991, p. 22). Theses representations vary from highly depoliticized to revolutionary representations. Joy James (1999) has written about the diversity of battles and political positions among Black women activists, noting that because of our ideological and economic diversity, Black women cannot be posited as a class:

> Black women activists and feminists are not uniformly progressive, although they all invariably face marginalization and opposition fueled by white supremacy, corporate capitalism, patriarchy, and homophobia. Radical or revolutionary black feminism also faces resistance from liberal and conservative feminisms and antiracism. (p. 4)

Gloria Joseph (1988) emphasized that Black-feminist perspectives are conceptual systems, and shaped by culture. Indeed, internationally, Black feminists underscore the considerable diversity of Black women's pedagogies and educational activism (Dolphyne, 1991; Imam, Mama, & Sow, 1997; Knowles & Mercer, 1992; Ogundipe-Leslie, 1993; Williams, 1993). Ghanaian linguist and women's activist Florence Abena Dolphyne (1991) reflects on her involvement with Western feminists at the mid-decade conference in Copenhagen in 1980. Western women wanted immediate legislation to eradicate traditional African practices such as polygamy and infibulation, whereas African women saw more sustained and systematic education and training as ways to slowly abolish practices grounded in the cultures. Dolphyne concludes:

> I have become more and more conscious of the difference in approach to women's issues between Western women, especially "feminists," and African women who are actively working for women's emancipation. (xiii)

Internationally, the activism and scholarship of Black women has advanced theory by raising critical questions about the complex and simultaneous systems of oppression—from the vantage points of Black women mentioned earlier—such as sexism, heterosexism, racism, classism, and ageism. Moreover, Black women's theorizing internationally has raised questions about colonialist and postcolonial relations, as well as the cultural and historical specificities of Black women (e.g., Walker & Parmar, 1993; Wane, Deliovsky, & Lawson, 2002) Black-feminist pedagogy rests on an epistemology that critiques American/Western education. It is pedagogy of liberation, a pedagogy of protest. The range of these pedagogies takes place in varied settings outside of formal classrooms, such as churches (Townes, 1995), homes (King & Mitchell, 1999), and community groups (Bryan, Dadzie, & Scafe, 1985; Hamer & Neville, 2001). However, in this discussion, I shall examine the contributions of some Black feminist/womanist theorists whose goal is to transform formal classrooms.

Black Women and Feminist Identity

Many Black women activists are reluctant to name themselves "feminist" for many reasons. Some feel that feminism is an academic (White) philosophy, or a denomination irrelevant to the realities of their specific lives. Many Black female scholars focus on gender without espousing a feminist standpoint or politics. Perhaps, as hooks (1994) argued, they are "uncertain about whether feminist movement could really change the lives of Black females in a meaningful way" (p. 126). Indeed, Florence Abena Dolphyne (1991) writes:

> I myself, as Vice-Chairman and later as Chairman of the National Council on Women and Development, the national machinery set up by the Ghana Government to ensure

that the objectives of International Women's Year and the subsequent United Nations Decade for Women are achieved in Ghana, always knew that I was working for the emancipation of women in Ghana. However, I never considered and still do not consider myself a "feminist." (p. xiii)

Sexism and patriarchal thinking in Black communities may prevent women from advocating feminist/women's issues in community political organizations. It may also produce tensions between Black men and women as well as amongst Black women, some of whom may view organizing as women to be unnecessary. Worn-out accusations of dividing the race, fragmenting struggles, or following White women serve to besmirch Black feminist projects that are, in reality, beneficial not only to Black women, but also to Black men, Black children, the community, and beyond. Revolutionary spaces can be created that enable Black people to fight together against racism, sexism, classism, homophobia, and so forth. I agree with Caroline Knowles and Sharmila Mercer (1992), who remind us that political struggles could more effectively be built around issues rather than biogenetics.

Patricia Hill Collins (1991) argues that Black feminism is a "process of self-conscious struggle that empowers women and men to actualize a humanist vision of community" (p. 39). Importantly, she emphasizes that, "In spite of the fact that Black women do not readily identify themselves as feminists, there is a high level of support for feminist issues" (Collins, 1991, p. 153). Barbara Omolade notes (1994) that "Black feminism is sometimes referred to as womanism because both are concerned with the struggles against sexism and racism by Black women who are themselves part of the community's efforts to achieve equity and liberty" (xx).[2] Womanist theologian Emilie Townes (1995) writes, "The womanist project is to take a fuller measure of the nature of injustice and inequities of human existence from the perspective of women, Black women" (p. 10). Womanism is not a fixed, closed conceptual system, but as Katie Cannon writes, it continually evolves through its rejection of all forms of oppression and commitment to social justice (Cannon, 1995, p. xx).

In this discussion, I shall refer to Black feminist and womanist writings under the rubric of Black-feminist scholarship, although I acknowledge that this terminological collapse may be problematic. Collins (2001) explains that this debate about nomenclature reflects the "basic challenge of accommodating diversity" (p. 9). Indeed, bell hooks argues that the term "womanism" deflects attention from feminism as a political struggle to end sexism and sexist domination, She argues that womanists prefer to focus on Black female cultural practice and lifestyle (Paris, 1993). Cheryl Sanders (1989) also agrees that womanism is more celebratory than critically reflective. However, I focus on those "womanist" writings that acknowledge the workings of sexism and sexist oppression. The womanists from whom I draw are Black women theologians (e.g., Cannon, 1995; Sanders, 1995; Thandeka, 1999; Townes, 1995), for their creative connections between spirituality, praxis, and social justice.

Black Feminist Pedagogy as a Critique of Traditional Education

In an important note about pedagogy: David Lusted (1986) argues that pedagogy involves the entire organization of practices between the teacher, the learner, and the knowledge they produce together. This interaction can change consciousness:

> To insist on the pedagogy of theory, as with the pedagogy of teaching, is to recognize a more transactional model whereby knowledge is produced not just at the researcher's desk nor at the lectern but in the consciousness, through the process of thought, discussion, writing, debate, exchange; in the social and internal, collective and isolated struggle for control of understanding, from engagement in the unfamiliar idea, the difficult formulation pressed at the limit of comprehension or energy; in the meeting of the deeply held with the casually dismissed; in the dramatic moment of realization that a scarcely regarded concern, an unarticulated desire, the barely assimilated, can come alive, make for a new sense of self, change commitments and activity. And these are also transformations which take place across all agencies in an educational process, regardless of their title as academic, critic, teacher, or learner. (p. 4)

It is precisely this change of consciousness and commitments that Gloria Joseph (1988) envisions as she names Black feminism a "philosophy of liberation of humankind," and its classroom practice "a pedagogy of liberation" (p. 177). Such practice critiques traditional educational discourses and practices. Throughout the world, patriarchal and colonialist thought have devalued, suppressed, and ignored women's alternative knowledge, women's ways of being, as well as their intellectual and political work. This process of subordination is accomplished, as Gloria Joseph (1988) argues, in the denial of equitable education for non-Whites, a process that is integral to the maintenance of the status quo, and to America as a racist society. Students from oppressed and marginalized social groups are denied the right to learn about their own cultures from critical, informed perspectives.

Similarly, Black women throughout African diaspora speak of how the political-economic system has a vested interest in creating unequal and hierarchical educational opportunities, and reinforcing domination (Brathwaite, 1991; Bryan, Dadzie, & Scafe, 1985; hooks, 1994; James, 1993; Joseph, 1988; Ogundipe-Leslie, 1993). Black women, as mothers, have a scathing educational critique: "The schools have kept our children at the bottom of the ladder of employability and laid the blame on us," write British Black activists Beverly, Bryan, Stella Dadzie, and Suzanne Scafe (1985). They note that

Black women's pedagogical activism has been part of a wider struggle for survival and wholeness for the Black community, while recognizing that "the campaigns we have taken up as mothers, teachers and schoolgirls have been given added strength and direction by the experience we have brought to them as women" (p. 59).

Barbara Omolade (1994) coordinated the Center for Worker Education, offering a Bachelor of Science in Education degree, and enabling childcare workers to become teachers. She argues for a theory of pedagogy that engages the dimensions of race, class, and gender. She notes that her working-class adult-female students were often required to separate their lived realities from classroom life, immersing themselves in the "sedentary activities of reading, writing, and speaking in a way that is structured by certain racial, gender, and class privileges" (p. 145). The language of academe caused them to "freeze up" and "never find a confident or powerful intellectual voice" (p. 149). She laments that although the unions and academy have worked together to provide adults with college degrees in centers for worker education, both the academy and the union support traditional liberal-arts and education courses that meet state licensing requirements, and conventional pedagogical methods. Thus, unions and schools promote the status quo:

> rather than expanding their own radical social change tradition. In addition, most union member students graduate without ever learning about labor, the history of workers' struggles, or radical education traditions. (p. 147)

Omolade's critique becomes more trenchant as she reflects upon the apolitical understandings of these Black female teacher graduates:

> Thus, what gets reproduced from the Center's B.S. education program are teachers unprepared to engage in serious intellectual discourse within the complex and combative environment of the public schools. . . . These programs offer Black women students access to a college education while teaching them to become even more ignorant of the significance of their own histories and experiences. . . . they have produced the same old technically skilled bureaucrats and teachers who lack intellectual breadth and imagination. Only this time, they are Black women. (p. 147–149)

Omolade (1994) further offers a critique of racism and gender. She critiques White patriarchal standards of beauty, which engender White teachers' inability to recognize Black female students' intelligence. They are negatively evaluated by other criteria such as their physical characteristics, hair texture, and social skills. These racist and sexist representations of the Black female are omnipresent at all levels of the schooling process (Evans, 1992; Fordham, 1993; Grant, 1984; Henry, 1998; Okazawa-Rey, Robinson, & Ward, 1987; Omolade, 1994; Osler & Vincent, 2003).

Black womanists/feminists who write about their classroom practice show that their pedagogy flows out of a political commitment that informs their curricula and classroom interactions. They argue for analyses of the social constructions of race, nationality, culture, gender, sexuality, and class as important for understanding Western patriarchy, and that these constructs remain central to understanding historical and societal phenomena. They also show us how these social and historical positions are present in the classroom and need to be addressed in our relationships with our students (Henry, 1993; 1996; 2001; James, 1993). Our very presence in the academy critiques White patriarchy; Black law professor Anita Allen (1994) recalls a young White male asking, "What gives you the right to teach this class?" (p.183)

The insights of Black women teachers on the epistemic margins, teaching from critical and feminist perspectives at the college and university levels, has exposed the complexities of teaching in counter-hegemonic and transgressive ways such as trying to articulate alternative visions along with students. Black feminists draw from a diversity of transformative and oppositional thinkers, both men and women, across cultures and margins. Black feminist educational critiques can be summarized under three main themes: (1) the dominant patriarchal educational system, which serves a White elite; (2) White academic feminist pedagogy, whose analyses of class and race are often irrelevant for the majority of Black women (hooks 1981); and (3) Black educational thought, which privileges masculinist discourse and ignores the educational concerns of Black women and girls (see Omolade, 1994).

Critique of Curricula

Apart from "women-worthies" (e.g., Ella Baker, Angela Davis)—rarely discussed from feminist/womanist perspectives in education classes—knowledge of and by Black women as intellectuals, social activists, liberators, or revolutionaries continues to be suppressed. Consider Pan-Africanist Marcus Garvey and Abolitionist Henry Bibb. Only Black feminist/womanist scholarship has informed us of the antiracist protest of Amy Garvey (Harley, 1993) and Mary Bibb (Cooper, 1991). The fact is, as Gerda Lerner (1973) writes, "there is a female aspect to all history, that women were there, and that their specific contribution to the building and shaping of society was different to that of men."

Historical and cross-cultural analyses show that education has been central to the lives of Black women, and Black women have been central protagonists in antiracist pedagogical practice (Bristow et al., 1994; Bryan, Dadzie & Scafe, 1985; Cooper, 1991; De Silva, 1992; Hamer & Neville, 2001; Steady, 1987; Theoharis, 2001). It is important to be informed about these "herstories," and about how those who came before us have struggled for social transformation. Of course, uncritical over-glorification of Black heroines serves little use. As Joseph (1988) exhorts, learning history helps "shatter the prevailing mythology that inhibits so many from acting more decisively for social change and the creation of a more just society and a viable future for all." (p. 176).

Feminist practice does not mean that the curriculum is uniquely about women. The subject matter (curriculum) could be about men, science, music, literature, or any number of themes. All topics can be studied in respect to women and girls or from feminist frameworks. The political analysis and thus one's feminist consciousness bring a particular lens and make a space for particular questions to be asked and investigated in one's classroom practice. In a political commitment to rectify curricular omissions and distortions, Black feminist teachers draw from a political-historical analysis of the social constructions that position us differentially, as defined by the power elite (e.g., economic, religious, cultural, physical, linguistic, ethnic, racial, sexual dimensions). Thus, feminist/womanist pedagogies invite critique and alternatives to traditional education by opening up new thinking about previously unexplored curricula; they also can advance new, alternative, and sometimes oppositional interpretations and analyses to help change students' consciousness. Gloria Joseph (1988) relates a class discussion of Eleanor Bumpers, a poor, elderly Black woman killed by a SWAT team because she owed $98 in rent payments. This example allowed her predominantly White, middle-class students to examine police brutality; racism; the treatment of the poor, elderly and Blacks; as well as the North American emphasis on money over human welfare and life.

As Black feminists point out, the distortions and omissions of traditional curricula damage not only Black people (by omission of their contributions, perspectives, and issues of concern to them), they also damage all people. Students lose the opportunity for growth and change if they cannot clearly examine and understand the historical dimensions of current societal dilemmas and oppressions or the ways in which they may help dismantle them. This lack of analysis misleads students to believe and accept that existing societal problems and educational inequities are in reality "natural," "inevitable," or due to the inherent characteristics of certain classes and cultures (e.g., high unemployment, crime, overpopulation, poverty, low test scores, high drop-out rates, underachievement, overrepresentation in Special Education.) It also perpetuates dichotomous thinking, which serves the dominant group (us-and-them politics). Many feminists and people of color have critiqued this binary Western masculinist thinking (e.g., Aguilar-San Juan, 1992; Butler, 1981; Collins,

1991; Cora, 1992; Du Bois, 1977; Gilroy, 1993; Fanon, 1967; Harding, 1991; Lather, 1991; Olguin, 1991; Spivak, 1986; Wright, 1953).

Curricular perspectives are still, for the most part, "White male studies," privileging Eurocentrism and patriarchy without a serious analysis of the cultures, experiences, and perspectives of women and people of color in a society based on oppressions through the dimensions noted above. In my classes, I encourage students to examine how institutional structures are soaked in power relations (sexual, economic, social, etc.). For example, in examining contemporary trade books and publishers' Web sites geared for teachers, undergraduate students are often seduced by beautiful, glossy images of women and people from diverse cultural groups. College course syllabi boast more "multicultural" texts than in recent years. One has to critically examine the discourses of diversity, critical pedagogy, and social justice in examples such as these, for the most part still anchored in traditional dominant narratives. However, whether elementary classrooms or graduate-school seminars, one must interrogate how power is created and sustained through texts and ideas.[3]

Discussions with my education students regarding *how* anti-discriminatory texts (such as "White Privilege" by Peggy McIntosh [1995]) were examined in many courses often reveal a disappointing set of common avoidances: (1) insufficient time to discuss the readings; (2) texts by people of color scheduled for the last class or only if time permitted; and (3) White students' therapeutic storytelling of White oppression without a critical analysis of race.

Pedagogical Processes

The traditional epistemic view in North American (Western) education casts knowledge as static; subject matter as objective and rational; and scientific truth as something to be mastered in one particular way, a way that serves Anglo-European patriarchal thought. There is only one "right answer"; knowledge is transmitted unidirectionally, from the teacher to the student; the teacher (as long as HE is White) is the expert. The traditional classroom continues to encourage competitive, individualistic, and hierarchical climates with winners and losers; often students become regurgitators, content to figure out how to "give the teacher what s/he wants." In this model, all students are assessed by the same external, pseudo-objective standards. The "science" of teaching, in this mechanistic view, is often reduced to "techniques" and "strategies." To the contrary, for feminist educators, pedagogy underscores the interconnectedness of student, teacher, and the entire knowledge-production processes within and outside of the classroom, as well as the power of pedagogy to change consciousness (hooks, 1994; Maher & Tetreault, 2001). Feminist models evoke the conceptualization of Lusted (1986) mentioned above.

Pedagogical practices reflect epistemological understandings. Black-feminist pedagogy challenges not only traditional content, but also the processes that structure learning in traditional classrooms. Gloria Joseph (1988) and Patricia Hill Collins (1991) have named the following commonalities in Black women's epistemologies: (1) the use of dialogue in assessing knowledge claims; (2) personal expressiveness; (3) personal accountability; (4) concrete experience as criterion of meaning; and (5) the ethic of caring. These epistemological underpinnings critique the positivistic foundation of traditional pedagogies (Collins, 1989).[4]

Feminists of all colors have critiqued the knowledge-production processes in classrooms. Feminists view students and teachers as reciprocal authorities who engage in dialogue and construct knowledge from multiple positions (Maher & Tetreault, 2001). Their pedagogies share principles with a number of progressive educators, whose epistemological positions and pedagogies strive for "holistic," "critical," "inquiry-based," and "democratic" approaches to teaching and learning (e.g., Freire, 1970; Graff, 2003; Ng, 2003).

Black feminist educators often write about the power of students radicalized with a critical analysis of society. They seek to work in ways that critically and actively engage students. They aim to help students unmask the often hidden dimensions of power and oppression in order to envision alternatives toward the well-being of all humanity (Cannon, 1995; hooks, 1994; 2003; James, 1993; Joseph, 1988). This area of feminist writing passionately depicts the emotional, psychological, professional and political struggles of this mission toward students' critical consciousness. For example, Joy James (1993) delineates a difficult and systematic guided transition toward new understandings of race, class, and gender devised for students with a group of scholars. The aim was to enable critical analyses of power and oppression in society by providing students with a language of critique, by carefully selecting and sequencing texts, by restructuring group/peer activities, and by creating collaborative activities including drawing and journal writing. Although progress was made, student resistance, stress, denial, anxiety, and hostility abounded.

To conduct an oppositional or transformational feminist pedagogy, one has to present an analysis of institutional and societal power, and structure the processes in nontraditional ways. bell hooks (1989) describes how she restructured her classes in ways that students can "come to voice" (p. 53). She writes:

> Everyone's voice is heard as students read paragraphs which may explore a particular issue. They do not have the opportunity to refuse to read paragraphs. When I hear their

voices, I become aware of information that they may not know that I can provide. Whether a class is large or small, I try to talk with all students individually or in small groups so that I have a sense of their needs. How can we transform consciousness if we do not have some sense of where the students are intellectually, psychically? (p. 54)

However, pedagogies that require students to engage in critical analysis can sometimes produce disturbingly strange harvests, especially when students are, as Lusted (1986) writes, "pressed at the limit of comprehension or energy" (p. 4): White women vomited after a class on African American women taught by bell hooks, in which Black female students were in the majority (De Danaan, 1990). While this example may seem rather extreme, it underscores the discomfort experienced by many White middle-class students whose privilege has always allowed them to see their realities at the center of curriculum discourse. Consequently, many of us as Black women professors contend with violent histrionics in relation to our practice: Here are some examples from my own teaching: a White student-teacher who was resistant to self-reflection regarding her White privilege reported to my superiors that my pedagogy was "ruining her self-esteem"; a young man labeled Joel Spring's text (2002) *American Education* biased, saying, "he writes about the internment of the Japanese but never the oppression of other groups, like the Germans. Germans have gone through a lot of oppression. They were interned also." In a response to another chapter, the same student contested any critique of the American educational system, by writing: "America must be a good country, YOU chose to come here. Then why aren't you teaching in central Africa, communist China or Equador?" A graduate student confronted me with the following: "You're the hardest professor around here. I guess you feel you have to prove you can do the job!" Lastly, a Black male, resistant to the critical Black feminist thinking required in a doctoral seminar on Black womanist research perspectives, entered my office claiming he had a gun to shoot me! (Henry, 1996)

Faced with these varying levels of resistance, it is important to envision one's pedagogical work as not only political but spiritual (Ani, 1994; Cliff, 1986; Sanders, 1995; Townes, 1995). bell hooks (1994) urges transformative educators to "transgress those boundaries that would confine each pupil to a rote, assembly-line approach to learning" (p. 13). She advocates a "holistic, engaged pedagogy," more demanding than traditional critical or feminist pedagogies, one in which all students can learn, and in which teaching is seen as spiritual practice. Black-female theologians offer another view of the spiritual, envisioning womanist practice as an ultimate expression of the love of God and others (Townes, 1995). For ethicist and theologian Katie Cannon (1995), womanist pedagogy:

emerges out of Black women challenging conventional and outmoded theological resources, problematizing the obvious . . . creat[ing] alternative ways of conceptualizing the "natural". . . . The imperative suggested by this pedagogy is an engaged scholarship that leads us to resist domination through mindful activism and helps all of us to live more faithfully the radicality of the gospel (pp. 137–138).

Gloria Joseph (1988) emphasizes the spiritual traditions that have sustained marginalized groups. She argues in favor of traditions that value interpersonal relations among people as opposed to material acquisitions:

There is an alternative way to view the world, and that will optimize experience. It certainly has allowed Black people to survive the most dreadful kind of slavery that has have been known to humankind. (p. 179)

For Marimba Ani (1994), the separation of the spiritual and the material in Western thinking denies Spirit, degrades nature, and produces self-alienation and the devaluation of the African self and African knowledge (Spirit). She argues that such thinking precipitated European imperialism, the objectification and rationalization of the universe and the domination of objects and others.

Concluding Remarks

My purpose has been to illustrate some ways in which Black feminists critique traditional curricula and practices. Black-feminist pedagogy is premised upon the possibility of social change. Black feminist educators posit alternative interpretations of society and history through Black women's experiences and analyses with oppression; they provide a lens to examine and change power relationships in the classroom and allow for alternative ways to teach and come to know about oneself and the world.

This brief discussion does not engender a broad analysis nor theoretical explanations in which various Black feminist/womanist perspectives are examined. Time and space do not allow for an explication of the specificities and interconnections in various geopolitical contexts. Indeed, there are many projects and political locations from which Black feminists work toward social change.

Black women represent various communities. The diagram on page 101 attempts to depict the interconnectedness of knowledge, theories, and practices; despite their boundaries and epistemic positions, feminisms/womanisms embrace overlapping issues and agendas. Hence, some spheres (representing various feminist positions and agendas) are within, others outside of the outer circle of feminism/womanism.

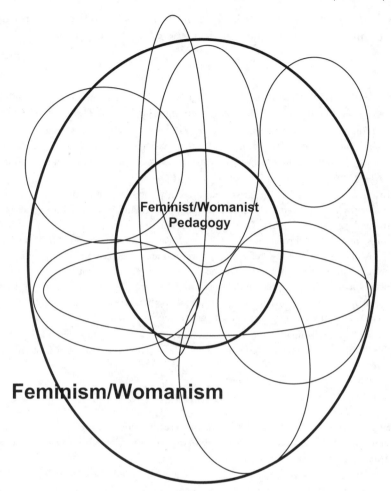

Feminist/Womanist
Pedagogy

Feminism/Womanism

Future Directions

This chapter examined Black-feminist practice in colleges and universities. In higher education and especially in colleges of education—institutions where pedagogy, educational policy, teacher education, and graduate educational scholarship are fostered and examined—the principles and practice of Black-feminist pedagogy have been largely ignored. These Black-feminist intellectual ideas can incite educational critiques regarding contemporary educational practices in contemporary classrooms along the dimensions of nationality, language background, race/ethnicity, class, sexuality, and gender. Although research and intellectual discussion regarding social justice perspectives abound, they do not incorporate Black-feminist lenses. I hope that this brief discussion has raised the awareness that Black-feminist analyses can provide critical lenses to examine theoretical and practical issues.

Notes

1. For a discussion of patriarchy, a term that carries a number of contested meanings, see Gordon and Hunter (1998), including their important analysis of the role of historicity.

2. A culturally specific term created by Alice Walker in the late 1970s. Derived from *womanish*, it is a reworking of the term *feminist* that takes into account the experiences of Black women. *Womanist* connotes a variety of meanings, see Walker (1983), pages x–xii, and 71–82.

3. In a sixth-grade social-studies classroom I recently observed, the students were using *World History* by Dianne Hart (1991). On the first page is a "multicultural" line-up of people at the polling station. A Black woman heads the queue. Pictures of people from diverse cultures are scattered throughout the text. Yet the analysis of women in "His-story" is grossly disappointing. The few references to women are trivialized and unproblematic, often collapsed into a "women-can-be-like-men" framework. The first written reference to women occurs in the fifth chapter, under a heading "Women in Egypt," where we learn that Egyptian women were respected as wives and mothers, could own property, divorce their husbands, testify in court, and become government officials.

4. I am not naturalizing identities or communities. A "Black women's epistemology" is a useful tool in conceptualizing consciousness and identities as shaped by subordination, race, culture, class, gender, and so forth.

References

Aguilar-San Juan, K. (1992). Exploding myths, creating consciousness: Toward a PanAsian unity. In M. Silvera (ed.), *Piece of a heart: A lesbian of color anthology*, pp. 185–192. Toronto: Sister Vision Press.

Allen, A. (1994). On being a role model. In D.T. Goldberg (ed.), *Multiculturalism: A critical reader*, pp. 180–199. Cambridge, Mass.: Blackwell.

Ani, M. (1994). *Yurugu: An African-centered critique of European cultural thought and behavior.* Trenton, N.J.: Africa World Press.

Brathwaite, K. (1991). The Black student and the school: A Canadian dilemma. In S. Waliaula Chilungu & S. Niang (eds.), *African continuities/L'héritage africain*, pp. 95–216. Toronto: Terebi.

Bristow, P., D. Brand, L. Carter, A. Cooper, S. Hamilton, & A. Shadd (eds.) (1994). *We're rooted here and they can't pull us up.* Toronto: University of Toronto Press.

Bryan, B., S. Dadzie, & S. Scafe (1985). *The heart of the race.* London: Virago.

Butler, J. (1981). *Black studies, pedagogy and revolution.* Washington, D.C.: University Press of America.

Cannon, K. (1995). *Katie's cannon: Womanism and the soul of the Black community.* New York: Continuum.

Carby, H. (1992). The multicultural wars. In G. Dent (ed.), *Black popular culture*, pp. 187–199. Seattle: Bay Press.

Cliff, M. (1986). I found God in myself and I loved her/I loved her fiercely: More thoughts on the work of Black women artists. *Journal of feminist studies in religion* 2(1): 7–39.

Collins, P. (1989). Comparison of two works on Black family life. *Signs* 14(4): 745–771.

———. (1991). *Black feminist thought: Knowledge, consciousness and pedagogy.* New York: Routledge.

———. (2001). What's in a name? Womanism, Black feminism, and beyond. *The black scholar* 26(1): 9–17.

Combahee River Collective (1982). A Black feminist statement. In G. Hull, P. Bell Scott, & B. Smith (eds.), *All the women are White, all the men are Black but some of us are brave.* Old Westbury, New York: Feminist Press.

Cooper, A. (1991). The search for Mary Elizabeth Miles Bibb Cary, Otherwise known as Mary Bibb, Black woman teacher in Canada West during the mid-nineteenth century. *Ontario history* 83(1): 39–56.

Cora, M. (1992). Dos culturas/two cultures. In M. Silvera (ed.), *Piece of my heart: A lesbian of colour anthology*, pp.193–196. Toronto: Cross Cultural Communication Centre.

De Danaan, L. (1990). Center to margin: Dynamics in a global classroom. *Women's studies quarterly* 1&2: 135–144.

De Silva, P. (1992). Black women teachers' resistance to racism in Saõ Carlos Saõ Paulo, Brazil. Paper presented at the annual conference of the American Educational Research Association. San Francisco, Calif.

Dolphyne, F. (1991). The emancipation of women: An African perspective. Accra: Ghana Universities Press.

Du Bois, W.E.B. (1977). *The education of Black people: Ten critiques, 1906–1960* (H. Apteker, ed.). New York: Monthly Review Press.

Evans, G. (1992). Those loud Black girls. In D. Spender and E. Sarah (eds.), *Learning to lose: Sexism and education*, 2nd ed., pp. 183–190. London: Women's Press.

Fanon, F. (1967). *Black skin, white masks.* New York: Grove Press.

Fordham, S. (1993). Those loud Black girls. *Anthropology and education* 24(1): 3–32.

Freire, P (1970). *Pedagogy of the oppressed.* New York: Herder and Herder.

Gordon, L., & A. Hunter (1998). Not all male dominance is patriarchal. *Radical history review* 71: 71–83.

Graff, G. (2003). *Clueless in academe: How schooling obscures the life of the mind.* New Haven: Yale University Press.

Grant, L. (1984). Black females' "place" in desegregated classrooms. *Sociology of education*, 57(2): 98–111.

Gilroy, P. (1993). *The Black Atlantic: Modernity and double consciousness.* Cambridge, Mass.: Harvard University Press.

Harding, S. (1991). *Whose science, whose knowledge.* Ithaca, N.Y.: Cornell University Press.

Harley, S. (1993, August). The silent voice: African American women in the Pan-Africanist movement. Unpublished paper presented at the National Council of Black Studies Annual Conference, National Theatre, Accra, Ghana, West Africa.

Hamer, J., & H. Neville (2001). Revolutionary Black feminism: Toward a theory of unity and liberation. *The black scholar* 28(4): 22–29.

Hart, D. (1991). *World History: Prehistoric times to the present.* New York: Janus.

Henry, A. (1993). There are no safe places: Pedagogy as powerful and dangerous terrain. *Action in teacher education* 15: 4–14.

———. (1996). A wha' dem a go on wid? (Poem) *Frontiers: A journal of women studies,* 16(1): 27–28.

———. (1998). Taking back control: African Canadian women teachers' lives and practice. New York: State University of New York Press.

———. (2001).The politics of unpredictability in a reading/writing discussion group with girls from the Caribbean. In C. Lewis & P. Enciso (eds), Special issue, Already reading: children, texts, and contexts, *Theory into practice* 40(3): 184–189.

hooks, bell. (1981). *Ain't I a woman.* Boston: South End Press.

———. (1984). *Feminist theory from margin to center.* Boston: South End Press.

———. (1992). *Black looks.* Boston: South End Press.

———. 1989). *Talking back: Thinking feminist thinking Black.* Toronto: Between the Lines.

———. (1994) *Teaching to transgress.* New York: Routledge.

———. (2003). *Teaching community: A pedagogy of hope.* New York: Routledge.

Imam, A., A. Mama, & F. Sow (1997). *Engendering African social sciences.* Dakar: CODESRIA.

James, J. (1993). Reflections on teaching: Gender, race, and class. *Feminist teacher* 5(3): 9–15.

James, J. (1999). Resting in gardens, battling in deserts: Black women's activism. *Black scholar* 29(4): 2–7.

Jordan, G., & C. Weedon (1995). *Cultural politics.* London: Blackwell.

Joseph, G. (1988). Black feminist pedagogy in Capitalist America. In M. Coles (ed.), *Bowles and Gintis revisited: Correspondence and contradiction in educational theory,* pp. 174–186. London: Falmer.

King, J., & C. Mitchell (1999). *Black mothers to sons.* New York: Peter Lang.

Knowles, C., & S. Mercer (1992). Feminism and antiracism: An exploration of the political possibilities. In J. Donald, & A. Rattansi (eds), *Race, culture and difference,* pp. 105–123. London: Open University and Sage Publications.

Lather, P. (1991). *Getting smart: Feminist research and pedagogy with/in the postmodern.* New York: Routledge.

Lerner, G. (1973). *Black women in White America: A documentary history.* New York: Oxford University Press.

Lorde, A. (1984). *Sister Outsider.* New York: The Crossing Press.

Lusted, D. (1986). Why pedagogy? *Screen,* 27(5): 2–14.

Maher, F., & M. Tetreault (2001). *The feminist classroom.* New York: Basic Books.

Martin, J. (1994). Methodological essentialism, false difference, and other dangerous traps. *Signs* 19(3): 630–657.

McIntosh, P. (1995). White privilege: Unpacking the invisible knapsack In M.L. Anderson and P.H. Collins (eds.), *Race, class and gender: An anthology,* pp. 70–81. Belmont, Calif.: Wadsworth.

Mirza, H. (1993). The social construction of Black womanhood in British educational research: Towards new understanding. In M. Arnot and K. Weiler (eds.), *Feminism and social justice education,* pp. 32–57. London: Falmer.

Ng, R. (2003). Toward an integrative approach to equity in education. In P. Trifonas (ed.), *Pedagogies of difference: Rethinking education for social change*, pp. 206–219. New York: Routledge-Falmer.

Ogundipe-Leslie, M. (1993). African women, culture and another development. In S. James & A. Busia, *Theorizing Black feminisms*, pp. 102–117. New York: Routledge.

Okazawa-Rey, M., T. Robinson, & J. Ward (1987). Black women and the politics of skin and hair. *Women and therapy* 6(1/2): 89–102.

Olguin, R.A. (1991). Towards an epistemology of ethnic studies: African American studies and Chicano studies contributions. In J. Butler & J.C. Walter, *Ethnic studies and women's studies*, pp. 149–168. Albany: State University of New York

Omolade, B. (1994). *The rising song of African American women*. New York: Routledge.

Osler, A., & K. Vincent (2003). *Girls and exclusion: Rethinking the agenda*. London: Routledge-Falmer.

Paris, P. (1993). From womanist thought to womanist action. *Journal of feminist studies in religion* 9: 115–125.

Sanders, C. (1989). Christian ethics and theology in womanist perspective. *Journal of feminist studies in religion* 5: 83–112.

———. (1995). *Living at the intersection: Womanism and afrocentrism in theology*. Minneapolis: Augsburg Fortress.

Smith, D. (1987). *The everyday world as problematic*. Boston: Northeastern University Press.

Spivak, G. (1986). Three women's texts and a critique of imperialism. In Henry Louis Gates (ed.), *Race, writing and difference*, pp. 262–280. Chicago: University of Chicago Press.

Spring, J. (2002). *American education*. 11th edition. New York: McGraw-Hill.

Steady, F. (1987). African feminism: A world wide perspective. In R. Terborg-Penn, S. Harley, & A. Rushing, (eds.) *Women in Africa and the African diaspora*. pp. 3–21. Washington, D.C.: Howard University Press.

Thandeka, (1999). *Learning to be white: Money, race, and God in America*. New York: Continuum.

Theoharis, J. (2001). "We saved the city": Black struggles for educational equality in Boston, 1960–1976. *Radical history review* 81: 61–93.

Townes, E. (1995). *In a blaze of glory: Womanist spirituaity as social witness*. Nashville: Abingdon Press.

Vogel, L. (2000). Domestic labor revisited. *Science & Society* 64(2): 151–170.

Walker, A. (1983). *In search of our mother's gardens*. San Diego: Harcourt Brace Jovanovich.

Walker, A., & P. Parmar (1993). Warrior marks: Female genital mutilation and the sexual blinding of women. New York: Harcourt Brace.

Wane, N., K. Deliovsky, & E. Lawson (2002). Back to the drawing board: African Canadian feminisms. Toronto: Sumach Press.

Williams, C. (1993). We are a natural part of many different struggles: Black women organizing. In W. James and C. Harris (eds.), *Inside Babylon: The Caribbean diaspora in Britain*, pp. 153–164. London: Verso.

Wright, R. (1953). *Outsider*. New York: Harper and Row.

Chapter Five

WILLIAM H. WATKINS

A Marxian and Radical Reconstructionist Critique of American Education
SEARCHING OUT BLACK VOICES

Introduction: A Bumpy Ride

The Cold War was the most extensive and expensive ideological and educational campaign of the twentieth century. Supported by big government, big business, and other interests vested in state monopoly capitalism, this sponsored curriculum reached deep into the mass media, public education, religion, families, and community life. Costing billions of dollars, its objectives were to halt the spread of Communism and to intellectually discredit Marxian-Socialist thought. Though tarnished and bloodied, Marxism just won't go away. Perhaps it won't go away because the economic and political contradictions Karl Marx described exist to this very day.

Exploring any (Black) Marxian-Socialist critique of public education in the United States is indeed a complicated and tricky endeavor. First and foremost, there are many varieties of Marxism. Aside from myriad ideological differences, there are vast continental, regional, and national differences alongside modern and postmodern renditions. The confusion thickens if we attempt to situate Trotskyists, Maoists, and assorted others into a Marxist typology. Because of the monumental difficulty in offering precise, even consensual definitions, I have added the word "radical" to the discussion. Similiarly, the word radical can also be vague and ambiguous. In this work, I use radical to mean a notion of dissent and protest thought that is antiracist, anticapitalist, and broadly Socialistic, favoring the reorganization of society along the lines of collectivism. I don't wish to play "name and claim" games, but rather to broaden the boundaries of discourse and research on race and education. Beyond the never-ending task of defining Marxism, the additional problem of understanding and discerning Socialism, and its relationship to Marxism, is equally daunting; this is particularly true in terms of American Socialism, which has often been anti-Communist.

Linking Black folks to the Marxian-Socialist framework is at least another lifetime's worth of work for all the same problems of definition. Scholarly and biographical work on Black Marxism continues to appear. Books by Robin D.G. Kelley (2002, 1994, 1990); Earl Ofari Hutchinson (1995); Nelson Peery (1994); Mark Naison (1984); Gerald Horne (1986); Cedric Robinson (1983); Harry Haywood (1978); and Benjamin J. Davis (1969) have enriched our understanding of African Americans and Marxism in general; however, the Black Marxian critique of education remains underresearched.

Within the United States, the Marxian critique of education could be discerned in the early 1930s. It was preceded by the ideas of "progressive" education early in the twentieth century. The Social Reconstructionists, radical progressive educators (Cremin, 1961), require our attention, although perhaps they did not reach the standards of orthodox Marxian critique (Stanley, 1992; Watkins, 1990; & Bowers, 1969).

As a professor of education specializing in curriculum studies, I have found over the last twenty years that my students, undergraduate and graduate, have very little background and foundation to understand Marxism. Because the monopoly capitalist state wishes to conceal the role of property and wealth, Marxian philosophy and political criticism has been relegated to the null curriculum, the wasteland of "illegitimate" and irrelevant knowledge. It is rare that students in our public educational system are exposed to Marxist social science. Hence, I am compelled to provide some introduction to this important body of (educational) protest thought.

I take on several tasks in this endeavor. First, I hope to briefly overview fundamentals of Marxian-Socialist theory. Next, I will survey the central points of the Marxian critique of public education. Third, I want to review the Social Reconstructionist movement and the contributions of Dr. W.E.B. Du Bois within that radical dialogue. Then, drawing from the sparse literature, I point to a Black Marxian critique of education in America. Finally, I call for more research and investigation into this relevant and important area in the present era of school politics.

Understanding Classical Marxian Socialism

Building on the intellectual foundations of Hegel's dialectic, St. Simon's philosophical materialism, and classical British economics (Feuer, 1959), Karl Marx (1818–1883) produced a criticism of capitalism that shook the world at its foundations. In his dense magnum opus, *Das Kapital* (1867), Marx demonstrated that the extraction of surplus value (profits) from human labor enriched the owning classes (Heilbroner, 1986). His monumental writings confronted the prevailing social science of the time. These writings include *The Poverty of Philosophy* (1847); with Engels, *The German Ideology* (1845–6); with Engels, *The Communist Manifesto* (1848); and *A Contribution to the Critique of Political Economy* (1859). Alongside his benefactor and lifelong colleague Frederick Engels (1820–1895), Marx argued that politics was the concentrated expression of economics. All of human history was driven by issues of property, wealth, and power. The propertied and the propertyless were locked in an irreconcilable struggle, in which those who worked the means of production would eventually control them. Social revolution was inevitable, and a new world would be constructed upon the ashes of the old.

Marx never saw his vision take shape. The Russian revolutionary Vladimir Ilyich Ulianov (1870–1924), better known as Lenin, emerged as the preeminent Marxist of the early twentieth century. His book *What Is to Be Done?* (1902), charted the seizure of power by the working class and peasantry. Another of his major works, *Imperialism: The Highest Stage of Capitalism* (1917), offered a treatise on modern colonialism. Here he argued that laissez-faire capitalism turned into its opposite, monopoly capitalism, and had expanded internationally where powerful nations now subjugated weaker countries. In that work he also noted the growing importance of banks and finance capital. In *State and Revolution* (1918), he examined the power dynamics of the modern nation-state and offered a general blueprint for insurrection. Conventional Marxists view Leninist theorizing as the expansion of Marxism in the early twentieth century.

Although unknown to many, Marx wrote on the political economy of Black labor in the United States. For example, in *The Poverty of Philosophy* (1847), he wrote:

> Direct slavery is just as much the pivot of bourgeois industry as machinery, credits, etc. Without slavery you have no cotton; without cotton you have no modern industry. It is slavery that has given the colonies their value; it is the colonies that have created world trade, and it is world trade that is the pre-condition of large-scale industry. Thus slavery is an economic category of the greatest importance. (pp. 356–7)

At the turn of the twentieth century, barely a handful of educated and literate African Americans, Dr. Du Bois among them, participated in limited discussions of Marxist theory.

The ABCs of Marxism

The one-hundred-year attack by Western social science, narrow nationalism, and right-wing conservatism has obfuscated and distorted rudimentary and classical Marxist theory. A brief summarization of several fundamental principles of Marxism-Leninism follows.

First, *historical materialism* describes the "laws" of history and socioeconomic formation. It suggests that there has been a historic progression from primitive communalism, the earliest human community, to primitive slavery, to feudalism, and to capitalism. It asserts that capitalism is but a stage of history, not humankind's permanent economic system; and that the propertyless will eventually seize the instruments of production and force the creation of a state organized around public property. Socialism is viewed as a historical inevitability. Human agency, especially the role of oppressed socioeconomic classes, is seen as the conscious and driving force in this process.

Second, *materialist dialectics* disputes the idealistic conceptions of cause and effect. Dialectics speaks of the universality of contradiction. It is a system of philosophic thought that views the unity and struggle of opposites as central to the processes of motion. It seeks out connectedness in phenomena. It builds upon the formula of thesis-antithesis-synthesis. Dialectics allows one to observe phenomena in their oppositionist aspects. It sees both universality and particularity of contradiction in phenomena. Dialectical analysis sees negation of phenomena and the subsequent negation of the negation. It also examines the processes whereby quantitative changes become qualitative changes. Dialectics posits that the objective contradictions within capitalism, thesis and antithesis, will lead to its negation and lead to a new social order, Socialism.

Marxian *political economy* attempts to explain capitalist economic and sociopolitical relationships. Based on Marx's *Das Kapital* (1867), *A Contribution to the Critique of Political Economy* (1859), and *Theories of Surplus Value* (1863), an attempt is made to explore the mechanics of commodity production, capitalist exploitation, surplus value, rent, primitive accumulation, monopoly, the reserve force of labor, wages, crises, overproduction, reproduction of labor, and the law of value. The focus is on the role of private property. A central thesis of Marxist political economy holds that the owners of industry, and the means of production, gain profit from the expropriated labor of their workers. Unpaid labor, or surplus value, is the basis of capital accumulation for the owners, and the motion toward impoverishment of the workers. The capitalist system experiences both cyclical and general crises. Cyclical crises are represented by frequent recessions and economic downturns. The general crisis is the historical demise of exploitation of man by man.

The theory of *imperialism*, contributed by Lenin, asserts that capitalism has reached its highest and final stage, that is, the development of international domination by monopolies. The monopolies have destroyed laissez-faire and competitive capitalism in favor of huge combines, interlocking directorates, cartels, trusts, and multinational corporations. In the process, finance capital has superceded industrial capital in a world where banks and finance shape economics. Imperialism suggests the concentration of wealth into the hands of a very few, the impoverishment of subject peoples and nations, uneven economic development, world power blocks, globalization, wild speculation, large-scale crises, and the necessity of militarism, war, and reaction. The central notion of imperialism is that it exists when capitalism reaches its final state of development.

The theory of classes and *class struggle* holds that, under capitalism, society is inextricably divided into socioeconomic classes. The bourgeois class owns the means of production, and is the organizer of the social and political processes. The working classes either work the means of production, or are held in reserve. Finally, the middle classes occupy managerial or small-scale entrepreneurial positions that are tenuous, as they are driven into the ranks below. The classes are thus locked into a mutually antagonistic struggle to control the means of production, and the accompanying state power. The theory holds that those who work the means of production will ultimately seize them in the name of all the toilers.

Marxism asserts a theory of *base and superstructure*, as articulated by Russian theorist Konstantinov (published 1955). This notion holds that the economic relations of production will shape, and provide context for, society's institutions. Hence, capitalist relationships and ideology dominate the social and ideological culture. While resistance is inevitable, the dominant ideas of any society are the ideas of its ruling class. Institutions reflect and reproduce dominant, that is, capitalist ideas. Schools would thus fall into the category of "reproductionist" institutions.

Next is the concept of the *state*. Marxists, neo-Marxists, and a variety of reformers have long argued about the nature and definition of the state. Many view the state as a mediator of societal differences. Classical Marxists view the state as a body of control, which combines both force and ideology. Hence, the state includes the army, police, courts, and jails. The ruling class, however, would prefer to operate peacefully. The recourse to force and coercion is maintained in reserve. The state ultimately changes hands, and is controlled by the economic class in power. The state is inextricably linked to the existence of classes. The state is essentially an instrument of domination, wherein the government serves the ruling class.

The end of the Cold War witnessed a furious intellectual attack against Marxism. Previous sympathizers and advocates raged against what they now viewed as dogmatic, doctrinaire, and outdated. It is far beyond the scope of this essay to fully discuss the critique of Marxism; however, a fundamental and recurring critique of Marxism is that it ignores human agency. Well-meaning interpreters of Marx insist the theory is mechanistic, top down, and deterministic. They argue that Marx didn't understand race, culture, oppositionism, and resistance from the bottom.

Marx and the Marxists: On Education

Approaching the Marxian analytical framework on schooling, several propositions are salient. First is the organization of society into irreconcilably antagonistic socioeconomic classes. Marxian outlooks assert that there is no compromise between the propertied and the propertyless. There is a life and death battle to be fought out in history and politics. Private ownership of property allows the ruling elite to order society and its institutions in favor of capital.

Mass public education, as we know it, didn't exist during Marx's lifetime. Hence, he did not write extensively nor did he directly address state schooling; however, his sketchy writings offered kernels of thinking for future theorists to embellish. Today's Marxian discourse explores the role of schools both in contemporary society and in social transformation. One widely embraced argument holds that schools are sites of ideological contestation and opposition, and hence, offer significant potential in social change and reform. Marx's focus on the relations of production led him to the industrial workers as the instrument of social transformation; therefore schools, as agents of the state, could not play a vital role (Liston, 1988).

Brosio (1994) offers a comprehensive description of Marx's views on the system of education:

> Marx did not write systematically about education but took the need for universal schooling seriously. He knew that the kind of education that he favored could not occur in a class-stratified society under capitalist aegis; however, he did promote certain kinds of reforms that could be said to represent the democratic imperative on schooling for his place and time. (p. 456)

Further:

> Marx proposed that education for the young consists of three closely related aspects: intellectual education, physical training or gymnastics and polytechnical training, by

which he meant instruction in the scientific principles underlying all production processes, together with instruction in the use of the tools of production. Marx realized that not only was schooling in the capitalist West for the most part a tool of the dominant class, but in addition it was and is the product of the classical philosophical dualism that separated mental and muscle, idea and action. (pp. 456–7)

With that ideological skeleton, the role of school in the modern capitalist state is at the heart of the dialogue of contemporary Marxist criticism. Beyond the widely discussed issues of equity, racial and gender discrimination, and social justice, more penetrating Marxian analysis explores and questions several relevant sub-issues related to education. Among them: education and the state, intelligence and testing, knowledge production, knowledge distribution, knowledge neutrality, and reproduction/correspondence.

For some time, theorists have been vexed by the inherent difficulty of framing a Marxian analysis and critique of public education in the United States. Many have chosen to utilize interpretations and interpreters of Marx for their analysis. Others, such as Strike (1989), have chosen to look directly to the writings of Marx. Although Marx could not have understood or foreseen how public education unfolded in twentieth-century America, he nevertheless offered relevant insights on capitalism and social motion, upon which we can construct analysis and exploration.

The Nature of the State

Defining the role of the state in an advanced capitalist society is at the heart of public and social theory. Conventional U.S. political theory suggests the political state is a mediating force that advances democracy, settles disputes, and balances countervailing forces. The state is presumed to be the arbiter of divergent interests, providing oversight and defending the greater good.

Marxists, on the other hand, don't see the state as neutral. As mentioned earlier, they see the state and its apparatus as under the control of the economic and hegemonic elite. The capitalist state protects the capitalists. It is concluded that education, as a state function, is charged with the ideological protection of the capitalist system. Ideas that do not conform to that objective are then either rejected or ignored.

Intelligence and Testing

Intelligence came to be a defining rationale for the social order in the early twentieth century (Gonzalez, 1982). Those in possession of knowledge were seen as more fit to manage the social order. Intelligence replaced work as the essence of human capital. The organization and leadership of society was to be placed in the hands of the intelligent. Intelligence came to be associated with leadership, property ownership, and worth.

I.Q. testing emerged as the "scientific" way of discerning intelligence. More importantly, I.Q. tests provided the "proof" of human difference. Difference emerged as the central organizing rationale of capitalism, and its system of public education in the United States, for all modernity. All could not, and would not, learn and achieve in the same way. Famed psychologist Edward Thorndike's book *Individuality* (1911) signaled the concretization of "differential psychology" (Clifford, 1968), which was built upon hereditarianism. This body of thought served as justification for why some children would achieve, and others would not. Thorndike wrote:

> The mental capacities of human beings at birth, or at conception, vary widely, probably as widely as their capacities to become tall or strong. Their original propensities or proclivities, or emotional and temperamental tendencies vary, and perhaps as widely as their facial contours or finger-prints. (cited in Clifford, 1968 pp. 314–5)

Thorndike became an adamant supporter of testing and measuring intelligence. His views were widely supported by American eugenicists, racists, and Aryan theorists. Harvard psychologist Hugo Musterberg effectively articulated the hereditarian-difference implication for education:

> We have brought the work of education under one formula. This is not meant to indicate that education should be uniform. Everybody ought to be made willing and able to realize ideal values, but everybody is called to do it in his own way. The child who comes from the slums, the child who never saw a green meadow, and the child who never saw a paved street, cannot be educated after a uniform pattern. The education of the boy cannot be the education of the girl, the education of the intelligent child must differ from that of the slow-minded child. . . . Yet still more important are the differences between the individual tasks which the life after school will put before the individuals. To make the child willing and able to realize ideal values, means also to secure the subtlest adjustment to these later differences. The laborer and the farmer, the banker and the doctor all must help in building up the realm of values. But they are equally prepared for it only if they are prepared for it in very different ways. (Cited in Gonzalez, 1982, p. 142)

Knowledge Production

Herbert Spencer (1861) raised the eternal question, "What knowledge is of most worth?" Marxian-oriented theorists have deepened that question. Apple (1979, 1983) helped formulate new questions for our consideration: Who produces knowledge in the stratified state? How is knowledge supported? What knowledge finds its way into acceptance? What ideas get into the classroom? Others, for example, Watkins (2001), Anderson (1980), and Arnove (1980), have explored how ideas and school-knowledge are funded by corporate philanthropic foundations.

Marxist-oriented thinkers are concerned about the privatization of knowledge. More specifically, how does knowledge support the capitalist values of individualism, competition, and the ideals of Western civilization? Price (1986) wrote:

> At the same time the countries of late capitalism are saturated with ideologies celebrating individualism and competition. Commodity production has extended into almost every aspect of society, However independent of the institutions of capitalism a producer of knowledge may be the pressure to produce in the commodity form is intense.
>
> Let us look next, in outline, at the institutions within which the production of knowledge may take place. Private capitalist firms employ large numbers of people in research and development, both directly and on a consultancy basis. Others are employed by the state. They may be employed directly in research institutions, in the universities and other colleges in the tertiary education sector, or they may work for national broadcasting organizations, or government "think tanks." The judiciary must not be forgotten in its role of knowledge creation, even if that is only a small part of its duties. (p. 60)

The management and production of knowledge have become a central focus of foundation life. Major foundations such as Ford, Rockefeller, Carnegie, Heritage, Sage, and many others, contain or support social-science institutes, which help to legitimize knowledge for mass distribution. These huge agencies, which operate without democratic deliberation, have become the brokers of ideas. Their influence reaches to textbook publishing, the print and electronic media, and ultimately to the very heart of our political culture.

Knowledge can serve as a regulator. It creates boundaries for discourse and understanding. Knowledge can either open up our world or close it down. Marxists are concerned that school-knowledge in the capitalist state restrains and restricts the re-creation of experiences, and our explanations of phenomenon. As an example, Marxists ask if poverty, unemployment, and war are explained as state policy, or simply as the uncontrollable natural unfolding of social life? The former explanation opens the door to more investigation, while the latter suggests such occurrences exist outside the will of human control.

The Distribution of Knowledge

Who knows what? Who learns what? How does knowledge circulate to people of different social classes, economic groups, racial groups, and gender groups? Do all students get the same exposure and impact from the school curriculum? These are but a few of the questions Marxists have raised in this area.

Marxists believe that knowledge is power. Marx argued that ideas, when gripped by the masses, become a material force. Thus, concepts such as the constitutional right to a job, the constitutional right to a home, state-sponsored university education, state-funded medical care for all, and state-owned utility companies, have galvanized people around the world; not simply because they relieve suffering and misery, but because they offer dreams, promises, and alternatives of a better life. Ideas contribute to the politics of possibility.

Marxists recognize the different types of knowledge imparted in both schools and the larger society. For the sake of simplicity, we may collapse two of the main categories into technical-scientific and sociopolitical. It has been argued that both of these categories of knowledge are unevenly distributed to varying economic, racial, and gender groups. Gutstein (2003) and Small (2001) have argued that math, for example, serves as a political gatekeeper, creating a major divide where the successful move onward and upward while the working classes and people of color are relegated to the ranks of low achievement.

Anyon's often-cited study (1981) offers a powerful argument about the distribution of sociopolitical knowledge in textbooks. Surveying widely used textbooks, she found few that were critical of social-class stratification, or of the uneven distribution of wealth. Moreover, she posited that school conceals or misrepresents socially and politically significant inequities of wealth and power. She concluded that despite claims to neutrality, the official school curriculum is ideologically biased.

Price (1986) suggests that three factors employed by the capitalist class impede the equitable distribution of knowledge: secrecy, censorship, and copyright. He cites Marx, who, in *A Contribution to the Critique of Hegel's Philosophy of Law* (1843) wrote: "the general spirit of the bureaucracy is the secret, the mystery, preserved within itself by the hierarchy and against the outside world" (p. 86).

Thus the bureaucracy of the political state creates official secrecy to protect the vested interests of those in power. Censorship may involve the official or unofficial recognition of knowledge. In schools, for example, labor studies and peace studies are rarely provided. Finally, the copyright commodifies ideas. It situates ideas as personal property requiring permission to share. All three of these barriers obstruct the free access to information.

Knowledge Neutrality

Socially consensual knowledge, especially school-knowledge, possesses the aura of eternal truth; that is why is it so accepted. The British sociology of education and curriculum school of thought initiated radical and Marxian-oriented thinking in this area. Michael F.D. Young, in his groundbreaking work, *Knowledge and Control* (1971), grappled with the idea of the social construction of knowledge. Young directs us to examine who controls the curriculum, from the state and publishers on down to the classroom teachers.

Arnove (1980) also helps us understand that acceptable social and political knowledge reflects the ideological interests of those in power. He wrote:

> Carnegie, Rockefeller, and Ford have a corrosive influence on a democratic society; they represent relatively unregulated and unaccountable concentrations of power and wealth which buy talent, promote causes, and in effect, establish an agenda of what merits society's attention. They serve as "cooling-out" agencies, delaying and preventing more radical, structural change. They help maintain an economic and political order, international in scope, which benefits the ruling-class interests of philanthropists and philanthropoids—a system which, as the various chapters document, has worked against the interests of minorities, the working class, and Third World peoples. (p. 1)

Reproduction and Correspondence Theory

Bowles and Gintis's *Schooling in Capitalist America* (1976) provided an invitation to explore how schools were intertwined with the hegemony of the ruling class. They argued that schools reproduced the capitalist economy by mechanically turning out new workers and new owners. They further argued that the social relations in school corresponded to the economic and social relationships of the larger capitalist society. School therefore was not a neutral agency forging democracy, but rather central to the schemes of labor exploitation and oppression. This happens through the development of assorted skills, the creation of human capital, and the cultivation of attitudes that prepare the student for the relationships of work. They describe the process of developing the consciousness for work.

Bowles and Gintis see production and the culture of production as an important developmental idea. Students must be readied for the social division of labor, stratified interpersonal relationships, and authoritarian hierarchy. They argue further that schools cultivate the myth of equal opportunity and access; but in reality, social status in life is tied more to other factors, such as hereditary wealth, than it is to school achievement. School does little to alter that arrangement. Quite the contrary, school reproduces it.

Their notion of correspondence holds that schools integrate students into the economic system by providing parallels for corresponding social relations. They write of the "personal demeanor," "modes of self-preservation," self-image," and "social class identifications" required by a stratified capitalist society, which are provided by schooling. Schools train people in the acceptable social relationships, say Bowles and Gintis. Schools train good employees.

Marxian Critique of State Education in the United States: An Overview

In general, Marxists believe that schools have an ideological purpose. Their job is to promote individualism, competition, worker loyalty, patriotism, and the support of Western civilization.

De Tocqueville-styled (1838/2000) classlessness, a pillar of Western social science, is aggressively promoted in American education. In this case, classlessness holds that America is not burdened with the rigid class stratification of other advanced industrial countries. Property ownership, governance, and opportunity are presumably accessible to all. The school curriculum cloaks the adversarial relations of production; instead suggesting that business and labor are equal partners. The partnership argument camouflages economic exploitation and the powerlessness of labor.

Secondly, schools support the legitimacy of inequities in wealth and status. Difference is part of the natural order. Gonzalez's (1982) harsh, summative Marxist critique of American education compels our attention:

> Education has a political task to accomplish, and in accomplishing it, it creates social problems manifested as dropouts, disinterest in formal learning, low reading and writing skills—all due to low self-esteem and negative self-concepts generated by educational techniques which emphasize individualism and inequality through tracking and curriculum differentiation according to levels of "intelligence" or "aptitude." Perhaps the most conspicuous aspect of education in the U.S. is not the high dropout rate or the functional illiteracy but the serious psychological damage perpetuated through teaching. Schools generally fail to develop confidence and motivation in students, because schools are responsible for developing a quiescent majority, politically manageable, if not apolitical. Elitism is fostered and this constantly divides students into the "thinkers" and "workers". . . .
>
> Antidemocracy in the schools is a necessary political device to resolve the class struggle. . . . Patterns of cultural discrimination, English as the "official" and exclusive language, and the denial of the nationalities' histories are but a few of the manifestations of antidemocracy. (p. 148)

The Marxian critique is accompanied by resistance and opposition to schools. At one level, theorists, intellectuals, and school teachers themselves have offered dissent. The Social Reconstructionist Movement was one example that combined these groups. Additionally, people of color, the working classes, and other alienated groups have provided more than a century of protest. The next section examines this spirited, sometimes confrontational, protest.

The Social Reconstructionist Movement

Origins

The Social Reconstructionist Movement of the 1930s was among the largest radical dissenting educational movements in the twentieth century. By the turn of the twentieth century, a new criticism was emerging in America's social-science community. Concern was being expressed about the inequities and impersonal nature of the then emergent corporate-industrial organization of society. Thorstein Veblen's *Theory of the Leisure Class* (1899), along with essays by muckraking journalists, dramatized social and economic problems in the midst of plenty. The emerging Progressive Movement, with its themes of democracy, humanism, and social reform, profoundly affected the educational community.

While progressive education made its influence felt in the post–World War I period, the Progressive Education Association (PEA) was never a strong centralized organization. It had no single voice (Bowers, 1969) and was always smaller than the National Education Association (NEA). By the mid 1930s, the intellectual climate of the country took a noticeable turn to the left, as the social criticism of the early 1900s expanded. A significant section of the intelligentsia and the politically conscious populace began to question the moral worth of the capitalist system; insisting that human rights take priority over property rights. The educational community was compelled to join this discourse.

A discernibly dissident group began to make their voices heard within the PEA. One rallying point for this group was the report of the Commission on the Social Studies within the American Historical Association (AHA). The report, funded by the Carnegie Foundation, was presented in seventeen volumes between the years 1932 and 1937. Among those who contributed to the project were well-known educators and social theorists like Charles A. Beard, Merle Curti, George S. Counts, and Jesse Newlon.

The year 1932 became eventful for this dissident group, which became known as Social Reconstructionists or Social Frontiersmen. While the PEA remained committed to child-centered education, the Reconstructionists wanted more of progressivism than the exaltation of the child. They wanted education to feature a "social point of view," that is, a descriptive and prescriptive examination of social problems.

When George S. Counts of the University of Chicago delivered his disturbing lecture "Dare Progressive Education Be Progressive?" to the PEA in April 1932, the new movement took on identity. Counts criticized the Progressive Education Movement as one of middle-class dilettantes. He stated:

The great weakness of Progressive Education lies in the fact that it has elaborated no theory of social welfare, unless it be that of anarchy or extreme individualism. In this, of course, it is but reflecting the viewpoint of the members of the liberal-minded upper middle class. (Counts, 1932a, p. 258)

Further in this lecture, which was greeted by a stunned silence that sent shockwaves through the Progressive education community, he suggested that these Progressives were romantic sentimentalists and not interested in addressing the economic and social crises. He called on Progressive educators to

face squarely and courageously every social issue, come to grips with life in all of its stark reality, establish an organic relation with the community, develop a realistic and comprehensive theory of welfare, fashion a compelling and challenging vision of human destiny, and become somewhat less frightened than it is today at the bogeys of imposition and indoctrination. (p. 259)

Counts continued to speak about how our competitive capitalist society "must be replaced by cooperation" and "some form of socialized economy." This blockbuster lecture, along with two others, "Freedom, Culture, Social Planning, and Leadership" and "Education Through Indoctrination," were issued in what R. Freeman Butts (1978, p. 385) called "perhaps the most widely discussed pamphlet in the history of American education, *Dare the School Build a New Social Order?*" (Counts, 1932). In this work, which became the blueprint for Social Reconstructionism, Counts challenged the educational community to bridge the gap between school and society; where schools should create a vision of a new world based on the principles of collectivism.

The works of Counts in 1932, combined with the publication of the Commission on the Social Studies in the Schools' *A Charter for the Social Sciences in the Schools* (1932), drafted by Charles A. Beard, served as a unifying framework to bring together such individuals as William Heard Kilpatrick, John L. Childs, R. Bruce Raup, and Harold Rugg. Additionally, other well-known progressives like John Dewey and Boyd H. Bode were attracted to the call of the Reconstructionists.

Social Reconstructionism: An Educational and Political Program

While the dissident Social Reconstructionists remained within the PEA and enjoyed a measure of support, it became clear that they had a different focus. In an effort to respond to the insurgents, particularly Counts, the PEA in 1932 established the Committee on Social and Economic Problems. This committee simultaneously served to rally the Reconstructionists and further split the ranks of the PEA. Between 1932 and 1934 the Reconstructionist position became more clearly defined and more radical. Two more books joined the essays of Counts to advance their cause. *A Call to the Teachers of the Nation* (1933) written by the PEA's Committee on Social and Economic Problems, summoned teachers to act, while *The Educational Frontier* (1933), edited and partially written by the respected William Heard Kilpatrick (1932), called for the politicization of education. The Social Reconstructionists now had their own identity.

As the Reconstructionists more forcefully asserted their position, the larger sentiment within the PEA reasserted itself. Though still not tightly administered, the PEA focused its commitment and its journal, *Progressive Education*, on child-centered classroom techniques. The Reconstructionists, experiencing increased difficulties getting published (Bowers, 1969), founded their own journal, *The Social Frontier*, which first appeared in October 1934. Now they could continue to develop their distinctive position. The "hard core" of the Reconstructionists, that is, Sidney Hook, Counts, Harold Rugg, Jesse Newlon, Goodwin Watson, and John Childs, best articulated their view. Three sociopolitical and educational propositions formed the foundation of Social Reconstructionism.

First, there was the advocacy of a "collectivist" society. The evil capitalist system was seen as the source of human misery, unemployment, and divisiveness. Capitalism was to be replaced by "economic collectivism." Though Hook was a Marxist, and Counts spoke of his serious study of Karl Marx, the beliefs and language of the Reconstructionists seldom suggested "proletarian" revolution as Marx had called for. The Reconstructionists instead spoke of evolutionary change. They, in fact, suggested that, given New Deal politics and the intellectual climate, the country had already evolved into an era of economic collectivism. For them, a benevolent and democratic Socialist collectivism represented desirable social development. A redistribution of the wealth and resources would allow public morality and cooperation to reshape society.

Second, the Reconstructionists called for linking education with (collectivist) political ideology. The attainment of a truly progressive society required an expanded role for education. Treating children humanistically was fine, but education must take on a major role in the plan to transform society. Education must be utilized to transform social institutions. Education should be viewed as a form of social action. Schools must take an active role in determining the new social order.

Third, schools should participate in reshaping society to realize the true mission of education. Kilpatrick argued that the worn socioeconomic system was making it difficult for schools to produce worthy citizens. Schools should foster a broader social responsibility and work for the common good. By helping to transform laissez-faire capitalism, education could help make society more humane. Education should be at the cutting edge of civilization. In short, the process of schooling should be inextricably linked to social progress.

Remaking the Curriculum

If education was going to significantly contribute to social change, schools must necessarily adopt a curriculum sufficiently critical of the old social order, while becoming supportive of the new collectivism. The Social Reconstructionists called on the curriculum community to support wholesale change in curriculum materials, activities, and outlooks.

A leading curriculum theoretician among the Reconstructionists was Professor Harold Rugg of Teachers College, Columbia University. Long committed to change, Rugg in *The Scientific Method in the Reconstruction of Elementary and Secondary School Subjects* (1921), argued for a curriculum that would combine critical sociopolitical inquiry with the life experience of the learner. Above all, Rugg wanted to guarantee that any new curriculum was pedagogically sound. In the early 1920s Rugg began to publish his own social studies pamphlets. In his series, published by Ginn, entitled "Man and His Changing Society," Rugg offered a comprehensive social science curriculum based on democratic and humanistic values.

In the October 1936 (Vol. III, No. 19) issue of *The Social Frontier*, Rugg challenged "commissioners, presidents, deans, superintendents, principals, supervisors, teachers . . . to stir the mass into action!" (p. 15). Rugg went on to blast "professional Directors of Curriculum and a powerful behind-the-scenes body of textbook writers and publishers who have controlled the program of American education . . . primarily in the interest of the status quo."

In his blueprint for a new curriculum, Rugg suggests that schools focus on the "social scene," a "new psychology," and a "syllabi of activities and materials directly out of the crucial conditions, problems and issues of our changing social order." He goes on to advocate confronting controversial issues, exploring alternative decision making, and teaching the basic issues of civilization in the classrooms.

The End of an Era

As the war years approached, radicalism gave way to patriotism. The fascist menace was so threatening it became the priority for conservatives and Socialists alike. The resignation of Counts from *The Social Frontier*'s editorial board in 1937 signaled the end of this energetic yet short-lived movement.

As the Reconstructionists began to lose momentum, the newly formed John Dewey Society began to attract many of the old forces and actually absorbed *The Social Frontier*. During the war years a few halfhearted efforts were undertaken, particularly by Rugg, to rekindle the old vigor, but without much success. By the mid 1950s even the PEA was in mortal decline.

It can be concluded that the Social Reconstruction Movement was very much a product of its time. While it attracted the attention of significant educational and curriculum thinkers, it never became the hoped-for mass movement of teachers. Though short lived, this body of thought left its indelible imprint on educational theorizing and curriculum reform.

Since World War II, scattered efforts, such as the work of Theodore Brameld (1956), the Society for Educational Reconstruction, and that of other individuals, have kept this once lively movement in our consciousness. Addressing issues of race and class, the Social Reconstructionists unleashed a qualitatively new critique of American public education. It can be argued that Dr. W.E.B. Du Bois was a Social Reconstructionist.

W.E.B. Du Bois: Radical Socialist Educator

Traditional curriculum scholarship has for too long overlooked the historical evolution of the "radical" Black pedagogy. Any cursory overview of the traditional scholarship reveals that historiographers and curriculum theorists alike have failed to explore the foundations of this body of thought. More importantly, critical Black pedagogy has often been viewed narrowly as protest thought. While there can be no doubt that the policies and practices of racialism have shaped Black intellectual life, there remains a body of inquiry that needs further examination.

Black and White pedagogy have been as disconnected as Black and White history. Typically the White radical intelligentsia is seen to have been concerned with sweeping economic, political, and social change, while the mostly overlooked Black radical thinkers are associated exclusively with Black liberation. Without question, there is a Black radical tradition within the education dialogue. W.E.B. Du Bois is a pioneer in that movement.

Though known in academia since the turn of the twentieth century, Du Bois has rarely been considered a force in the curriculum dialogue. While he lived through, and was influenced by, sweeping social transformations such as the Progressive Movement and the radicalism of the 1930s, seldom is his contribution included as a factor in the discourse of his day. We have not yet come to fully appreciate or understand the work of this man who was so passionately concerned with the aims of education (Provenzo, 2002).

If we proclaim Du Bois as the father of radical Black pedagogy, it can be said that his is an outgrowth of late-nineteenth-century sociological inquiry.

Early on, pioneer Black scholars such as George Washington Williams and T.T. Fortune examined the conditions of Blacks in the reconstructed South. Du Bois, already committed to activism and social change, linked social criticism to the emerging examination of Black life. Armed with an education from Fisk, Harvard, and the University of Berlin, Du Bois was well prepared to take his place as a social theorist, social critic, and radical educator.

Having visited the Soviet Union in 1926, and again in 1936, Du Bois began to reexamine his views on Marxism. With the Russian solution looking more and more attractive to many in the United States, Du Bois wanted to consider the possibility of class struggle aimed at social justice, racial equity, and international cooperation. Marable (1986) says of Du Bois in the 1930s:

> . . . Du Bois began to make a serious study of Marx's writings and moved further left. In May 1933, he observed that Marx was a "colossal genius of infinite sacrifice and monumental industry, and with a mind of extraordinary logical keenness and grasp." Marxism had a direct bearing on the liberation of Afro-Americans. Du Bois noted that "the shrill cry" of American Communists was not "listened to," but he believed that some form of "modified" Marxism philosophy did have relevance to the United States. "In the hearts of black laborers," Du Bois wrote, "lie those ideals of democracy in politics and industry which may in time make the workers of the world effective dictators of civilization." In the summer of 1933, he taught a course, "Karl Marx and the Negro," at Atlanta University. (p. 137)

The educational views of Du Bois should be examined within the context of his time in order to understand their true impact.

The Progressives advanced a new examination and critique of the dynamics of schooling. They began to look at school as a social and political construct. The more radical Progressives began to explain schooling in terms of power and ideology. They viewed schools as linked to dominant political and economic ideologies, that is, the corporate state and its narrow objectives. It was at this chronological and political juncture that the interests of Du Bois overlapped with those of the Progressive educational community in general, and the Social Reconstructionists in particular.

Du Bois and Social Reconstructionism: Common Origins, Common Views

Though the Social Reconstructionists never claimed Du Bois, nor did he claim them, they were undeniably linked by virtue of their history, pedagogy, and views on the nature of society, Socialism, and reform. While segregation dominated our sociopolitical processes, racial politics also influenced radical social theory.

The Communist Party of the 1930s actively worked for Negro equality and the militant organizing of Black sharecroppers in the South, and unskilled Black labor in the North. At the same time, non-Communist, and often anti-Communist, radical leftists recognized the struggles of Blacks, but did not support that position in deeds.

Progressivism represented the common historical thread between Du Bois and the Reconstructionists. The Democratic-Socialist views of the left wing of the Progressive Movement were consistent with Du Bois's views between 1910 and 1930. A collectivist economic order, without revolution, is what Du Bois had long advocated. Consistently supporting and being supported by such progressives as Walter Lippmann, Jane Addams, and many others, Du Bois was comfortable with this company. Additionally, he was an unyielding supporter of educational reform, the suffrage movement, and trade unionism, all of which were progressive platform issues. Marable (1986) says of Du Bois's association with progressivism:

> He sought to advance theoretical concepts on the meaning of each movement to the reconstruction of American democracy. But as a Negro, Du Bois was always aware of the veil of color that inhibited many white radicals from pursuing creative reform strategies challenging racial inequality. He believed that the central contradiction in democratic society was the barrier of racism, and that if left unchallenged, racial prejudice would compromise the goals of social reformers. (p. 84)

Du Bois: A Pedagogy for Social Reconstruction

Because of Du Bois's intense concern with questions of race and class, his views on education are often overshadowed. It will be argued that Du Bois's views on the purposes of education coincide with those of George S. Counts, Harold Rugg, Sidney Hook, Theodore Brameld, and others associated with the heyday of Social Reconstructionism during the 1930s.

While Du Bois wrote widely on character training and Black college issues, the Reconstructionists did not. In the remaining areas, education for social change and the aims of education, the views of Du Bois are almost indistinguishable from those of Rugg and Counts and other Reconstructionists during the early 1930s.

In regard to the purposes of education, Du Bois becomes the consummate Social Reconstructionist. Beyond cognitive development, the Reconstructionists saw a special role for schooling. That role was to assist the evolution of a new enlightenment and even a new social order. By virtue of their positioning in society, confrontation with ideas, dynamic nature, and the perceived leadership role of teachers, schools were to be viewed as having revolutionary possibilities.

Du Bois consistently upheld the notion that schooling was both personally and socially emancipatory. He noted that education should "give to our youth a training designed above all to make them men of power." Du Bois often said that education must prepare one to do the "world's work." What was the world's work? Du Bois (in Aptheker, 1973) answers thus:

> The world compels us today as never before to examine and re-examine the problem of democracy. In theory we know it by heart: all men are equal and should have equal voice in their own government. This dictum has been vigorously attacked. All men are not equal. Ignorance cannot speak logically or clearly even when given voice. If sloth, dullness and mediocrity hold power, civilization is diluted and lowered, and government approaches anarchy. The mob cannot rule itself and will not choose the wise and able and give them the power to rule. (p. 118)

Education, for Du Bois, becomes social capital, which can be utilized to influence society. In an eloquent summary of his views on the power of education, Du Bois (in Aptheker, 1973) noted:

> We are going to force ourselves in by organized far-seeing effort—by outthinking and outflanking the owners of the world today who are too drunk with their own arrogance and power successfully to oppose us. (p. 77)

Du Bois and Democratic Socialism

Ultimately, the Social Reconstructivist aspect of Du Bois rests with his political and social philosophy. Like his radical counterparts in the 1930s, Du Bois advocated a (collectivist) democratic-Socialist organization of society's wealth, resources, and knowledge. He argued in 1942 (in Weinberg, 1970):

> In the period between 1860 and 1914, capitalism had come to its highest development in the European world, and its development meant the control of economic life and with that the domination of political life by the great aggregation of capital. It became, therefore, increasingly clear, as Karl Marx emphasized at the beginning of the era, that there could be no real democracy unless there was greater economic equality. (p. 196)

Du Bois, the Socialist, looked for a vehicle for social reform. He, like many others, concluded that the dynamic nature of ideas and ideology could prompt change. For Du Bois, there was an undying belief that ideas, when adopted by people, became a force in the real world. It is that belief that, in the search for change, continues to point reformers and radicals to the schools.

Other Black Voices

While data is scarce and the scholarship is limited, there exists a Black Marxian and neo-Marxian radical critique of American public education beyond that of

Du Bois. Scattered writings in *The Social Frontier*, the ongoing activities of Harlem activists, and the widely known "local control" movement in New York during the late 1960s provide examples for consideration.

Social Frontiersman

The previously discussed Social Reconstructionists published their own journal. Initially called *The Social Frontier*, the name changed in October 1939 to *Frontiers of Democracy*. The April 15, 1940, issue was dedicated to the race question. Articles by well-known scholars such as Margaret Mead, William Heard Kilpatrick, and Eugene L. Horowitz bemoaned the social inequality of the races, and attempted to excavate the social roots of prejudice. Black philosopher Alain Locke offered a contribution entitled "With Science as His Shield: The Educator Must Bridge Our 'Great Divides.'" Beyond the standard denunciation of segregation, Locke explored possibilities for the curriculum. He called for intercultural studies; arguing that students needed a broader social science and social studies ideology that would support tolerance, democracy, and humanity. He wrote:

> Presumably there would be a more humane and tolerant sense of solidarity in a society permeated with such social intelligence and less need and demand for the intolerant and chauvinistic varieties of patriotism and other group loyalties. The school, after all, cannot alone create democracy or be primarily responsible for it. (p. 210)

The Frontiersmen had a wide but short-lived audience. Their larger work suggests interest in the "Negro question" and specifically the education of Blacks. Theirs was a radical voice that attempted to connect with the Black radical voice of the time. Beyond intellectual work, the militant Black critique of public education was heard in the community.

Harlem: Hotbed of Education Dissent

Two groups exemplified the Black radical protest of public education in Harlem during the 1930s: the Harlem Committee for Better Schools and the Teacher's Union (TU). The Committee for Better Schools was a mass organization that included parents, teachers, churches, and community reformers. Indignant about Harlem's neglected and deteriorating schools, these activists recruited and attracted Black teachers and radicals. Allied with the Teachers Union, they worked for the physical improvements of schools, free lunches, and better working conditions for teachers (Naison, 1984).

An incident in 1936 where a burly White school principal physically attacked a fourteen-year-old black schoolboy sparked community action. Here is how Naison (1984) describes the outrage:

The Committee for Better Schools, with the aid of seasoned Communist street speakers like Audley Moore and Richard Moore, immediately established picket lines at the school and organized demonstrations designed to force Schoenchen's expulsion from the school system. These protests attracted thousands of participants, ranging from Harlem parents to top-ranking black politicians, to leaders of the Harlem branch of the NAACP, and culminated in a mass trial of the School Board at Abyssinian Baptist Church. Three months after the incident, Schoenchen was transferred to a school outside Harlem. (p. 215)

Naison looks back at the work of the committee:

In cooperation with the Teacher's Union, the committee sponsored workshops and forums on black accomplishments in American life and fought to remove racist textbooks from the city school system. Condemning the practice of channeling blacks away from academic careers, they agitated for the right of black students to participate in college-bound programs and to attend high schools out of the Harlem district.

The Party's presence pervaded the committee. Theodore Bassett, its secretary, and Emmet May, its vice-chairman, were both Party members, and conducted most of the committee's administrative tasks. Born in the south and trained as schoolteachers, they did their work with a quiet efficiency that won the respect of the black ministers and schoolteachers who composed the group's other leaders. In addition, Party neighborhood branches participated actively in the committee's work. Communists served as members of PTA's in most Harlem schools and placed their best street speakers at the Committee's disposal when it organized demonstrations. (p. 216)

The Teacher's Union

Founded in 1916 by the children of unionists committed to unionism (Markowitz, 1993), Local 5, Teacher's Union (TU) of the American Federation of Teachers was formed in New York City. During the 1920s the aggressive and expanding TU took up bread-and-butter issues such as salaries and working conditions, as well as the broader issues of academic freedom, church-state relationships, and the "democratization" of the schools (Markowitz, 1993). By the 1930s the TU counted many Communists and Socialists in its ranks. It became an active part of the broad social movement against Fascism and reaction. As the hard Left gained power within the TU, those opposing their views split and formed the Teacher Guild in 1935.

The more-radical TU participated in campaigns against poverty, unemployment, and teacher firings. Markowitz (1993) attempts to assess the level of radicalism among New York teachers during the Depression Era:

As for the political beliefs of the city's teachers, while a number of Communist party members did teach in the city's schools, according to most accounts, including several of those interviewed, they apparently constituted only a very small portion of the teaching staff. . . . The results of a questionnaire for city teachers sponsored by the John Dewey Society for the Study of Education in 1936 showed that the general tendency of teachers was "leftish" with "pale pink" rather than "red" coloring. The study found that while there was predominance of teachers holding Socialist convictions, only a small group actually voted for the Socialist party. This study noted that while the great majority of teachers saw the need for far-reaching economic and social reforms, their dissent from the status quo was of a gradualist rather than revolutionary approach. (p. 158)

The Scottsboro Boys case led to Communist Party recruitment of, and alliances with, African Americans. Segregated and inferior schools had long plagued urban and rural Black education. By the mid 1930s, public school-teachers who were Communist Party members readily joined the community struggles of Black schools. In Harlem, for example, largely Jewish female and African American Communist Party members joined with a broader number of teachers and parents to protest inferior schools. Markowitz (1993) chronicles the activities of teachers Alice Citron, Dorothy Rose, Mildred Flacks, Celia Zitron, and Minnie Gutride among others in this effort.

Containing both Black and White Communists and radicals, the Teachers Union continued its activities despite being battered by government red baiting and defections. In the early 1950s they ambitiously challenged the established school curriculum. While it is difficult to sort out the exact role of Black people, they were clearly an integral part of this endeavor. Here is how Biondi (2003) describes the event:

> In 1951 the left-wing Teacher's Union, with which the board had broken relations after its expulsion from the CIO, produced a remarkable study of textbooks currently in use in the public schools. In "Bias and Prejudice in Textbooks in Use in New York City Schools: An Indictment," the union took pains to clarify why its review did not constitute censorship. The Teachers' Union "makes a sharp distinction between censorship—which it opposes—and the elimination of material containing racist stereotypes, distortion of historical and scientific fact, and bias, whether conscious of unconscious, toward allegedly 'inferior' peoples." Prepared by the Harlem Committee of the Teachers' Union, the report reflected scholarship in U.S. history that had been ignored by the mainstream academy, and it anticipated the revisionism of the next generation of historians who came of age during the civil rights movement. (pp. 244–5)

Thus we observe that one of the first movements to revise racist curriculum included Black voices. Biondi (2003) continues:

> To compensate for the deficient materials used in city schools, the Teachers' Union created its own Black history curriculum, including "The Negro in New York, 1626–1865: A Study for Teachers." While this guide was not adopted by the board, it is possible that individual teachers used it. It began: "In New York City the Negro people constitute more than 10% of the city population. This is probably the largest Negro community of any city in the world with great and growing influence on the social and cultural life of the city and of national importance because of its leadership in the fight for civil rights throughout the country. (p. 246)

Local Control in New York: The Radical Influence

In the context of expanding national affluence for some, differentiated and seg-regated schooling remained a target of Marxists and radicals throughout the 1950s. Unequal schools were viewed as symptomatic of the unequal society. On the heels of *Brown v. Board of Education* and McCarthyism, radical agita-tion for improved schools continued and even intensified in many areas of the nation. The school wars described by Danns (2003) in Chicago suggest con-tinued widespread discontent with public education by people of color.

Every aspect of the "great divide," that is, the contradictions between Black and White, affluent and poor, powerful and powerless, city and suburb, exist-ed in New York City in the 1960s. Within education, concerns about racism, the achievement gap, relevant curriculum, effective teaching, and governance boiled over in Ocean Hill–Brownsville. Its advocates saw the demand for local control of schools as empowering, liberating, and democratizing the schools.

The politics of this movement attracted an assortment of radicals, Black and White, to the cause. Taylor (1997) argues that Marxists and Marxism were prominent in the Ocean Hill–Brownsville project. He suggests that the leader, Rev. Milton Galamison, worked with and was influenced by Marxists. He writes:

> Using Karl Marx's notion of superstructure, i.e., political, religious, and cultural insti-tutions support the capitalist economic order, Galamison argued that individuals, the dominant culture, the state and its leaders, including the Protestant church in America, had all perpetuated class and race inequality and war. (p. 35)

Galamison emphasized Christian social obligation, telling his congregation that the dire situation created by class exploitation had created a special need for Christians. Followers of Christ must fight all forms of inequality, Galamison stated; if one professes to be a Christian, one cannot sit idly by and allow inno-cent human beings to suffer from poverty, racism, and war. True Christians should be vehicles for change and social redemption.

Further:

> Ideologically, Galamison felt connected to progressives and radicals, they worked for the same goals and criticized the same targets: the state and church. . . . On occasions he even praised Marxism. According to the Presbyterian minister, Socialism has been an important "historic force." It has been a "definite attempt to define the nature of man. The ideas of human dignity and justice are the basis of Marx's writings and these ideas created modern Socialism and Russian Communism." Galamison argued that the power that defined the Russian Revolution was a "concept of man: Faith in oneself, faith in the common man, in his ideas, his power, in his rights . . .

Galamison defended communists from red-baiting, noting enemies of change often scapegoated communism. "Communism, as the story goes, is responsible for all the world's woes." Galamison claimed that using communists as scapegoats was a diversion that takes people's minds off the real issues. (pp. 36–7)

Reclaiming Marxism in African American Protest Thought

The conservative restoration, the collapse of the Soviet Union, and the increasing theoretical assault on "materialist" conceptions of society have all served as distractions to Marxian thought in recent years. This generation of racial protest is saturated with racial determinism and identity politics. Popular culturalist themes assert the primacy of race over class, and often dismiss Marxian thought as Eurocentric or irrelevant. The African-centered themes enjoy widespread popularity in this environment.

Many culturalists and cultural theorists reject class struggle in favor of romantic reifications of racial unity and cultural bonding. Vague notions of cooperation are favored over labor-market theories and historical materialism. Despite the current employment displacements, significant transference of wealth from poor to rich, government "take-backs," and desperate new poverty, Marxian notions of class struggle and property ownership are under persistent assault.

Some Black culturalists have been virulent and strident in their criticism of Marxism. Many refuse to connect racial oppression to the expropriation of labor and property ownership.

The significant embrace of Marxism by African Americans dates to the aforementioned Scottsboro Boys case of the early 1930s, where nine Black youth were falsely accused of raping a White woman in Alabama. It was the Communist Party that spearheaded their public defense and protest. Additionally, the Communist Party organized mass protests against unemployment, evictions, and repossessions, thus attracting Blacks to their ranks. Between the world wars, Blacks were active in the Communist Party throughout the rural South, northern cities, and especially New York.

The Black Marxian tradition is indeed a rich one. It traces from the days of Cyril Briggs and the African Blood Brotherhood, to Angelo Hearndon, and the Sharecroppers movements in the South, to the many Black Marxists of the Harlem Renaissance, all the way through Angela Davis and the Black Panther Party.

Such a history should be embraced, shared, and reinforced. The Black Marxian tradition is hardly an aberration: Its roots lie deep within the voices of an oppressed people screaming for justice and equality.

Final Reflections

Several summative thoughts and questions occur as I have attempted to cull some of the existing scholarship in this area. Much remains to be done. Further exploration of primary source data, as well as more exhaustive scholarship on radical African American educational dissent, needs to take place for the following reasons:

First, contemporary popular school criticism, especially in urban education, has turned our attention to mediocrity. The mediocrity argument suggests that urban schools suffer from permissiveness, poor funding, social promotion, denied access, indifferent teachers, exoticized curriculum, limited home experiences, and lack of school choice. While many of these points are indisputable, they are simplistic and reductionist as an explanation. The mediocrity thesis doesn't encourage a historicized and politicized excavation of schooling. The resulting "reform" movement simply calls for the reversal of the aforementioned maladies. "Back to basics" and increased standardized testing are hardly remedies for structured inequity. We don't have enough informed public dialogue that locates schools squarely within the context of power, ideology, property, and partisanship. The state function of education must not be obfuscated as it was in the early twentieth century.

Second, popular criticism of urban schools focuses primarily on race. Even the well-articulated reproduction arguments rarely join race to class. The Black radical and Marxian examination of schools are more likely to identify the intersection of race and class oppression within the capitalist system as problematic. Many related questions cry out for illumination. Do "antiracist pedagogy" and multicultural education have any real teeth in this environment? How can we explore race and schooling in association with labor economics? What do the new demographics mean to public schooling? How do we understand urban renewal and regentrification in the postindustrial society?

Finally, I'm concerned about the marginalization of Marxian social science as an explanatory tool. Our society and our world are very complex. Social institutions, including schools, are shaped by power and ideology. Marxian critique is a valuable, if not indispensable, tool in exploring the dynamics of power, race, ideology, subservience, equity, gender discrimination, and hegemony.

References

Anderson, J.D. (1980). Philanthropic control over private Black higher education. In R.F. Arnove, ed., *Philanthropy and cultural imperialism: The foundations at home and abroad.* Bloomington: Indiana University Press, pp. 147–177.

Anyon, J. (1981). Social class and school knowledge. In *Curriculum inquiry* 11, number 1 Spring 1981 p. 27.

Apple, M. (1983). *Education and power*. Boston: Ark Paperbacks.

Apple, M. (1979). *Ideology and curriculum*. London: Routledge & Kegan Paul.

Aptheker, H. ed., (1973). *The education of Black people: Ten critiques, 1906–1960*. by Du Bois, W.E.B. New York: Monthly Review Press.

Arnove, R. ed., (1980). *Philanthropy and cultural imperialism: The foundations at home and abroad*. Bloomington: Indiana University Press.

Biondi, M. (2003). *To stand and fight: The struggle for civil rights in postwar New York City*. Cambridge, MA: Harvard University Press.

Bowers, C.A. (1969). *The progressive educator and the depression: The radical years*. New York: Random House.

Bowles, S., & H. Gintis (1976). *Schooling in capitalist America: Educational reform and the contradictions of economic life*. New York: Basic Books.

Brameld, T. B. (1956). *Toward a reconstructed philosophy of education*. New York: Dryden Press.

Brosio, R.A. (1994). *A radical democratic critique of capitalist education*. New York: Peter Lang.

Butts, R.F. (1978). *Public education in the United States: From revolution to reform*. New York: Holt Rinehart & Winston.

Clifford, G.J. (1968). *Edward L. Thorndike: The sane positivist*. Middletown, CT: Wesleyan University Press.

Commission on the Social Studies in the Schools (1932). *A Charter for the Social Sciences in the Schools*. American Historical Association.

Counts, G.S. (1932). *Dare the schools build a new social order?* New York: John Day.

Counts, G.S. (1932a). Dare the progressives be progressive? *Progressive Education* 9, pp. 257–263.

Cremin, L.A. (1961). *The transformation of the school: Progressivism in American education 1876–1957*. New York: Alfred A. Knopf.

Danns, D (2003). *Something better for our children: Black organizing in Chicago public schools, 1963–1971*. New York: Routledge.

Davis, B.J. (1969). *Communist councilman from Harlem: Autobiographical notes written in a federal penitentiary*. New York: International Publishers.

de Tocqueville, A.B. (1838/2000). *Democracy in America*. Chicago: University of Chicago Press.

Feuer, L.S. ed., (1959). *Marx & Engels: Basic writings on politics & philosophy*. Garden City, NY: Anchor Books Doubleday & Co.

Foner, P.S. ed., (1970). *W.E.B. Du Bois speaks: Speeches and addresses 1920–1963*. New York: Pathfinder Press.

Foner, P.S. ed., (1970). *W.E.B. Du Bois speaks: Speeches and addresses 1890–1919*. New York: Pathfinder Press.

Gonzalez, G.G. (1982). *Progressive education: A Marxist interpretation*. Minneapolis: Marxist Educational Press.

Gutstein, E. (2003). Teaching and learning mathematics for social justice in an urban Latino school. In *Journal for Research in Mathematics Education* 34, pp. 37–73

Haywood, H. (1978). *Black Bolshevik: Autobiography of an Afro-American Communist*. Chicago: Liberator Press.

Heilbroner, R. (1986). *The worldly philosophers: The lives, times and ideas of the great economic thinkers*. New York: Simon & Schuster-Touchstone Books.

Horne, G. (1986). *Black and red. W.E.B. Du Bois and the Afro-American response to the Cold War*. Albany: State University of New York Press.

Hutchinson, E.O. (1995). *Blacks and reds: Race and class in conflict 1919–1990*. East Lansing: Michigan State University Press.

Kelley, R.D.G. (2002). *Freedom dreams: The Black radical imagination*. Boston: Beacon Press.

Kelley, R.D.G. (1994). *Race rebels: Culture, politics, and the Black working class*. New York: The Free Press.

Kelley, R.D.G. (1990). *Hammer and hoe: Alabama Communists during the Great Depression*. Chapel Hill: University of North Carolina Press.

Kilpatrick, W.H. ed., (1933). *The educational frontier*. New York: Appleton-Century-Crofts.

Kilpatrick, W.H. (1932). *Education and the social crises*. New York: Liverright.

Konstantivov, F. (1955). *Basis and superstructure*. Moscow: (published by govt.)

Lenin, V.I. (1918). *State and revolution*. Petrograd: Martin Lawrence Ltd.

Lenin, V.I. (1917). *Imperialism: The highest stage of capitalism*. Petrograd: Martin Lawrence Ltd.

Lenin, V.I. (1902). *What is to be done?* (1931) English Edition London: Martin Lawrence Ltd.

Liston. D.P. (1988). *Capitalist schools: Explanation and ethics in radical studies of schooling*. New York: Routledge

Locke, A. (1940). With science as his shield: The educator must bridge our "great divides." In *Frontiers of Democracy* 6(53), April 13, 1940, pp. 208–210.

Marable, M. (1986). *W.E.B. Du Bois: Black radical democrat*. Boston: Twayne Publishers.

Markowitz, R. J. (1993). *My daughter, the teacher: Jewish teachers in the New York City schools*. New Brunswick, NJ: Rutgers University Press.

Marx, K. (1867). *Das kapital*. Published in English (1886). Chicago: Charles H. Kerr & Co.

Marx, K. (1863). *Theories of surplus value*. Published as Marx, K. (1963–71) *Theories of surplus value. Volumes 1–3*. Edited by S. Ryazanskaya. Moscow: Foreign Languages Publishing House.

Marx, K. (1859). Published (1904) *A contribution to the critique of political economy*. Chicago: Charles H. Kerr & Co.

Marx, K. (1847). *The poverty of philosophy*. (1935) English edition. London: Martin Lawrence Ltd.

Marx, K. (1843). *A contribution to the critique of Hegel's philosophy of law*. Cited in Price, R.F. (1986) p. 86.

Marx, K., & F. Engels (1848). *The Communist manifesto*. Petrograd: Martin Lawrence Ltd.

Marx, K., & Engels, F. (1845–6). *The German ideology*. Moscow: Marx-Engels Institute.

Naison, M. (1984). *Communists in Harlem during the Depression*. Urbana: University of Illinois Press.

Podair, J.E. (2002). *The strike that changed New York: Blacks, Whites, and the Ocean Hill–Brownsville crises*. New Haven: Yale University Press.

Peery, N. (1994). *Black fire: The making of an American revolutionary.* New York: The New Press.

Price, R. F. (1986). *Marx and education in late capitalism.* Totowa, NJ: Barnes & Noble Books.

Progressive Education Association's Committee on Social and Economic Problems (1933). *A call to the teachers of the nation.* New York: John Day.

Provenzo Jr., E.G., ed. (2002). *Du Bois on education.* Walnut Creek, CA: AltaMira Press.

Robinson, C.J. (1983). *Black Marxism: The making of the Black radical tradition.* Chapel Hill: University of North Carolina Press.

Rugg, H.O. (1936). *In Social Frontier,* Vol 3 No. 19 p.15.

Rugg, H.O. (1932). *Social reconstruction through education. Progressive Education,* 9(8), 11–8.

Rugg, H.O. (1921). *The scientific method in the reconstruction of elementary and secondary school subjects.*

Small, M. (2001). *Whose ideas count: Ideology and politics in teachers' struggles for mathematics education reform.* Unpublished Ph.D. Dissertation. University of Illinois at Chicago.

Spencer, H. (1861). *Education: Intellectual, moral and physical.* New York: D. Appleton.

Stanley, W.B. (1992). *Curriculum for utopia: Social reconstructionism and critical pedagogy in the postmodern era.* Albany: State University of New York Press.

Strike, K. (1989). *Liberal justice and the Marxist critique of education: A study of conflicting research programs.* New York: Routledge.

Taylor, C. (1997). *Knocking at our own door: Milton A. Galamison and the struggle to integrate New York City schools.* New York: Columbia University Press.

Thorndike E. (1911). *Individuality.* Boston: Houghton Miflin.

Veblen, T. (1899). *Theory of the leisure class: An economic study in the evolution of institutions.* New York: The Macmillan Co.

Watkins, W.H. (2001). *The White architects of Black education: Ideology and power in America, 1865–1954.* New York: Teachers College Press.

Watkins, W.H. (1990). The social reconstructionists. In T. Husen & T.N. Postlethwaite, eds., *The international encyclopedia of education,* Supplementary Volume Two. London: Pergamon Press. Reprinted in Lewy, A. ed., (1992), *The international encyclopedia of curriculum.* London: Pergamon Press.

Weinburg, M. (1970). *W.E.B. Du Bois: A reader.* New York: Harper Torchbook.

Young, M.F.D. (1971). *Knowledge and control: New directions for the sociology of education.* London: Collier-Macmillan

Chapter Six

JOY ANN WILLIAMSON

Community Control with a Black Nationalist Twist

THE BLACK PANTHER PARTY'S EDUCATIONAL PROGRAMS

African Americans have long linked education with liberation. When Whites thwarted their efforts to be educated—and free—African Americans devised creative solutions. Black men and women in the antebellum South created clandestine schools that taught reading skills to enable students to digest the Bible for themselves. In the North, they petitioned for public funds to support separate schools since desegregation was usually out of the question. After the Civil War, African Americans continued to create alternative venues for education since Whites—both in the North and South—refused to desegregate schools and usually relegated Black children to second-class and vocational forms of education. The 1954 *Brown v. Board of Education* decision struck down racial segregation in schools, but the decision met with heavy resistance and little immediate success in the South. Northern states were not bound by the decision, and racial segregation in northern schools continued. African Americans did not necessarily equate desegregation with equality of education, nor did they sit idly by and allow their children to remain uneducated when the Whites in power refused to practice what the Fourteenth Amendment to the Constitution promised: that "No State shall make or enforce any law which shall abridge the privileges or immunities of citizens of the United States . . . nor deny to any person within its jurisdiction the equal protection of the laws." African Americans continued to operate separate schools while attempting to gain access to mainstream education *and* strengthening their own schools.

American schools continued to be a battleground in the late 1950s and early 1960s. The *Brown* decision did not launch the Civil Rights Movement, but the decision did provide fodder for Movement projects like school desegregation. As the tide shifted from Civil Rights to Black Power, the majority of U.S. schools remained racially segregated, and Black schools were largely (though not always) inferior. African Americans continued to indict the U.S. school system for its failure to properly educate Black children. African Americans in the late 1960s refocused their energy on community institutions, including schools, and entertained community solutions. According to Black Power advocates, desegregated mainstream schools harmed Black students more than they helped them. These schools and their educational professionals never expected Black children to learn, and too often subscribed to various genetic and cultural-deprivation or deficit theories that blamed Black culture, family structure, and neighborhoods for the academic underachievement of Black children.[1] Black Power–minded critics were not the first or only group to find fault with such theories and indict public schools, but the climate of the late 1960s provided different options for different solutions. The school-decentralization movement emerged from this ethos and combined Black Nationalism, community control, and pedagogically progressive educational ideas (i.e., using the students' background to inspire learning, linking schools to the outside world, and promoting active problem solving) in the conceptualization of a "good" school.[2] The definition of liberation shifted, but education, as a means to achieve it, remained constant.

The Black Panther Party was born in this context. Like other Black social-protest groups, Panthers maintained faith in the liberatory power of education, and established both formal and informal educational opportunities. In particular, Panthers believed that exploited and oppressed people deserved an education that provided them with the tools to critically examine the capitalist structure, understand their reality as Blacks in America, and then plot a course for change. Panther educational ideals did not always translate into practice; however, their educational programs represent an important moment in Black educational reform, where radical solutions to Black America's problems seemed possible. It is tempting to ask whether Panther educational efforts were a success or a failure, but the purpose of this piece is not to judge the educational inputs and outcomes of Panther education. Rather, this chapter means to insert the Black Panther Party in the historiography of the community-control movement, and offer fodder for those contemporary reform movements that seek to integrate the cultural-racial background of students, high academic standards, and closer school-community relationships.

Contextualizing Panther Education Initiatives

After decades of attempting to force their way into the existing social order, only to meet intense White resistance and repression, African Americans became disillusioned with the tactics and goals of the Civil Rights Movement. Many questioned the federal government's dedication to improving the conditions of African Americans, were suspicious of the extent to which White liberals could be considered true allies, and examined the large discrepancy between expected results and actual achievements. This reevaluation resulted in a shift in ideas on the definition of Black Liberation. Many African Americans grew frustrated with the pace of change and began to demand more power, real power, Black Power. Rather than continued attempts to desegregate facilities, including schools, African Americans were called to unite: "Before a group can enter the open society, it must first close ranks. By this we mean that group solidarity is necessary before a group can operate effectively from a bargaining position of strength in a pluralistic society."[3] Under the banner of Blackness, African Americans could address their grievances and demand equal participation and representation in American society.

At the same time, the issue of community control in public schools began to gain attention and support. School desegregation was supposed to equalize Black and White academic achievement but did not produce the expected (or at least, hoped for) results. Educational researchers documented the intense alienation, dissatisfaction, low academic achievement, and sense of inferiority experienced by Black pupils and pondered how best to increase the academic achievement of Black students.[4] Increased community control of schools became one proposed solution.[5] A thoroughly democratic idea, community control allowed community residents to participate in policymaking and more fully link the school to the community. Such schools sought to improve education by diversifying content and enriching the affective schooling experience. Through the inclusion of Black-centered materials, use of students' backgrounds as a springboard for learning, incorporation of different perspectives of reality into the classroom, and connection of education to real-life situations and the community, students gained self-esteem, feelings of belonging, and cultural pride—all of which were lacking in mainstream schools. Such an education produced a well-rounded and intelligent individual ready to use his or her knowledge to initiate social reform and improve the conditions of the community from which he/she came. In theory, some educational reformers supported decentralization efforts and ideas on how to improve Black education. However, the Black Nationalist ethos dominant in certain educational reforms made teachers' unions and other educational professionals wary.[6]

The Black Panther Party, organized in 1966 in Oakland, California, emerged during the same time that the Black Power Movement and the notion of community control become popular. However, theirs was a unique criticism of the U.S. system, which translated into a particular kind of educational ideology and set of goals. The organization denounced the Civil Rights Movement as a movement interested in middle-class advancement rather than community uplift and adopted a mix of Black Power ideology and socialism in their analysis of societal stratification. Rather than using race as the only framework with which to understand stratification, they believed that economic class held the key to understanding oppression and looked to Karl Marx to inform their analysis. Like Marx, the Panthers believed in a dichotomy of classes: the bourgeoisie and the proletariat, the oppressor and the oppressed. In such a society, the ruling class and the working class maintained different motivations and goals, which led them into contradiction. To reduce this tension, socialism—the collective ownership and administration of means of production and distribution of goods—had to be instituted. If the struggle against capitalism and the ruling class intensified, Panthers believed "we will reach a point where the equilibrium of forces will change and there will be a qualitative leap into a new situation with a new social equilibrium."[7] In other words, capitalism would die and socialism would emerge. They conceded that racism and sexism would exist in the early stages of socialism, but asserted that community control of the means of production and the media would eradicate such kinds of oppression.

Though they relied on an economic analysis of U.S. stratification, Panthers addressed the fact that a disproportionate number of those in the working class were people of color. Specifically, Panthers explained why African Americans were so highly represented near the bottom of the economic scale, rather than evenly divided between all economic classes. To remedy this perceived dissonance, Panthers recognized two types of oppression: exploitation and colonization. Exploitation constituted the economic rape of a people. Colonization included economic rape and the destruction of a people's culture, language, history, and humanity. Poor Whites were in the lower class because rich Whites exploited them. African Americans were in the lower class because they were exploited *and* colonized. Racism was an evil particular to the colony, while capitalism was the evil of the entire mother country. According to Eldridge Cleaver, Minister of Information, the power structure used race and ethnicity as a pawn to exploit and distract workers from the reality of capitalist exploitation. But, Cleaver declared, "as we tear down the walls of the colony . . . we feel that what will then become most important will be the general grievances that are shared by all of the oppressed peoples in America. And I think we are reaching that point."[8]

The Panther Party's educational mission grew out of this ideology, and the organization heavily and aggressively criticized the public-school system. Though Black children attended school, theirs was not "education" in the Panther sense of the word. Panthers, like other African American protest groups and those in the community-control movement, understood education as a political enterprise. Eldridge Cleaver defined the role of education as passing "the heritage, learning, the wisdom and the technology of human history to the coming generations."[9] However, Panthers believed this knowledge was passed only to a small segment of society, while the masses received a watered-down and largely irrelevant education. This type of education achieved a specific purpose: to maintain the status quo in a socially stratified society. According to Cleaver, those in power "know that it is necessary for them to control the learning process in order to brainwash people, in order to camouflage the true nature of society."[10] The ruling-class elites tricked the masses into accepting the unequal distribution of tangibles and intangibles as legitimate, which in turn led the masses to believe they deserved their lowly positions in society. Further, teachers and professors who supported the interests of the ruling class lulled students into inaction. *Real* education was impossible under the current system. "What [the ruling class] has been providing is universal brainwashing that masquerades as universal education."[11]

Panthers proposed that the learning, the wisdom, and the technology of human history be distributed more broadly. The duty of society was to invest *all* individuals with the whole of the human heritage. Education was not an instrument with which to socialize young adults into the dominant culture, but an instrument through which oppressed peoples could learn how to change society. As the fifth point in their Ten Point Platform and Program, Panthers proposed an "education for our people that exposes the true nature of this decadent American society. We want education that teaches us our true history and our role in present-day society. We believe in an educational system that will give to our people a knowledge of self. If a man does not have knowledge of himself and his position in society and the world, then he has little chance to relate to anything else."[12] A revolutionary purpose for education remained in direct opposition to the rulers' purpose. Panthers considered it their duty to teach the masses how to recognize oppression and to overcome it: "the exploited and oppressed people have [a vested] interest in exposing the true nature of the society and in educating ourselves and our children on the nature of the struggle and in transferring to them the means for waging the struggle so they can be aware of the level of the struggle, of the progress and the history of the struggle and the nature of the enemy and the true vulnerability of the enemy. In other words, we want to be able to teach ourselves and our children the necessity for struggling against this ruling class."[13]

The intersection of economic class and race meant that the study of Black history and use of Black culture in the emancipatory process remained a constant in Panther proposals for a proper education. Though their primary focus continued to be economic-class stratification and oppression, race did remain an important factor in Panther critiques of the U.S. system. In fact, many of their educational programs sought primarily to educate Blacks. Panthers continued to emphasize knowledge of history and culture as a source of strength and as a tool for liberation, though they did begin to shift to an emphasis on revolutionary culture, rather than Black culture, during a certain period of their existence. Regardless, the Panthers recognized the necessity and importance of transferring the cultural knowledge—whether African American or revolutionary—to future generations. Such an education allowed African Americans to situate themselves in history and use their knowledge to combat oppression.

Panthers fully believed that community control of schools enabled this type of education to exist, but they often focused on emancipatory content at the expense of teacher practice. In other words, they sought to incorporate Black culture in their brand of education, but their teaching techniques revealed little faith in the Black masses to reach the proper conclusions about the revolution: "If the party isn't going to make the people aware of the tools of liberation and the strategic method that is to be used, there will be no means by which the people will be mobilized properly."[14] Panther writings revealed the tension between allowing the masses to come to their own conclusions, and overt instruction in the proper understanding of society's problems. Both attitudes were evident in the work of Huey P. Newton, Minister of Defense. On one hand, Newton believed that "the sleeping masses must be bombarded with the correct approach to the struggle."[15] On the other hand, he used a metaphor to explain more subtle educational methods: "Imagine people living in a cave. They've been there all their lives. At the end of the cave shines a light. Now one person among them knows the light is the sun. The rest are afraid of the light. Now let's say the person who knows about the light tells them it's not evil and tries to lead them out of the cave. They'll fight and probably overpower and maybe even kill him. . . . So instead he has to gradually lead them toward the light. Well, it's the same with knowledge. Gradually you have to lead people toward an understanding of what's happening. . . . One never drops a flowerpot on the head of the masses."[16]

Depending on the particular educational initiative and its specific purpose, Panthers used one of two teaching approaches: teacher-centered pedagogy that allowed for little discussion, or student-centered instruction that allowed students to drive both the pace and content in the classroom. They did attempt to use the schools to inspire social action, link the school to the community, and use student backgrounds and experiences to inform school curriculum—though they achieved these aims to varying degrees. Their failure to translate pedagogical theory into practice was not an issue exclusive to the Panthers.[17] Also, Panthers never pretended to subscribe to a notion of education that supported particular pedagogical techniques, and pedagogical questions did not occupy much of their time or energy. Locating Panther educational projects squarely in the community-control movement is more useful than judging their success or failure. In this context, Panther educational ideas are less easily dismissed as fringe proposals. Their critiques of the system were part of a chorus demanding immediate solutions to Black America's problems. Like other Black Power–minded educators, Panthers believed that combining Black Nationalism and community control could be a powerful tool to liberate the masses. Their ideological notions and educational proposals riled critics, but mounting educational research corroborated their indictment of the public-school system.

Panther Educational Proposals for Youth

The Panthers created educational initiatives inside and outside the public-school system. Both types of initiatives sought to provide an education that exposed the racist and classist nature of U.S. society. But, the initiatives outside the school system, including the Free Breakfast Program and the Liberation Schools, maintained a more overtly political agenda and teaching techniques. Panthers sponsored the Free Breakfast Program during the academic year, where students received free food and Panthers took advantage of a makeshift early-morning education opportunity. In the summer, children in Liberation Schools learned about the history of the oppressed in the United States from a Panther point of view. The morning-long Liberation Schools began in June 1969, and replaced the Free Breakfast Program sponsored during the academic year. Panthers initiated the first of such schools in Berkeley, Oakland, and San Francisco, California, but the concept soon spread to affiliates across the nation.[18] Though Panthers used the phrase "Big Family" in the classroom, as a tool to teach the students about their interconnectedness with other oppressed people across the globe, the Liberation Schools remained primarily Black in attendance.[19]

Children attending the Berkeley Liberation School ranged in age from two to thirteen. In Omaha, Nebraska, eight to twelve students attended the Panther Liberation School; in Des Moines, Iowa, between twelve and twenty elementary-aged students attended.[20] Bobby Seale, chairman of the Black Panther Party, described the Liberation School curriculum as steeped in an understanding of class struggle in terms of Black history.[21] Further, Panthers stated that, "the curriculum is designed to meet the needs of the youth, to guide them in their search for revolutionary truths and principles."[22] Students engaged in learning activities such as talks, songs, films, field trips, and exercise programs; and according to Val Douglas, an assistant teacher in the Berkeley school, students could self-direct some of their learning by choosing local or world events of interest for class study. Douglas remembered that a mother of one of the children was impressed by the fact that "their work shows that they can relate to what is happening to them and to other poor people in the world."[23]

Very little information exists on what exactly occurred in either the Free Breakfast Programs or the Liberation Schools, though Panthers published excerpts of the curricula in their newspaper, and the House Committee on Internal Security (HCIS), a congressional body that closely monitored Panther activities, conducted a thorough investigation of both programs. What can be gleaned from the evidence is that the curriculum was political in nature and sought to educate students about the evils of capitalism. A typical week at the Berkeley school included:

Monday: Revolutionary History Day
Tuesday: Revolutionary Culture Day
Wednesday: Current Events Day
Thursday: Movie Day
Friday: Field Trip Day[24]

According to the Panthers, the varied curriculum and mode of instruction kept students interested. Also, their daily activities linked the Liberation School directly to the community. The Breakfast Programs sought the same ends as the Liberation Schools, and employed overt teaching techniques including recitation drills. A drill used in the Seattle program clearly demonstrated the Panther agenda:

PANTHER: What do the Panthers believe?
CHILDREN: All power to the people.
PANTHER: Who are the capitalists?
CHILDREN: They are the pigs who control the country.
PANTHER: What do the capitalists do?
CHILDREN: They steal from the poor.
PANTHER: How do they steal from the poor?

CHILDREN: They make the poor pay taxes and this makes the capitalists richer and the poor poorer.
PANTHER: What should happen with capitalists?
CHILDREN: Off the pig. . . .
PANTHER: What do the Panthers believe?
CHILDREN: Off the pig.
PANTHER: Why are the pigs going to kill Bob Seale?
CHILDREN: Because he wants freedom for all people.
PANTHER: Why do the Panthers kill pigs?
CHILDREN: Because they want freedom for all people[25]

The Free Breakfast Program's implementation was spotty. Likewise, the Liberation Schools were somewhat sparse and short-lived. The HCIS survey revealed that seven of twenty-seven active Panther chapters and ten of fifteen inactive chapters, in 1970, operated or had operated a Liberation School.[26] For various reasons, very few Liberation Schools existed for any length of time. The lack of financial resources necessarily restricted both the proliferation of Liberation Schools and their longevity. Dependence on donations and fundraising meant monetary assistance was unreliable. Also, the United States government, in the form of intimidation, rumor, and violence, contributed to the closing of various schools. According to the final report of the Select Committee to Study Governmental Operations with Respect to Intelligence Activities (also known as the Church Report), the San Francisco Field Office of the Federal Bureau of Investigation identified the Panther Free Breakfast Program—which was closely related to the Liberation Schools—as a prime target because of its "potentially successful effort . . . to teach children to hate police and to spread 'anti-white propaganda.'"[27] Various agents sought to discredit the Panthers (and intimidate financial contributors) in an effort to undermine support and attendance in the schools. As a result, the Liberation School in Omaha lasted one week; in San Francisco, it lasted one day; and in Richmond, California, the school closed after an hour and a half.

Also, accusations of indoctrination from inside and outside the Black community precipitated the closing of many schools. As educational initiatives outside the public-school system, the Free Breakfast Program and Liberation Schools contained overtly hostile rhetoric unacceptable in a public school. The HCIS found that in cities like Kansas City, Des Moines, and Seattle, parents protested the use of posters, songs, and chants meant to teach the children that "police officers are 'pigs' who should be 'offed' because they mistreat black citizens and help to preserve an inhuman capitalist society in America."[28] Black adults initially may have been attracted to the Free Breakfast Program and Liberation Schools for a variety of reasons, but many parents found the Panther's combination of political content and teaching strategy objectionable.

Though Panthers sought to serve the community with these educational opportunities, the schools were not community initiated. In this instance, the Panthers misjudged the community's interests.

The link between Black Nationalism, community control, and pedagogical progressivism was most fully realized in the Panther-sponsored Oakland Community School. Operational from 1971 to 1982, OCS was a primary school that ran year-round and educated hundreds of students in its lifetime. The mission of the school, from its inception to its demise, was "to build a model school, provide a *real* education to Black kids," and prove Black children were educable.[29] OCS opened with twenty-five Panther children in attendance, but by the late 1970s, upwards of 120 students attended during an academic year. Most students were African American, though a few Chicano/a students also attended.[30] The staff included sixteen credentialed teachers and fifteen volunteer aides who taught the students grouped by ability rather than age. This guaranteed that students remained in a class until they mastered the material.[31]

The increased enrollment at the school corresponded with a shift in the school's focus and a shift in Panther leadership. By the mid 1970s, Elaine Brown, the new Panther chairman, and Ericka Huggins, OCS director 1973–1981 and a Panther member, played a large role in legitimizing the school as it dissociated itself with its Panther roots and became more mainstream in its curriculum and less overt in its pedagogy.[32] OCS's status as an accredited school with credentialed teaching staff and its longevity as an institution necessarily influenced school policy, content, and pedagogy. The particulars of Panther ideology disappeared, but emancipatory intent remained. OCS, even after it became mainstream in certain ways, continued to implement pedagogically progressive ideas with a Black-centered twist. It also expanded the concept of educating the whole child by providing not just a schooling experience but three meals a day, busses to carry students through dangerous neighborhoods to the school, books and supplies, and transportation to medical and dental services.[33] The school drew recognition from Black community members, lawmakers, and an assemblyman; and in 1977, California Governor Edmund "Jerry" Brown issued OCS a commendation for its admirable efforts.[34]

The school followed a standard elementary-school curriculum with language arts (including Spanish instruction), math, science, social science, performing arts, visual arts, physical education, and environmental studies. However, the 1979 OCS Handbook included lessons laced with emancipatory ideas and practices. The "school philosophy is to show children how and not what to think. . . . Instructors do not give opinions in passing on information;

instead, facts are shared and information discussed while conclusions are reached by the children themselves."[35] Instructors endeavored to use the students' experience as a springboard for learning about the world: "The children will begin with an investigation of *their* history and immediate environment and expand their investigations outward to include the world at large."[36] (italics mine) Also, the teachers were told that they must not "pre-arrange what is 'best.'" Rather, teachers acted as resources for students and offered various points of view. According to the Instructor Handbook, when studying religion, students intentionally were exposed to a variety of faiths, including Christianity, Buddhism, and Islam. Similarly, the study of important figures in history ranged from Harriet Tubman to Julius Caesar.[37] Teaching practices in the classroom may have been very different from the handbook's instructions, but the explicit nature of the handbook revealed a concern with pedagogy absent from previous Panther educational initiatives.

Other OCS content revealed the unique mix of Black culture as a springboard for learning and a global understanding of oppression. In 1980, students in a social-science class queried the history of their families, the school, and African Americans from 1619 to the present. Others performed a play entitled *Pass the Freedom, Please,* which depicted African American efforts to obtain justice and freedom and included students dressed as famous Black Americans. Another class studied units on the Civil Rights Movement, working conditions of miners, railroad workers, and factory workers at the turn of the century, and the music of Mexico, India, and the American South. A language-arts field trip took them to a local Black newspaper; a physical-education class attended a martial-arts tournament; a math class visited a local food store and a supermarket in another neighborhood to compare the cost of certain items. Also, the school celebrated various special days, including Cinco de Mayo, International Women's Day, May Day, and the birthdays of Dr. Martin Luther King Jr. and Malcolm X.[38]

OCS was the longest-lasting Panther educational initiative. It also achieved the greatest success at merging community control, pedagogically progressive education, and Black Nationalism. The Black community heavily critiqued the Free Breakfast Program and Liberation Schools, but OCS more closely reflected the Black community's desires for education in Oakland. Stripped of Panther socialist, militant rhetoric, OCS maintained an emancipatory mission. It managed to function as a Black-centered accredited school, which received the support of the Black community as well as recognition from the State of California. With the limited amount of materials that exist, it is impossible to examine the type of education that occurred in the OCS classrooms or to make a detailed case study of OCS. But, its existence lends fodder to those interested in the possibilities of community control, progressive pedagogical techniques, and culturally responsive curricula.

Panther Educational Proposals for Adults

The community-control movement focused on primary and secondary schools, but Panthers refused to wait for the youngest generation to precipitate reform when adults could take the reins immediately. To this end, Panthers initiated adult political-education classes, which formally began in 1968. Across the nation, in cities including Indianapolis, Seattle, Kansas City, and Philadelphia, Panthers used such classes for both internal and external purposes. Internally, the initiation of political-education classes marked the reorientation of the Panthers from a focus on military preparations to an effort to build a successful political party. "A 'unified political ideology' was to be transmitted by the national leadership to members throughout the country" via the classes.[39] Externally, the classes were used as a means to teach adult nonmembers about capitalism, Panther goals and objectives, class struggle, and basic reading and writing skills. Those adults interested in becoming Panthers received mandatory study kits that included revolutionary writings "relevant to the Black situation in America." The reading list included *Quotations from Chairman Mao Tse-tung* (heavily sampled to demonstrate the necessity for self-discipline), Huey Newton's essays on the colonial status of African Americans, Frantz Fanon's *Wretched of the Earth*, two books on Malcolm X, Karl Marx and Friedrich Engels's *The Communist Manifesto*, and other works by Kwame Nkrumah, Vladimir Lenin, and Che Guevara.[40] At least one Panther chapter required knowledge of the revolutions in the Soviet Union, China, Cuba, Algeria, other African nations, the Philippines, and Indonesia.[41] Panthers used the diverse set of readings to demonstrate the global nature of class struggle and offer fodder for social change in the United States.

The HCIS found that nine of twenty-seven active Panther chapters and fourteen of fifteen inactive chapters, in 1970, sponsored or had sponsored political-education classes.[42] The short life span of the political-education classes, the lack of a detailed curriculum, and the absence of a long-range educational program make the quality of Panther adult education difficult to assess. But if their newspaper, *The Black Panther*, is understood as part of their adult-education mission, their impact on adults becomes more powerful. The newspaper reached a weekly circulation of 140,000 in the United States in 1970, and the staff sent a smaller number of papers to subscribers in different countries.[43] The newspaper offered the Panther perspective on different community issues and occasionally carried excerpts from various revolutionary writings. Together, the political-education classes and the *Black Panther* used revolutionary culture as a basis for learning, exposed adults to a broad sampling of works with which to critique the capitalist and exploitative world around them, and promoted social action—all of which were ingredients in emancipatory education. Whether they allowed students to arrive at their own conclusions is debatable, but that was not their goal. Panthers believed they correctly analyzed the U.S. social structure and that their solutions were the appropriate solutions. With the urgent nature of Black America's plight, Panthers moved quickly to transmit their understanding to the masses.

As the Panthers entertained notions of community control and education for liberation, Black and White college students also pondered the notion of decentralization and defined education as a political enterprise. At campuses across the nation, students demanded a voice in campus policymaking, a more relevant curriculum, and a closer relationship between the campus and the community. The Panthers fully supported the efforts of these students, and individual Panther activism on college campuses can be traced to the attendance of Huey Newton and Bobby Seale at Merritt College, a California junior college. While attending Merritt—and prior to the organization of the Black Panther Party—Newton and Seale joined the Afro-American Association, a Black student group whose purpose, according to Newton, was "to develop a sense of pride among Black people for their heritage, their history, and their contributions to culture and society."[44] They soon left the organization due to conflicts with its leader, and the fact that it did not speak to the link between capitalist exploitation and racism. Later, they joined the Soul Students Advisory Council. The organization's main objective included forcing the administration and faculty to integrate a course in Black history into the curriculum. Their efforts prevailed, but Newton and Seale left the organization disillusioned, and founded the Black Panther Party.

Panther interest in the education offered at predominantly White institutions continued after Newton and Seale left Merritt College and Panther numbers grew. Panthers served in an advisory and supportive capacity for the Black Student Union at the University of California at Los Angeles, which demanded certain concessions from the administration including a Black Studies program. Elaine Brown recounted how Black students asked various Panthers to serve on a committee representing the general Black student population in their dealings with the administration. With Panther support, the committee demanded the administration involve them in the development of Black Studies, a voice in the disbursement of program funds, and a more relevant general education.[45]

Panthers played more tangential roles on college campuses as well. The Illinois Black Panther Party chapter was chartered in late 1968, and headquartered in Chicago. A year earlier, Black students at the University of Illinois at Urbana-Champaign (UIUC) organized the Black Students Association (BSA). From Chicago, less than two hours away, various members of the Illinois Panther chapter traveled to the UIUC campus at BSA's request in 1969 and 1970. In January 1969, invited by BSA and Students for a Democratic Society, Illinois Deputy Chairman Fred Hampton, Deputy Minister of Defense Bobby Rush, and member Diane Dunne spoke to UIUC students about the approaching revolution, and the need for the Black community to arm itself. Approximately one month later, on February 7, 1969, police arrested two Illinois Black Panthers at the Student Union. The next day, police arrested a group of eleven African Americans thirty miles from the UIUC campus. Nine of the eleven were suspected members of the Black Panther Party, and two were UIUC students and BSA members.[46] Former students also remembered being influenced and strengthened by the Panthers' example as they devised demands and tactics for changing their campus reality. Panther attitudes toward societal reformation informed the Black student fight for Black Studies, a Black cultural center, increased Black enrollment, and other programs and policies meant to alleviate alienation and promote Black consciousness.[47]

The combination of Panther–Black Nationalist tendencies and economic analysis of American stratification meant that Panthers encouraged alliances between Black and White student groups on college campuses. According to the Panthers, the focus on racial difference masked the true root of social stratification and oppression: economic class. The enemy sought to control education to ensure dependence and inaction, regardless of race or ethnicity. Panthers admonished groups that proposed Black Studies programs solely for the purpose of educating Black students because they ignored the fact that other non-Black students suffered oppression. During a speech to students at San Francisco State College, David Hilliard, chief of staff, commented on the Party's position regarding cross-racial alliances on college campuses. Hilliard suggested an expansion of the emerging Black Student Unions "so that we can usurp all the revolutionary individuals, all the organizations, and put together a more formidable force so that we can withstand the repression that's being meted out against us. That's the only way that we're going to make the American revolution."[48] Hilliard proposed the formation of a multiracial group, instead of separate ethnic organizations, and asserted that such an alliance did not hinder the Black student struggle but strengthened it. It meant more energy, more ideas, and more power. Hilliard recognized the strength in numbers and prodded students to use it to their best advantage. The rise of the ideal educational institution—one that taught socialism as the key in lifting the United

States out of its oppressive roots and allowing its citizens to realize their potential—necessitated such coalitions.

Panther attempts to unite different ethnic groups on college campuses failed, and their efforts often were met with intense resistance. At San Francisco State College, Newton noted "almost all the students' questions and criticisms were directed at the Black Panthers' willingness to work in coalition with white groups. . . . [T]he students were opposed to working with white groups, or, for that matter, almost anyone but Blacks."[49] Instead, many Black student unions took a decidedly race-based focus more consistent with Black Power ideology. At San Francisco State College, the same venue where Hilliard spoke on the advantages of cross-race alliances and where Newton noted harsh criticism, the Black student union became the first to successfully demand that Black Studies be initiated on campus. The first director, Nathan Hare, described Black Studies programs without a grounding in Black Nationalism as "quite profoundly irrelevant" and demanded that the courses at his institution be taught from a Black perspective.[50] Like-minded Black Studies departments and programs, which resolved to use the Black American historical and cultural experience as a basis for study and understanding, quickly spread across the country to other predominantly White institutions. The nature of the emerging Black Studies departments and programs was not completely inconsistent with Panther educational proposals, but the lack of a class analysis, the demands to restrict Black Studies to Black students *only*, and the resistance to cross-race alliances contradicted Panther ideology.

Panthers did not necessarily revoke support from Black student unions that adopted a race-based understanding of Black oppression and made no overtures to White students for alliances. After all, Panthers themselves used Black culture and history as a basis for instruction in their Free Breakfast Program, Liberation Schools, OCS, and political-education classes. Also, Panthers supported Black and White student critiques of U.S. higher education and demands for free speech, decentralization of power, coursework relevant to 1960s America, and meaningful links between the campus and the community. The Panthers were not the only, or even the most important, influence on Black student attitudes and tactics at college campuses, but the students did derive strength from their example. Panthers and other significant figures and ideologies of the late 1960s contributed to the students' understanding of their role in society, the goals of an emancipatory education, and the possibilities of a relevant education. Many students then took this understanding and demanded that their campuses provide the tools necessary to critically analyze their reality in order to act upon it. Though somewhat inconsistent with Panther ideology, Black students and Black Panthers sought similar ends—Black liberation and control of their own destiny.

Conclusion

Robert Lowe and Harvey Kantor point out that the historiography of 1960s educational reforms disconnects Black demands for increased community control of schools from the larger context of Black social movements and struggles for societal change.[51] Also, discussions of the community-control movement ignore the demands for immediate solutions to Black academic underachievement and reduce the call for control to political jockeying and attempts to use the schools for a Black separatist agenda. In the 1970s, many critics of community control believed that "the search for political 'liberation' of black Americans has no place in the schools" and that decentralization would "institutionalize the separation of the races."[52] Thirty years later, Diane Ravitch faulted community control advocates "for failing to understand that the interests of their people would be best advanced by breaking down the barriers of race and class, and by overcoming the self-limitations of separatism."[53] The community-control movement and its Black Nationalist origins flew in the face of desegregation efforts, and instead pondered radical solutions that made conservatives, and even liberals, anxious. Educational professionals vowed to protect public schooling from the Black particularistic agenda and keep politics out of schools. But these critics missed the fact that community control was but one cog in the wheel of collective racial (and societal) uplift, and that a fundamental aim of community control was to increase Black academic achievement. With the redefinition of education as political, the two ends—a high-quality education and Black liberation—occurred simultaneously. Liberation necessitated education.

In the story of the 1960s, the Black Panthers are situated even more peripherally than the community-control movement, and the Panther's educational programs are not discussed in relation to the movement for community control.[54] Radical solutions to improve education, particularly those initiated by African Americans, provoked the ire of educational professionals for as long as African Americans attempted to determine the path of their own education. The Panther's socialist ideology and prescriptions placed them on the fringe of even the radical solutions. Whereas the Black community-control movement was indicted for attempting to hijack public education for political purposes, the Black Panther Party's programs were considered a threat to national security.[55] Educational professionals and educational historians are quick to throw the proverbial baby out with the bath water and refuse to acknowledge the fact that Black Power–era critiques of education, including Panther criticisms, were legitimate. Panther educational initiatives usually were short-lived and certainly left room for improvement, but they represented an important wing of the school-decentralization efforts of the Black Power era. They sought to improve Black education by linking schools to the community, using students' backgrounds as a conduit for learning, infusing Black-centered content and themes in the curriculum, demanding communal control of the schools, and encouraging social action. Positioned alongside other Black Power–era school-reform efforts, the Panthers and their educational proposals are not so easily dismissed.

An examination of Panther programs, including their shortcomings, can be useful to contemporary reform movements that seek to improve the quality of Black education. Educational reformers continue to ask the question: Can pedagogically progressive education with a Black sensibility work? Multicultural education and Afrocentric education seek some of the same aims as the 1960s community-control movement and the Oakland Community School. Like their predecessors, these 21st-century reformers critique the public-school system as Eurocentric, patriarchal, and anachronistic in its one-size-fits-all approach to education in a diverse society.[56] In its place, multicultural and Afrocentric advocates argue for a different type of education that diversifies classroom materials, exposes students to alternative perspectives on reality, embraces different learning styles and language characteristics, and prepares students to become social-change agents.[57] Like their predecessors, such reform efforts encounter opposition. Their critics attack the reforms as a dilution of the academic curriculum that will sacrifice excellence for the sake of self-esteem, and fracture the American public into ethnic enclaves.[58] Inside schools, the reforms are often reduced to a celebration of an ethnic holiday or a special unit on a famous African American.[59] Critics also characterize these Black-inspired reforms as political maneuvers, rather than honest attempts to devise creative and even legitimate solutions to Black underachievement. The baby, once again, goes overboard.

Educators, parents, community members, and others continue to, as David Tyack and Larry Cuban put it, "tinker toward utopia" as they attempt to reconcile their faith in education with the glacial pace of educational reform.[60] Educational reformers created the public-school system to act as the great equalizer, where children from different ethnicities, races, language groups, and economic classes received an equal educational opportunity. Over time, this common-school mission received heavy scrutiny for its homogenization efforts, but the America's faith in public schools as institutions remained relatively constant.[61] The Black community, often outside the educational centers of power as well as the public-school system itself, also tinkered toward utopia. During the Black Power era, when their attempts to force their way into the public schools failed or when their children received substandard education in desegregated schools, they tinkered with alternative educational reforms and pondered solutions outside the norm. Like other Americans, the Black community in general and the Black Panther Party in particular maintained faith in the power of education. African Americans, however, merged cultural pride, academic achievement, and social reform—a combination antithetical to the mission of the common school. If public schools cannot reconcile these different opinions on the nature and purpose of schooling, the African American community will continue to set up alternative educational opportunities, as they tinker toward their own definition of utopia.

Notes

1. A federal-government report, known as the Coleman Report, found that achievement was related more closely with a student's family background than the quality of the school the student attended. In many ways it absolved schools for the low academic achievement and social status of African Americans. James Coleman, et al., *Equality of Educational Opportunity* (Washington, D.C.: Government Printing Office, 1966); and Fredrick Mosteller and Daniel P. Moynihan, *On Equality of Educational Opportunity: Papers Deriving from the Harvard University Faculty Seminar on the Coleman Report* (New York: Random House, 1972).

2. I am using the phrase "progressive education" to denote the pedagogical progressivism of which John Dewey is considered the spokesperson. See John Dewey, *Democracy and Education* (New York: Free Press, 1966), and *The School and Society* (Chicago: University of Chicago Press, 1990).

3. Stokely Carmichael and Charles V. Hamilton, *Black Power: The Politics of Liberation in America* (New York: Dial Press, 1967), 44.

4. See Kenneth Clark, *Dark Ghetto* (New York: Harper and Row, 1965); Jonathan Kozol, *Death at an Early Age: The Destruction of the Hearts and Minds of Negro Children in the Boston Public Schools* (New York: Houghton Mifflin, 1967); and Herbert Kohl, *36 Children* (New York: New American Library, 1967).

5. This chapter will not discuss the community-control movement in depth. For a more thorough treatment of the issues, including opinions on both sides of the debate, see Henry Levin, ed., *Community Control of Schools* (Washington, D.C.: Brookings Institution, 1970).

6. The 1968 Ocean Hill-Brownsville teacher's strikes in New York City are the most famous example of a community-control experiment that pitted the Black community against school professionals, including the powerful teacher's union, the United Federation of Teachers. See Maurice Berube and Marilyn Gittell, eds., *Confrontation at Ocean Hill-Brownsville: The New York School Strikes of 1968* (New York: Praeger, 1969); and Jerald Podair, *The Strike that Changed New York: Blacks, Whites, and the Ocean Hill-Brownsville Crisis* (New Haven: Yale University Press, 2002).

7. Huey P. Newton, "Intercommunalism," in *In Search of Common Ground: Conversations with Erik H. Erikson and Huey P. Newton,* edited by Kai T. Erikson (New York: W.W. Norton, 1973), 25.

8. Lee Lockwood, ed., *Conversations with Eldridge Cleaver: Algiers* (New York: McGraw-Hill Book Company, 1970), 107.

9. Eldridge Cleaver, *Education and Revolution* (Washington, D.C.: Center for Educational Reform, 1970), 1.

10. Ibid., 6.

11. Ibid., 16.

12. "October 1966 Black Panther Party Platform and Program," cited in *Off the Pigs! The History and Literature of the Black Panther Party,* edited by G. Louis Heath (Metuchen, N.J.: The Scarecrow Press, 1976), 249.

13. Cleaver, *Education and Revolution,* 6.

14. Huey P. Newton, "The Correct Handling of a Revolution," *The Black Panther,* 18 May 1968, cited in *The Black Panthers Speak,* edited by Philip S. Foner (New York: Da Capo, 1995), 43.

15. Ibid.

16. David Hilliard and Lewis Cole, *This Side of Glory: The Autobiography of David Hilliard and the Story of the Black Panther Party* (Boston: Little, Brown and Company, 1993), 121.

17. Larry Cuban discusses obstacles to pedagogically progressive ideas inside the mainstream classroom in *How Teachers Taught: Constancy and Change in American Classrooms, 1890–1990* (New York: Teachers College Press, 1993).

18. Heath, *Off the Pigs,* 107.

19. "Liberation Schools," *The Black Panther,* 5 July 1969; Foner, *The Black Panthers Speak,* 171.

20. Heath, *Off the Pigs,* 107–108, citing evidence gathered from the House Committee on Internal Security hearings on the Black Panther Party, part 4 and part 3, 1970 (hereafter cited as HCIS).

21. Bobby Seale, statements made at a press conference, *The Black Panther,* 21 June 1969, 14, cited in Heath, *Off the Pigs,* 107.

22. "Liberation Schools," 170.

23. Val Douglas, "The Youth Make the Revolution," *The Black Panther,* 2 August 1969, cited in Foner, *The Black Panthers Speak,* 172.

24. Ibid.

25. Heath, *Off the Pigs,* 101–102, citing HCIS.

26. Heath, *Off the Pigs,* 115 note 66.

27. United States Senate, *Final Report of the Select Committee to Study Governmental Operations with Respect to Intelligence Activities,* report no. 94–755, 94th Congress, 2d session (Washington, D.C.: U.S. Government Printing Office, 1976), 210. The charge of spreading anti-White propaganda is interesting since the Panthers were vocal advocates of cross-race alliances and repeatedly demonstrated their willingness to engage in such relationships.

28. Heath, *Off the Pigs,* 102, citing HCIS.

29. Elaine Brown, *A Taste of Power: A Black Woman's Story* (New York: Pantheon Books, 1992), 392–393.

30. JoNina M. Abron, "'Serving the People': The Survival Programs of the Black Panther Party" in *The Black Panther Party Reconsidered,* edited by Charles E. Jones (Baltimore: Black Classic Press, 1998), 186; and "The Oakland Community School," brochure, 1977, series 2, box 16, folder 2, Huey P. Newton Papers, Black Panther Party Programs, Stanford University Archives (all archived material is gathered from this source; therefore, all subsequent citations will be represented as HPN Papers, BBP Programs with the appropriate series, box, and folder).

31. "Oakland Community School Instructor Handbook," 1976, series 2, box 17, folder 1, HPN Papers, BBP Programs.

32. Originally, the school was known as the Intercommunal Youth Institute. The name change to the Oakland Community School marked the shift in ideology and leadership as well as the drive toward legitimacy. Elaine Brown discusses OCS in her autobiography, *A Taste of Power.*

33. Brown, *A Taste of Power,* 393.

34. Ibid., 439, and "The Oakland Community School," brochure, 1977.

35. "About the Oakland Community School," flyer, 1979, series 2, box 16, folder 2, HPN Papers, BBP Programs.

36. "OCS Instructor Handbook."

37. Ibid.

38. *Oakland Community Learning Center News,* volume IV, no. 5 (February–March 1980), series 2, box 16, folder 2, HPN Papers, BBP Programs.

39. Earl Anthony, *Picking Up the Gun: A Report on the Black Panthers* (New York: Dial Press, 1970), cited in Heath, *Off the Pigs,* 148.

40. Heath, *Off the Pigs,* 149, citing HCIS, part 3, exhibit 11.

41. Ibid., 195 note 2, citing HCIS. The Panther chapter referenced was located in Indianapolis, Indiana.

42. Ibid., 108, citing HCIS.

43. Heath, *Off the Pigs,* 141, citing HCIS investigations. Craig Peck discusses the Black Panther newspaper as an educative device in "Educate to Liberate: The Black Panther Party and Political Education" (Ph.D. diss., Stanford University, 2001).

44. Huey P. Newton, *Revolutionary Suicide* (New York: Writers and Readers, 1973), 62–63.

45. Brown, *A Taste of Power,* 160–164.

46. Black Students Association Publications, 1967-, file number 41/66/826, University of Illinois at Urbana-Champaign Archives.

47. This is discussed more fully in Joy Ann Williamson, *Black Power on Campus: The University of Illinois, 1965–1975* (Urbana: University of Illinois Press, 2003), especially Chapter 2.

48. David Hilliard, "Black Student Unions," *The Black Panther,* 27 December 1969, cited in Foner, *The Black Panthers Speak,* 125.

49. Newton, *Revolutionary Suicide,* 172.

50. Nathan Hare, "The Case for Separatism: 'Black Perspective,'" in *Black Power and Student Rebellion Conflict on the American Campus,* edited by James McEvoy and Abraham Miller (Belmont, Calif.: Wadsworth, 1969), 234.

51. Robert Lowe and Harvey Kantor, "Considerations on Writing the History of Educational Reform in the 1960s," *Educational Theory* 39, no. 1 (1989): 1–9.

52. Henry Levin, "Summary of Conference Discussion," in Levin, *Community Control of Schools*, 282. Levin identifies these sentiments as part of the main criticism of community control that arose from a Brookings Institution–sponsored conference held in December 1968.

53. Diane Ravitch, *The Great School Wars: A History of the New York City Public Schools* (Baltimore: Johns Hopkins University Press, 2000), 378. Ravitch is referring to the Ocean Hill–Brownsville situation with this critique.

54. Only one piece I have found included the Panthers alongside community-control issues. However, only the Panther's support of the Black community in the Ocean Hill–Brownsville events is mentioned (D. Crystal Byndloss, "Revisiting Paradigms in Black Education: Community Control and African-Centered Schools," *Education and Urban Society* 34, no. 1 [November 2001], 91). For a discussion of the peripheral treatment of the Panthers in 1960s U.S. history in general, see Nikhil Pal Singh, "The Black Panthers and the 'Undeveloped Country' of the Left," in Jones, *The Black Panther Party Reconsidered*.

55. United States Senate, *Final Report of the Select Committee*.

56. Both James Banks and Christine Sleeter, two of the most prolific advocates of multicultural education, offer such critiques. See James Banks, "Multicultural Education: Historical Development, Dimensions, and Practice," in *Handbook of Research on Multicultural Education,* edited by James Banks and Cherry McGee Banks (New York: MacMillian, 1995); and Christine Sleeter, *Multiculturalism as Social Activism* (Albany: State University of New York, 1996).

57. James Banks, "Multicultural Education," and Molefi Kete Asante, "The Afrocentric Idea in Education," *Journal of Negro Education* 60 no. 2 (Spring 1991), 170–180.

58. In particular, E.D. Hirsch, Diane Ravitch, and Arthur Schlesinger Jr. lament the multicultural ethos that exists in some schools, and interpret the drive for equality as inimical to academic excellence. See E.D. Hirsch, *The Dictionary of Cultural Literacy* (Boston: Houghton Miflin, 1988); Diane Ravitch, *The Troubled Crusade: American Education, 1945–1980* (New York: Basic Books, 1983); Diane Ravitch, "Multiculturalism: E Pluribus Plures," *The America Scholar* (Summer 1990), 337–354; and Arthur Schlesinger Jr., *The Disuniting of America* (New York: W.W. Norton, 1992).

59. James Banks, "Multicultural Education"; Joan Davis Ratteray and Mwalimu Shujaa, *Dare to Choose: Parental Choice at Independent Neighborhood Schools* (Washington, D.C.: U.S. Department of Education, 1987); and Kofi Lomotey and C. Brookins, "Independent Black Institutions: A Cultural Perspective," in *Visible Now: Blacks in Private Schools,* edited by Diana Slaughter and Deborah Johnson (New York: Greenwood Press, 1988).

60. David Tyack and Larry Cuban, *Tinkering toward Utopia: A Century of Public School Reform* (Cambridge: Harvard University Press, 1995).

61. Carl Kaestle discusses the common school and its legacy in *Pillars of the Republic: Common Schools and American Society, 1780–1860* (New York: Hill and Wang, 1983).

Chapter Seven

BEVERLY M. GORDON

Leadership, the Cultural Other, and Education in the New Millennium

Introduction: The Fear Factor

In many interesting ways, the American psyche has changed drastically since 9/11. Having been attacked, the United States is now on the offense fighting a war against "terrorism" by invading Afghanistan, and now fighting an ongoing guerilla war in Iraq. We watch as the current Bush administration performs Michael Jackson's "moon walk" dance step, having proclaimed to the world on May 1, 2003, "mission accomplished." For this author, the war and now occupation in Iraq is more than an altruistic move by the United States to free the Iraqi people from a horrific dictator and his family, or even a grab for control over oil reserves and other markets (B. Gordon, 2003a). As I reflect on this war, it is emblematic of a growing concern in the West about control and domination of people of color, who constitute the majority world population. Western global hegemony is being challenged, not only by people of color struggling against continued Western, particularly U.S., global imperialism, but also by the ever-increasing global population of people of color. Lest the reader feel unconvinced of this, look at Patrick Buchanan's argument about the population decline of the West, and the ever-increasing "alien" population (Buchanan, 2002). While Buchanan is talking about the United States, the argument is of global proportion. There is a sense of fear, "white fear" (B. Gordon, 2003b), of the numerical and therefore political, influential, controlling ascendance of those whom some Whites perceive as "other." The U.S. fear factor is the umbilical cord from being White to maintaining control, even if it runs counter to common sense. This is the same fear that Welsing speaks of; that is, White fear of White genetic annihilation. (Welsing, 1991).[1] Are these recent events other variations of "Willy Horton"—not the man, but his cynical use by politicians? The unspeakable unspoken message—fear of the dangerous "other"—worked for George Bush Sr., as it is working now.

Fear and aversion of "other" is critical to the discussion of education. Fear coupled with the need for domination and control is precisely the tension between racialized groups, which impacts the images this society formulates regarding people "other" than themselves. Based on fear and the need for domination and control, the dominant society develops a normative world view of the "other" compared to themselves. This normative view is used as the basis to define perceptions, evaluations, assumptions, and beliefs. Moreover, if the dominant society conceptualizes itself as being in competition with those deemed "other" (e.g., regarding numerical majority, or societal control), it will respond defensively, in an effort to maintain its domination, control, and its perceived "need" for survival.

Education, as a societal institution, is a key means for that society to disseminate the knowledge, culture, and information to future generations so that they have the necessary tools and predisposition to maintain its power and status within its own shores and the global community. Is it the case that the current mode of operation is doing what it was designed to do, namely, maintain control and domination? Certain segments of the population receive an abundance of excellent educational opportunities and preparation, while "other" segments receive inadequate educational opportunities and education. Ironically, this unequal distribution of intellectual capital is maintained by entrenched hierarchical structures, even though it may not be in the best interest of society at large. These race- and class-based structures may contribute to the reduction of the number of citizens needed to maintain the economic and social health of the society. As the baby boomers retire, there is a concern that there will be too few new adults capable of entering into the workforce to support the retirement system.[2]

Why would a society continue to operate like this? Might it be that fear of "others," who may be in direct competition with that society, and the need for control and power, is driving society to operate in ways that is against its own long-term vested interests? Might it be that this fear is symptomatic of a national "dysconscious racism" (J. King, 1991) awakening to a global majority of people of color?

A New Millennium Begging for New Ideas

The entire field of education is confronted with persistent and contested issues such as the 2001 No Child Left Behind legislation, looming threats of a national curriculum and assessment, school choice, voucher plans, busing, and achievement testing; as well as new challenges such as the corporate running of school districts, and shrinking federal, state, and local financial support. African Americans[3] are confronted with those issues and the struggle for adequate educational opportunities and education, and against the unequal distribution of intellectual capital.[4] Sixty percent of African Americans are urban dwellers who form a Black underclass in which African American children are three times as likely as their White counterparts to live in a single-female-parent household, and where African American men experience higher levels of joblessness and much lower wages than their White male counterparts (Strickland & Ascher, 1992). Urban Black student populations are still attending segregated schools, and more often than not, "desegregated" schools are resegregated along racial and economic class lines. Most dishearteningly, justifications[5] for why low-income Black and Brown children are at risk are ever present (Strickland & Ascher, p. 614).

Even in this new millennium, the dominant society's rationale for the continuing poverty and despair within a majority of the Black and Brown urban populations has remained virtually the same. Societal change is seen in the form of a nation or state becoming increasingly more punitive in its legislative policies and judicial practices toward the disenfranchised. The economic, political, and social conditions that produce societal malaise have been rendered invisible. Community crises in the form of the working poor, drugs and violence, homelessness, and hopelessness manifested in "the cultural other" are borne by the people enslaved within that community.

When research is begun with assumptions and perceptions grounded in this fear of "other" and its resulting images and normative views that the group being studied is problematic, such assumptions speak volumes about the perspectives and paradigms employed to study the problem, as well as the probable outcomes, findings, policies, and implications of the work. The pejorative conceptualization of African American students as problematic is so much a part of the dominant beliefs in education that it has become taken for granted. In fact, critiques of deviancy theories are often ignored because conceptualizing the African American student as a problem has been normalized as common-sense thinking (B. Gordon, 1979; Kambon, 1992; Wilson, 1993). Community crisis is born out of the hierarchical structuring, the system of symbolic meanings, and the societal action that constitutes the dominant canon; and is reified through the societal order, political arrangements, and economic policies and practices. Since political and economic arrangements in society have a profound impact on the community, it is appropriate to question the political, social, and economic leadership in the community.

Leadership and the Resurgence of "The New Negro"

One question rarely heard in educational discussions is: Who constitutes the leadership in the African American community, and what are their positions on critical issues confronting African Americans in the new millennium? I am concerned about the danger of the African American community splintering into a working-poor underclass constituency, and an ever-more distant and estranged middle- and upper-middle-class constituency. Given that the emergence of the concept of a multiracial middle-class majority united by common language, culture, and customs is already being discussed, such a concern is valid (Lind, 1995). Issues of national and local leadership in and of the Black community are serious points of ideological contestation that impact on education; such as the tension between "community nominated" (Foster, 1990) and dominant-society–"appointed" leadership, and how these competing forms of leadership impact on the direction of the African American community (Gordon, 1997, p. 237).

The struggle to identify leadership figures in and for the African American community, and the impact of leadership on community life and institutions, have been historical struggles against the dominant society's hegemonic influence on Black society. In the field of education, for example, Anderson (1988) and Watkins (2001) have documented the historical struggle of African Americans against intellectual hegemony, and the imposition of appointed leadership, both Black and White, by White philanthropists and other powerful decision makers, in Black educational institutions since the late 19th century. In contemporary society, there has been an upsurge in the prominence of Black conservative leadership appointed or promoted by powerful White conservatives. Some of the more illustrative examples could include, but are not limited to: former ambassador and presidential candidate Alan Keyes, Supreme Court Justice Clarence Thomas, National Security Advisor Condoleezza Rice, Secretary of State Colin Powell, Secretary of Education Ron Paige, and authors Thomas Sowell and Shelby Steele. Juxtaposed with these are the "community"-chosen and appreciated leaders, including, but not limited to: university professors Patricia Hill Collins, Michael Eric Dyson, Toni Morrison, and Cornell West; law professors Lani Guinier and Christopher Edley; entertainer Bill Cosby; journalist Tony Brown; radio talk-show hosts Tom Joyner and Tavis Smiley; Reverend Jesse Jackson; Reverend Al Sharpton; and Minister Louis Farrakhan. Locally elected community leaders would include the Black mayors of Philadelphia and Detroit, as well as those serving on city councils, school boards, etc., throughout the country. Nationally recognized elected community leaders would include Senator Barack Obama, Congresswomen Maxine Waters, former congresswoman and presidential candidate Carol Mosley Braun, and Congressmen Charles Rangel and Ron Dellums.

The appointed leaders are, for the most part, promoted by Whites, as demonstrated in the appointments of Rice, Paige, and Powell by the current Republican administration of George W. Bush. Do these individuals have allegiance to, connectedness with, or influential symbolic capital in the African American community at large? By their actions, one could wonder out loud if they are exemplars of new-millennium "New Negroes" (B. Gordon, 1997). New Negroes are African American men and women who attained their status and social standing during the late 1950s through the 1960s, 1970s, and even 1980s, because of the struggle for Civil Rights, affirmative-action policies, and federally or privately sponsored higher-education programs that provided them access to privileged White institutions. (For example, Clarence Thomas did not attend Yale University because his family were alumni or had such wealth and influence that they could afford to gain him entrance and pay for his education.) In turn, New Negroes are now actively advocating and setting into place laws and future policies that would limit the access and opportunities for other African Americans (Owens, 2003). New Negroes view affirmative-action policy and helping programs as forms of "preferential treatment" for otherwise "unqualified" and "under-qualified" individuals (Painter, 1991).

"The New Negro" is, of course, a term borrowed from Alaine Locke, a contributing force in and during the Harlem Renaissance, whose classic work is of the same title (Locke, 1925[1980]). During the 1920s, the New Negro was viewed as extraordinary. Through the use of art and intellectual work as a means of demonstrating his or her humanity, the New Negro would not be stereotyped as Uncle Tom and Aunt Sally; the New Negro stood in accordance with her or his own individual merit. The New Negro perceived race as a hindrance, and believed that the poor were poor because they were caught in a cycle of poverty. At the very least, the New Negro did not see the plight of poor Black people through sympathetic eyes. In contemporary times, New Negroes resemble colonial intellectuals who have adopted and internalized the ideological and political perspectives as well as "the correct answers and ready solution" learned in formal education (Fasheh, 1990):

> Generally speaking, hegemonic education produces intellectuals who have lost their power base in their own culture and society and who have been provided with a foreign culture and ideology, but without a power base in the hegemonic society. (p. 25)

Current Black conservatives who are being appointed to some of the most powerful and influential positions in U.S. society will have a direct impact on African American issues. What is most disconcerting is that the majority of African Americans do not share most of the values, beliefs, and perspectives of New Negro leadership. The New Negroes, like Fasheh's (1990) colonial intellectuals are, in a real sense, alienated "from their own culture, history and people" (p. 25). My worry is that, to some extent, these New Negroes view their Black brethren with contempt and distain. More worrisome still is the question of how, then, do these New Negroes view themselves within the context of their Black community roots—with love and sensitivity, and a sense of service and upliftment, or with contempt, self-hatred and loathing, or even indifference? While it is not the scope of this particular work to explore the psychological and emotional attachments of New Negroes to the African American community at large, such a query is necessary in order to more fully understand what Fanon (1967) identified as the "black skin, white mask" phenomenon.

There are great opportunities and great dangers for the African American community entering the 21st century. One danger is that the dominant society selects our leaders and sets the agenda for the direction of the African American society. Another may be the dominant society's effort to pit one group of people of color against another. An even greater danger is that subsequent generations in the Black community will know less and less of their history, and be lulled into believing that being emulsified into the dominant society will equal acceptance. However, the greatest danger confronting the Black community is allowing the miseducation that alienates some of our best and brightest and isolates them from subsequent generations of their own people. Carter G. Woodson (Woodson, 1933[1977]) warned of this more than 60 years ago and the warning needs to be heeded, particularly now.

One example of how we Black folk can begin to heal ourselves, and stretch out our hands to other people of color in the global community, is to reconceptualize how we see ourselves in relation to American society and the world at large. Our goal should be to build collaborations and shared leadership with other people of color throughout the world. One way of achieving this would be to begin a conversation that brings together a vision of humanity as being symbolically kin related.

Framing Cultural Questions, Cultural Knowledge, and Cultural Models

> One cannot extirpate from the mind of the colonized man the culture which has been imposed upon him and which has poisoned him, except by offering him a substitute culture, namely his own culture, which implies an action to restore to life, re-valorize and popularize that culture. (Tourè, 1969)

Reclaiming one's cultural ways of being is an essential aspect of an authentic being. Culture has the capacity to serve as a weapon of liberation (Tourè, 1969). While the dominant society uses its culture, science, art, technology, and so on to justify and perpetuate its domination, it is still possible for a community to use its cultural meanings, values, beliefs, and artifacts as a prophylactic against ideological domination. The power of these cultural meanings and artifacts is that they are autochthonous to the real world, as opposed to being situated in the artificial and ideological environment of schools or other social institutions. Language has shared cultural context through which different groups express their specific group interests; and more important, the terrain of language is a terrain of power relations (Carby, 1987).

In light of this author's desire to dislodge prevailing discourses that perpetuate dominant social structure and power relations, and to engage alternative conceptions and practices, I find utility in the way in which the Black Studies Cultural Model (BSCM) conceptualizes humanity, because it speaks to understanding the world outside of traditional Western conceptual systems (Wynter, 1991, July 27). The BSCM also assists my own thinking about cultural knowledge[6] (B. Gordon, 1982, 1985, 1995), what cultural models mean for the African American community, and how cultural knowledge and cultural models might inform classroom pedagogy and school policy.

The Black Studies Cultural Model of human development argues for a cultural conceptualization of humankind (Wynter, 1991, July 27). This cultural model counters hierarchical views of humankind by proposing that being human constitutes more than existence as a biological, genetically preprogrammed organism. Humans were preprogrammed to be human, and came into being human simultaneously with their discourse, language, and meanings. Humankind is unique among all other animals because we live symbolic modes of being. There are no gradations within the human species (Wynter, 1990, September).

The Black Studies Cultural Model of human development, at its essence, argues for a conceptual system in which human beings are viewed not as genetically bonded and separated, but as symbolically kin related in the sense of treating "others," or "other people's children," as if they were part of one's own family, clan, or village. This cultural model fits the definition of autochthonous science in that it originates from the particular perspective of the African American reality, part of which includes the preservation of African conceptualizations and ways of thought and living, in effect, its *lieu de memoire* (B. Gordon, 1995).

At the dawning of the 21st century, the United States is emerging as a unique entity in a world undergoing global transformations and realignments of allegiance and power, particularly within the Third World (Wynter, 1991). In light of the United States' world prominence, and in the context of the previous discussion about "White fear," we must ask whether the United States is willing to reinvent itself into a democratic egalitarian society or whether it will remain as it was originally invented—as a hierarchical society based on a structure of domination and subjugation (Wynter, 1990, September). Clearly, there will be resistance to any change that challenges the current power configuration. Yet the stakes are so high that we must insist change occur as a matter of human rights and ecological survival. In the wake of possible global warming, and contestation about the depletion of the ozone layer, the realization that the West, particularly the United States, uses far more than its fair share of natural planetary resources, and other environmental concerns, it is fair to posit that the planetary environment is at risk of being destroyed because of the logic directing the collective behaviors and beliefs that characterize Western conceptions of science and humankind (Wynter, 1990, September).

The contemporary challenge for the curriculum field and educational policy is the deconstruction and the reinvention of schooling in a way that reflects the vision of humanity, in the emergent popular and intellectual culture, as being symbolically kin related. Lind (1995) talks about the emergence of a republic based on class. A cultural model would encourage the emergence of a culture based on the interrelatedness of humanity. Societal institutions such as schools, the media, and the justice system contribute to the socialization of youth in contemporary society. As demonstrated by increasing sense of youth alienation and crime rates, communities of children and youth have surmised that their social caste in this society is that of fringe dwellers, with very little at stake in the maintenance of the societal status quo. With regard to African American communities, from the upper-middle-class and middle-class neighborhoods to those of the working poor, young people not only see and experience disparity and injustice, but are questioning and even rejecting current societal values and beliefs. Simultaneously, they are constructing their own cultural contexts, often without knowledge of their cultural history. While African American, or any, popular youth culture is by no means monolithic, as demonstrated in the various controversies involving rap artists, the texts of their music, and public appearances (Baker, 1993; B. Gordon, 2003b; Lusane, 1993; Powell, 1991; Rose, 1991), popular youth culture posits a political view that challenges the dominant society (Hall, 1992). The cultural artifacts with which African American youth resonate (i.e., rap, music, fashion, film, politics) challenge the current systems and institutions of U.S. society by imploring students not to participate in U.S. domination and subordination of other people (Powell, 1991; Rose, 1991). The images, therefore, that Black youth are exposed to are critical in shaping their consciousness of themselves in society and the world. African American youth as well as their global-community cousins, who may be ambivalent about great Western work (Bloom 1988; (Hirsch, 1987), know the difference between the political ideologies espoused by Malcolm X and Martin Luther King Jr., and by and large, they are choosing Malcolm X's notion of obtaining justice "by any means necessary," partly because of their dawning awareness of the reality in which they live. Repeated scenarios of social injustice and inequity for African Americans, especially in urban areas in the United States, and other people of color, albeit in the Middle East, Australia, Africa, and South America, result in cynicism. For urban Black youth, cynicism, coupled with a dawning awareness that their chances of success in receiving justice, parity, or real power and control of capital in the current social, economic, and political configurations are slim, disintegrates into hopelessness. Such hopelessness results in both rage and defeatism. Youth rage explodes, more often than not, within their own communities and on each other—resulting in crime, drugs, and death, which in turn feeds the penal system and keeps it as a growth industry, even into this 21st century. The defeatism results in their rejection of the idea of "whiteness" as either a conceptual system or an institutional system. Yet, as they reject whiteness but value the symbols of White success and happiness, they pursue these symbols. Thus, capitalism thrives on them.

The danger remains that in urban Black youths' alienation from and rejection of whiteness, and for those who equate and reject rigorous academic preparation as "acting White," these students contribute to their own lack of skills and devaluation in society, to their own detriment, because they do desire to be part of the social order that currently exists (Fasheh, 1990; Fordham, 1988; Fordham & Ogbu, 1986; Willis, 1977). If urban Black youth have rejected the legitimated means of access to social rewards, because they perceive the social system to be biased against them, why would they seek inclusion in a society that devalues and is punitive to them? By the same token, if given a reason to do so, Black youth can become engaged in a society that provides equitable and real opportunities for them to develop to their fullest potential. There are at least three issues here regarding African American youth that must be addressed: ahistoric popular culture; youth rejection of the prescribed means of access to social rewards; and youth acceptance of these social rewards as having value despite their rejection of the legitimated means of achieving them. The critical theorizing and knowledge construction affecting the education of children of color in Western societies like the United States, as well as in the Third World, is a struggle over *ideology* rather than pedagogy (Fuller, 1991; Troyna & Hatcher, 1992).

Reconstructing Curriculum Discourse: Cultural Implications for Policy and Pedagogy

Two important sets of questions arise from this discussion. First, what must be the regime of truth operating in school curriculum that manages to produce and reproduce, regularly and precisely, the racial stratification between and among groups in U.S. society? (Wynter, 1991, July 27). Second, in whose interest, and for what purpose, are African American children and other children of color in the United States educated? Will that education function as a mode of ideological domination, working to co-opt Black students to the current societal hierarchy, or will it function as a force of social reconstruction to help them redefine the nature of their own lives? As an autochthonous critique, the cultural model aptly challenges this current regime of truth. However, critique alone will not change conceptual systems by arguing they work in the interest of some particular groups as opposed to other groups. We know that children must be encouraged to play with knowledge, to manipulate it, and to analyze ideas. They must also be encouraged to employ reading, writing, mathematics, science, history, etc., in order to solve problems and create new knowledge. Moreover, pedagogical and conceptual practices must include the exploration of the ethical issues and moral imperatives that come with the acquisition of knowledge, particularly advancing scientific and technological knowledge.

For teacher education and curriculum development, this means learning from and applying the numerous exemplars of African American scholarship on formal and informal learning (e.g., Crichlow, Goodwin, Shakes, & Swartz, 1990; Delpit, 1995; B. Gordon, 1982; L. R. Gordon, 1995a; Henry, 1992; Hilliard, 1992; Hollins & Spencer, 1990; Jansen, 1990; J. E. King, 1992, 1992 April; Ladson-Billings, 1992; Ladson-Billings & Henry, 1990; Lee, Lomotey, & Shujaa, 1990; Oldendorf, 1993). These citations represent a huge body of knowledge generated by African American and African Caribbean scholars and practitioners that gives the Black experience meaning and context, because they are situated in societies structured in dominance by race, class, and gender. How might the curriculum field employ these conceptualizations and pedagogy in a learning environment that encourages Black children to play with knowledge, and manipulate and analyze ideas to create new knowledge? How might children of color come to understand that while there are "intellectual, moral and humanitarian dimensions" of knowledge, knowledge also has as a central function of "creating power" (Fasheh, 1990, p. 23), giving those who possess it the ability to dominate those who do not have it? The single most important question is: why has change not occurred in light of the knowledge base generated by African Americans for the education of their children? What is working against implementing these curricular and pedagogical changes? For teacher educators and teachers alike, what might it mean to explore a different conceptualization of humanity? Specifically, what might it mean for educational institutions to define humankind as symbolically kin related?

Most teachers are decent human beings doing a very tough job, and are caught between multitudes of competing pressures. On one hand, teachers are at the mercy of school levies, state budget cuts, and federal mandates with little financial support, and now, increasingly by, political pressure to teach to tests in the name of raising national standards. On the other hand, we come to the profession with our own historical and cultural baggage and ideology. Unfortunately, in many instances, the perspective disseminated to preservice and in-service teachers unwittingly reinforces stereotypes and prejudices about students based on race, class, and gender. With regard to issues related to urban African American students, segments of the White teaching profession (who make up the majority of educators teaching children of color in K–12 schools) may need to unpack the everyday ways that make racism so normative that it becomes the transparent-invisible lens through which they view the world, never realizing the distortion of the lens. Such a conversation might assist teachers in identifying how "dysconscious racism" (J. King, 1991) manifests itself, providing ideas about how to define and identify racism, and repositioning themselves toward an "anti-black racism posture" (L. R. Gordon, 1995a, 1995b).

In the real world, it is in this nation's long-term interest to have an educated population that has a stake in the well-being of their community and society at large. And clearly, the future is pointed toward a technologically and scientifically advanced society, which will demand a more educated, highly skilled, and diversified workforce that is interested in advancement, but is ecologically minded. There will need to be a balance between caring for and preserving the integrity of the global environment, while addressing the needs and desires of humankind. The curriculum field and educational policy must be forward looking, to conceptualize possibilities and then to work toward the realization of those possibilities. The following are some suggestions for further discussion and consideration.

Those who write, guide, and influence curriculum development and educational policy must be mindful of future trends in the growth and direction of scientific and social knowledge, and the implications of ever-advancing knowledge and technology. As Fasheh (1990) discovered, science and mathematics can be used for purposes of domination as well as for the exploration toward new meanings and understandings of the physical environment.

Furthermore, issues surrounding accessibility to advanced levels of knowledge also need to be addressed. Curriculum and policymakers are encouraged to employ the works of African American scholars as suggested in this essay.

Finally, educational policymakers particularly must support efforts that effectively and expeditiously address issues of fiscal inequity and physical-facility disparities, among schools and school districts. As computer literacy and access to technology become more of a norm in the education of children, policymakers, curriculum planners, and the community will be required to work together to ensure that all segments of the population are computer literate.

Several of the issues and concerns that confront urban children are not remarkable to suburban African Americans. By the same token, the Black community is not homogenous, but is a dynamic, diverse, and heterogeneous community. Elsewhere as an author I have focused on the African American suburban educational experience (B. Gordon, 2001). While African American children face challenges unique to the suburban experience, some of their challenges are the same as their urban counterparts. How racism is manifested in both urban and suburban boundaries, or the ways communities operate and configure themselves in suburbia, is informative (B. Gordon, 2001). Moreover, such inquiry may be an easier starting point for teachers to reflect on and critique their own ideological baggage.

The assaults on affirmative action in higher-education admissions policies are clearly ominous developments and will make it even more difficult for African American students to gain access into predominantly White colleges and universities; nevertheless, these racist actions might have a silver lining, particularly at the undergraduate level. The cultural and community experiences of attending a historically Black college or university (HBCU) will help center and ground our youth in a way that is mostly lost in predominantly White institutions. The African American community must seriously consider returning their children *en masse* to HBCUs for at least some portion if not all of their undergraduate experiences. Furthermore, beyond the formal classroom and closer to home, there are opportunities for community education. As noted earlier, the African American community's autochthonous models of self-help and service have uplifted and improved the community (B. Gordon, 1985). Community education will allow people to: find their own voices and speak; reclaim their self-worth, their lives and ways of doing things; and "facilitate their ability to articulate what they do and think about in order to provide a foundation for autonomous action" (Fasheh, 1990, p. 26). A classic example of community education would be the work done by Bernice Robinson, under the guidance of Septima Clark and Myles Horton of the Highlander School, in the South Carolina Sea Island Citizenship schools (Oldendorf, 1993). Begun in 1954, these schools had their genesis in the need to register African Americans to vote, and the need of African Americans to become enfranchised and self-reliant. Pedagogically speaking, teacher and supervisor Bernice Robinson asked the students what it was that they wanted to learn and needed to know, so that she could develop materials to meet their needs. These adult learners wanted to "fill out order blanks from catalogues, read the newspaper, read letters from their children, do simple arithmetic, read the Bible, and register to vote" (Oldendorf, 1993, p. 172).

The Citizenship School model and the 1964 Mississippi Freedom School model (Radical Teacher, 1991) are examples of many possibilities for community work. Efforts such as Saturday schools, private or independent African American institutions, parent and community workshops, continued voter-registration drives, and church-based academic tutorial initiatives have long been part of the landscape of applied research and educational activism in the African American community (Anderson, 1988; Henry, 1992; J. E. King, 1992, 1992 April; Lee et al., 1990). The idea of kin relatedness, or as Henry says, "other mothering," is an essential feature of this educational activism in the African American community. Furthermore, with the push to dismantle mandated busing for desegregation, it is incumbent upon the community, parent by parent, to be involved in neighborhood schools. Community relations must also include ongoing efforts to build relationships, lines of communication, and collaboration with other people of color in their communities.

Public schools should be engaged in the neighborhoods they serve, by facilitating, for example, community-school projects. More precisely, administrators and teachers need to be connected to the neighborhoods they serve in ways that demonstrate a vested interest in the health and well-being of those communities. This could include, for example, participating in community activities, attending church or community events, collaborating with community groups and organizations, patronizing local stores. Obviously, any policy that requires such connectedness may be met with a variety of responses that will also be instructive and awakening. Nevertheless, schools must be stakeholders in the well-being of the neighborhoods they serve.

Colleges of education should provide students with full current and future demographic information so that they are better informed about local, state, and national population shifts. Preservice and in-service teachers need information to help them assess the landscape of the teaching profession with regard to their "ideal dream teaching or administrative job" versus the projected job-related needs within education. Teachers and administrators who work in urban schools should do so because they want to teach in them, and not because of a lack of job availability elsewhere.

Finally, African Americans must be vigilant about the formal academic and social education given to our children, as we prepare for subsequent generations of leaders, scholars, popular artists, business people, scientists, and more. African Americans must ultimately take responsibility for the education that our children do or do not receive. Just as important, the African American community is also responsible for providing its children with cultural knowledge as an academic tutorial initiative and a deliberate assault on miseducation.

Community participatory action, or service to the community, a strong component in African American culture, comes in many forms: from work through African American philanthropic organizations, to attendance at school-board forums, to engagements in other community activities. African American communities should continue to develop and participate in after-school and Saturday activities, in cultural schools, and in volunteer tutorial programs, etc. Community participatory action also includes African Americans allowing their economic resources to work for the community, whenever possible, by patronizing black businesses and professionals such as architects, barbers, clothing shops and beauty parlors, commercial or residential contractors, funeral parlors, realtors/brokers, florists, health-care providers, dentists, physicians, attorneys, engineers, etc. Albeit diversified, the African American community is a dynamic force with great potential.

Final Thoughts: The Challenge to African American Leadership

Referring back to the earlier discussion, it is appropriate to ask what happened to the 1920s New Negro movement. The demise of the Harlem Renaissance and this New Negro movement were linked to the economic Depression of the 1920s and 1930s, the dispersal of key figures within the movement, and an end to the Harlem nightlife that flourished until the repeal of the Volstead Act to end Prohibition in 1933 (Watson, 1995). The most compelling reason for the demise of the New Negro movement resided in its being "torn apart by internal contradictions (Niggerati [interested Whites] versus the Talented Tenth, politics versus art, race-building versus literature), and its external dependence for support by the Harlemania and Negrotarians. . . . [In short,] the New Negroes mistook art for power" (Watson, 1995, p.159).[7] As he ended his editorship of *The Crisis*, Du Bois was queried as to why the Harlem Renaissance never took root. His response is instructive: "[The Harlem Renaissance] was a transplanted and exotic thing. It was a literature written for the benefit of White people and at the behest of White readers, and starting out privately from the white point of view" (Watson, 1995, p. 159). Could it be that the New Negroes of this new millennium are mistaking their adoption and internalization of dominant (right-wing) ideology and political perspectives for acceptance? Is the New Negro a variation of Professor Gleason Golightly (Bell, 1992),[8] the truly colonized man? (Fanon, 1967).

In this advancing, technological, and postmodern U.S. society of the 21st century, the most critical educational struggle for people of color will be for the control over the academic, intellectual, and political development of their children. This struggle is compounded by the economics of the new world order, the downsizing of the blue- and white-collar workforce, restructuring of the U.S. economy, and the emergence of the Third World as an influential global force; thus the question of what type of education that African American youth receive is absolutely critical. The conceptual systems that govern the production of knowledge and that regulate educational discourse, meaning, and the resulting societal behaviors and configurations, will no doubt be marshaled to control autochthonous critiques and social action. However, the brute force of domination alone will not quell, let alone resolve, social and, more specifically, pedagogical rebellion.

In this 21st century, the African American community must build on its strengths, confront its weaknesses, and reach beyond its borders into the global African Diaspora. The issues confronting future generations of African American youth are great. Urban youth are in crisis in their schools and their cities, while suburban Black youth are confronted with the "black skin, white mask" phenomenon (B. Gordon, 2001). Getting Black youth involved and engaged with the future and its possibilities will take strength, leadership, and grassroots efforts. In the curriculum field and in educational policy, there are opportunities to view and understand classroom pedagogy and transform it from a logical-positivistic competitive environment to an intrinsically motivated and engaging world. Most important, in the curriculum field, there is a great opportunity to challenge the regimes of truth, while simultaneously viewing humanity anew. All of this will take commitment and leadership.

The tensions between community-nominated and the society-appointed, right-wing conservative leadership may well be irreconcilable. They represent two fundamentally different conceptualizations of African Americans in and of American society. Leadership must represent the autochthonous and not the imported; an inauthentic person or ideology can never operate for the benefit of the community. In fact, the lack of authenticity of the New Negro makes their positions antithetical to the long-term survival of the community as a whole. Leadership speaks to guidance and understanding, a commitment to the educational advancement of the community, real but compassionate tough love, facilitating economic accessibility into business and industrial enterprises, the political savvy to engage in social action for the improvement and advancement of the community, and the ability to engage in national and global dialogues that require critique and social action.

The challenge for the African American community will be to see that future generations of African American leadership are not alienated from their community and therefore will not operate "with a foreign culture and ideology." The leadership needed will be one that provides guidance and strategic plans for the future life and well-being of the community, with compassion and a vision of what could be. Let us work toward generations of African American leaders who have a dream, and the action plan to move us forward.

Notes

1. Ironically, at the same time, the U.S. economy is suffering because international corporations are taking white- and blue-collar jobs oversees where the costs are less and the profits are better. *But only to a point,* because the attention span/patience of people unemployed or downsized in a struggling economy is getting shorter, in particular when they will be asked to pay billions more for the occupation and reconstruction of a nation, and where U.S. soldiers and personnel are being killed on a regular basis. In the six-month period from the start of the war until May 1, 2003, when the President declared "mission accomplished," more than 117 U.S. service personnel were killed and wounded, as well as several U.S.-appointed Iraqi officials and police officers.

2. This concern about the declining population may also be part of the push to rescind legalized abortions. While a full discussion of this topic is not in the scope of this work, such a query is necessary.

3. This category also includes people of color, home and abroad, as well as poor and working-class Whites, who cannot allow themselves to be identified with people of color because of their allegiance to the race card.

4. These issues include: lower rates of achievement, learning and behavioral labeling, tracking systems, and relatively contemporary issues such as computer illiteracy and lack of access to technology.

5. The justifications include: IQ, genetic differences, linguistic differences, cultural dissonance, societal racism, poverty, and inferior education.

6. Cultural knowledge is the *lieux de memorie* (collective memory) of a people. When speaking of African American cultural knowledge, the emphasis is on "African" and "knowledge." "Knowledge" is a socially constructed system of meanings and understandings that frames our living, values, world view, and belief systems. It is a collective wisdom that gives guidance about living, seeing, and being in the world. African American cultural knowledge is autochthonous to the African Diaspora in the Americas. Cultural knowledge is manifested in the popular and intellectual artifacts of the African American existential condition, reflecting the cultural, social, economic, historical, and political experience. This experience is mediated and disseminated through the academic, folk, and popular forms of literary arts, dance, film, spirituality and/or religion, music, philosophy, athletics, organizations, style, and so

forth. For people of the African Diaspora in the Americas, cultural knowledge has its roots and *lieux de memoire* in Africa. As a dynamic force, it continues to influence and transform the American experience.

7. According to Watson, Zora Neale Hurston coined the term "Negrotarians." The Negrotarians were those whose "ranks were united in little but their whiteness and their vaguely progressive beliefs; they encompassed two generations and both sexes, Jews, Christians, immigrants and land gentry. Their conceptions of African Americans varied widely. To different factions the Negro represented a revolutionary political recruit, a naturally sensuous animal, an indigenously spiritual being, an authentic American artist, a victim of civil rights abuse" (Watson, 1995, p. 95). The Harlemaniacs were an international high-bohemian group of Whites who were fascinated with Harlem (Watson, 1995, p.104).

8. Professor Gleason Golightly is a fictitious character in Bell's chapter entitled, "The Space Traders." Golightly is a conservative African American economist serving as an advisor to a conservative White president. Golightly believed his conservative stance held him and his opinions in high regard with the president. When intergalactic beings arrive and offer the United States gold, an unlimited supply of clean environmentally safe energy in trade for every African American, over Golightly protestations, the president and congress agree to the terms. While some African Americans are able to escape to Canada, all must go, including Golightly himself and his wife who are turned away at the Canadian border, even though he had been promised safe passage out of the country.

References

Anderson, J. D. (1988). *The education of Blacks in the South, 1860–1935.* Chapel Hill and London: University of North Carolina Press.

Baker, H. A., Jr. (1993). *Black studies, rap and the academy.* Chicago: The University of Chicago Press.

Bell, D. (1992). *Faces at the bottom of the well: The permanence of racism.* New York: Basic Books.

Bloom, A. (1998). *The closing of the American mind.* New York: Simon & Schuster.

Buchanan, P. J. (2002). *The death of the West: How dying populations and immigrant invasions imperil our country and civilization* (1st ed.). New York: Thomas Dunne Books/St. Martin's Press.

Carby, H. V. (1987). *Reconstructing womanhood: The emergence of the Afro-American woman novelist.* New York and Oxford: Oxford University Press.

Crichlow, W., Goodwin, S., Shakes, G., & Swartz, E. (1990). Multicultural ways of knowing: Implications for practice. *Journal of Education, 172*(2), 101–117.

Delpit, L. (1995). *Other people's children: Cultural conflict in the classroom.* New York: The New Press.

Fanon, F. (1967). *Black skin, white masks.* New York: Grove Press.

Fasheh, M. (1990). Community education: To reclaim and transform what has been made invisible. *Harvard Educational Review, 60*(1), 19–35.

Fordham, S. (1988). Racelessness as a strategy in Black students' school success: Pragmatic victory or pyrrhic victory? *Harvard Educational Review, 58*(1), 54–84.

Fordham, S., & Ogbu, J. U. (1986). Black students' school success: Coping with the burden of "acting White." *The Urban Review, 18*, 176–206.

Foster, M. (1990). The politics of race: Through the eyes of African-American teachers. *Journal of Education. Special Issue: History and Voice in African-American Pedagogy, 172*(3), 123–141.

Fuller, B. (1991). *Growing-up modern: The Western state builds third world schools.* New York: Routledge, Chapman & Hall.

Gordon, B. (1997). Curriculum, policy and African American cultural knowledge: Challenges and possibilities for the year 2000 and beyond. *Educational Policy, 11*(2), 227–242.

Gordon, B. (2001). *Race in Middle Class Life: The Educational Experiences of Middle class Suburban Black Families.* Madison, Wisconsin: Visiting Minority Scholar Lecture Series. Sponsored by University of Wisconsin School of Education and the Wisconsin Center for Education Research.

Gordon, B. (1979). *The educational life histories of nine high school drop-outs.* Unpublished Ph.D. Thesis, University of Wisconsin.

Gordon, B. (1995). The fringe dwellers: African-American women scholars in the postmodern era. In B. Kanpol & P. McLaren (Eds.), *Education, democracy and the voice of the other.* Boston: South End Press.

Gordon, B. (2003a). *The impact of the war in Iraq on education and educational research.* Paper presented at the American Educational Research Association Annual Meeting, Chicago, Illinois.

Gordon, B. (1982). Towards a theory of knowledge acquisition for Black children. *Journal of Education, 164*(1), 90–108.

Gordon, B. (1985). Toward emancipation in citizenship education: The case of African-American cultural knowledge. *Theory and Research in Social Education, 12*(4), 1–23.

Gordon, B. (2003b). *White fear, war and Black resolve. Some challenges, potentialities and possibilities of what Black folk face in the 21st century.* Unpublished manuscript.

Gordon, L. R. (1995a). *Bad faith and antiblack racism.* Atlantic Highlands, New Jersey: Humanities Press International, Inc.

Gordon, L. R. (1995b). *Fanon and the crisis of European man—an essay on philosophy and the human sciences.* New York and London: Routledge.

Hall, S. (1992). What is the "Black" in Black popular culture? In G. Dent (Ed.), *Black Popular Culture: A Project by Michelle Wallace.* (pp.21–33) Seattly: NBay Press.

Henry, A. (1992). African Canadian women teachers' activism: Recreating communities of caring and resistance. *Journal of Negro Education, 61*(3), 392–404.

Hilliard, A. G. III. (1992). Behavioral style, culture, and teaching and learning. *Journal of Negro Education, 61*(3), 370–377.

Hirsch, E. D. (1987). *Cultural literacy: What every American needs to know.* Boston: Houghton Mifflin.

Hollins, E. R., & Spencer, K. (1990). Restructuring schools for cultural inclusion: Changing the schooling process for African-American youngsters. *Journal of Education, 172*(2), 89–100.

Jansen, J. (1990). In search of liberation pedagogy in South Africa. *Journal of Education, 172*(3), 62–71.

Kambon, K. (1992). *The African personality in America: An African centered framework.* Tallahassee: Nubian Nation Publications.

King, J. (1991). Dysconscious racism: Ideology, identity and the miseducation of teachers. *The Journal of Negro Education, 60,* 133–146.

King, J. E. (1992). Diaspora literacy and consciousness in the struggle against miseducation in the Black community. *Journal of Negro Education, 61*(3), 317–340.

King, J. E. (1992, April). *The middle passage revisited: Diaspora literacy and consciousness in the struggle against "miseducation" in the Black community.* Paper presented at a symposium on "New Challenges to the 'Regimes of Truth': Toward a New Intellectual Order," at the annual meeting of the American Educational Research Association, San Francisco, California.

Ladson-Billings, G. (1992). Liberatory consequences of literacy: A case of culturally relevant instruction for African-American students. *Journal of Negro Education, 61*(3), 378–391.

Ladson-Billings, G., & Henry, A. (1990). Blurring the borders: Voices of African liberatory pedagogy in the United States and Canada. *Journal of Education, 721*(2), 72–88.

Lee, C. D., Lomotey, K., & Shujaa, M. (1990). How shall we sing our sacred song in a strange land? The dilemma of double consciousness and the complexities of an African-centered pedagogy. *Journal of Education, 172*(2), 45–62.

Lind, M. (1995). *The next American nation. The new nationalism and the fourth American revolution.* New York, London, Toronto, Sydney, Tokyo, and Singapore: The Free Press.

Locke, A. (Ed.). (1925 [1980]). *The New Negro.* New York: Athenaeum.

Lusane, C. (1993). Rap, race, and politics. *Race and Class, 35*(1), 41–56.

Oldendorf, S. B. (1993). The South Carolina Sea Island citizenship schools. In V. L. Crawford, J. A. Rouse & B. Woods (Eds.), *Women in the Civil Rights Movement* (pp. 169–182). Bloomington and Indianapolis: Indiana University Press.

Owens, K. (2003, October). Connerly's crusade. He gained notoriety in California with the controversial Prop. 209. Now anti-affirmative action crusader Ward Connerly looks to go national. First stop: Michigan. *Savoy, 03,* 47–50.

Painter, N. I. (1991). Whites say I must be on Easy Street. In *The eyes on the prize Civil Rights reader* (pp. 651–656). New York: Penguin Books.

Powell, C. T. (1991). Rap music: An education with a beat from the street. *Journal of Education, 60*(3), 245–259.

Radical Teacher. (1991). *Mississippi freedom schools* (pp. 1–46). W. Somerville, Massachusetts: Boston Women's Teachers' Group, Inc.

Rose, P. (1991). "Fear of a Black planet": Rap music and Black cultural politics in the 1990s. *Journal of Negro Education, 60*(3), 276–290.

Strickland, D., & Ascher, C. (1992). Low income African-American children and public schooling. In P. W. Jackson (Ed.), *Handbook of research on curriculum* (pp. 609–625). New York, Toronto, and Oxford: Macmillan Publishing Company.

Tourè, S. (1969). A dialectical approach to culture. *The Black Scholar, 1*(1), 11–26.

Troyna, B., & Hatcher, R. (1992). *Racism in children's lives.* London: Routledge, Chapman & Hall.

Watkins, W. (2001). *The white architects of black education: Ideology and power in America, 1865-1954.* New York: Teachers College Press.

Watson, S. (1995). *The Harlem Renaissance—hub of African American culture, 1920–1930.* New York: Pantheon.

Welsing, F. C. (1991). *The Isis (Yssis) papers* (1st ed.). Chicago: Third World Press.

Willis, P. (1977). *Learning to labour: How working-class kids get work-class jobs.* Westmead, Farnborough, Hants., England: Saxon House, Teakfield Limited.

Wilson, A. (1993). *The falsification of Afrikan consciousness: Eurocentric history, psychiatry and the politics of white supremacy.* New York: Afrikan World Information Systems.

Woodson, C. G. (1933 [1977]). *The miseducation of the Negro* (2nd ed.). New York: AMS Press.

Wynter, S. (1990, September). *America as a "world": A Black studies perspective and "cultural model" framework*: A letter to the California State Board of Education.

Wynter, S. (1991, July 27). *Plenary session: Diaspora literacy and the Black studies perspective in curriculum change.* Paper presented at the Diaspora Literacy, Santa Clara University, Santa Clara, California.

Chapter Eight

DIONNE DANNS

Chicago Teacher Reform Efforts and the Politics of Educational Change

During the decades of the 1960s and 1970s, African Americans became increasingly fed up with their repressed existence in American society, and rebelled in a variety of ways in an effort to challenge their subjugation. Their liberation efforts were part of, and inspired by, the freedom struggles world-wide, as oppressed peoples fought colonial and other systems of repressive rule. The struggles by African Americans during these eventful decades became known as the Civil Rights and Black Power Movements. During the Civil Rights Movement, integration and equality were sought through the courts, on the streets, at lunch counters, on public transportation, and in education-al facilities. As the Movement evolved, its leaders marched and demonstrated for legislative changes. Even after civil and voting rights legislation were passed, leaders had to organize marches and demonstrations to ensure com-pliance (Payne, 1995). Radical activists of the Movement believed that with-out power, societal changes would not occur to the extent that they wished. By 1966, young militant leaders ushered in the Black Power era as they began to shift their ideology, and pushed for control of institutions in Black commu-nities rather than integration.

This chapter is about teachers in Chicago organizing a movement to change the curriculum, quality of education, and power dynamics within the public-school system. While the educational movement in Chicago was wide-spread, this inquiry is a case study of Black teachers at Farragut High School. Farragut teachers issued demands to the school administrators in September 1968, and protested in various ways, yet their demands were largely ignored. They concluded that the only way to advance their cause would be to oust the principal and take over the school. Their school takeover lasted from 1970 until 1971. The protest organized at Farragut provides lessons about teacher dissent and community control. It also highlights the limitations of educational reform, particularly at individual schools, as bureaucratic mechanisms in the educational system serve to limit the possibilities of change (Tyack, 1977).

There are some limitations to this study. Methodologically, the events at Farragut are largely dependent on three oral-history interviews and a firsthand account in an article. These sources document the struggle at Farragut, and each source serves to corroborate the others. Hannibal Afrik (formerly Harold Charles) is a central character, and coverage of his ideas and participation are semibiographical. His interview reveals the protest thought of the teachers. As a leader of the teacher movement at Farragut, it may be inferred that his ideas at least encompassed the core group of Black teachers who created the demands. In his interview, Afrik's statement supports this notion: "Because I had obtained the signatures of nearly all of the black teachers in that school . . . their signature was their commitment and their code." The interview with Lois Travillion, one of the Black teachers who helped create the "Black Manifesto," offers a glimpse at the low expectations for Black students at Farragut. An interview with White district superintendent Joseph Rosen confirms statements by Travillion and Afrik. Elizabeth Anders's (1971) "Everybody Run Farragut," is her firsthand, chronological account of the events at Farragut. As a White teacher, her article provides much of the details about the struggle at Farragut, and gives a glimpse of the principal's leadership and the reasons why White teachers joined the struggle.

This study is also limited to teachers at Farragut High School. Teachers, students, and community members throughout Chicago and Farragut were organizing protests and issuing demands. Their combined actions pushed the centralized educational system of control closer to the community. The author has documented these protests in other publications. The Farragut movement is highlighted here specifically because of the teachers' leadership and success in establishing temporary community control.

Framing the Discussion

David Tyack (1974) traced the evolution of the disconnected, often politically controlled, decentralized U.S. educational system to a centralized bureaucracy at the turn of the twentieth century. Reformers at the time believed that this "one best system" was an efficient way of installing a more meritocratic system, socializing children for their role in the corporate society, standardizing curricula, and limiting the control of schools to the hands of experts. Tyack

(1974) contends that the myth of education being above politics "served to obscure actual alignment of power and patterns of privilege" (p.11). Reformers, claiming to create a more democratic system that would limit political patronage, essentially took control away from local people (Tyack, 1977). Superintendents and central boards of education with ties to the business community maintained power. These bureaucracies, ensnarled with red tape, made it difficult to institute changes that were not derived from the top levels of administration.

As the "one best system" was being created, issues of culture, race, and class were effectively marginalized. African American education took on a different, separate development where centralized control stripped Black schools of financial equality. James D. Anderson (1988) chronicled the desire of African Americans to acquire education in the South at the end of and immediately following the Civil War. Anderson writes, "The foundation of the freedmen's educational movement was their self-reliance and deep-seated desire to control and sustain schools for themselves and their children" (p. 5). While Blacks in the South began to create schools for themselves, White northerners and southerners had their own agenda for the education of the freedmen and women (Watkins, 2001; Anderson, 1988). Northern White philanthropists and southern educational reformers were financial and ideological supporters of the Hampton model. Developed by Samuel Chapman Armstrong, the Hampton model of industrial education for Black students severely limited academic courses and effectively prepared African Americans for their continued menial role in the southern labor market, and steered them away from questioning political and social injustice (Watkins, 2001; Anderson, 1988). Black educational efforts supported by northern missionaries and Black religious organizations, however, stressed a broader academic curriculum.

Two different ideologies emerged in the education of African Americans: one meant to keep Blacks in their place, and a second meant to elevate their status within the American society. White southerners established universal education in the South on the educational foundation that African Americans had developed and then attempted to severely restrict the quality of education that Blacks received. After the 1896 *Plessy v. Ferguson* Supreme Court decision, a separate and inherently unequal education was maintained for African Americans. Once southern Whites controlled the system of education for Blacks, Black teachers were paid lower salaries than White teachers, and Black schools received disproportionately low funding, despite the taxes African Americans paid (Anderson, 1988).

The Civil Rights Movement and the 1954 *Brown v. Board of Education* Supreme Court ruling sought to eradicate the history of exclusion and inequality in education, housing, and public accommodations, etc. The quest for Civil Rights in Chicago featured an educational movement, as activists pushed for desegregation of the city's public schools. The desire for desegregation in Chicago was met with half-hearted efforts by the schools' governing board of education, despite school boycotts and demonstrations. Civil rights advocates had fought a series of battles with the Chicago Board of Education and Superintendent Benjamin Willis in their attempts to achieve school desegregation. Their battles included three boycotts, sit-ins, and a Title VI complaint to the United States Office of Education in the U.S. Department of Health, Education, and Welfare (Danns, 2003b; Ralph, 1993; Anderson and Pickering, 1986). The Coordinating Council of Community Organizations (CCCO) documented the severe inequalities that occurred as a result of segregation. Despite their gallant efforts, the city had vested financial and political interests in maintaining its White middle-class population, and therefore, school officials did not give in to the CCCO demands (Timuel Black, personal communication, June 16, 2000; Vrame, 1970).

With the failure of desegregation, particularly in northern urban areas, those on the front lines for the battle against social injustice recognized their powerlessness. Shujaa and Afrik (1996) argue that the *Brown v. Board of Education* Supreme Court decision did not change the power relations that existed. As a result, the same school leaders in authority before *Brown* continued to make decisions about how, when, and where desegregation would take place. Hannibal Afrik, a Farragut High School teacher for thirty years, offered this view of power within public schools:

> In the white community, white people make all of the decisions about their schools. They determine the curriculum, the physical materials, teacher selection, principal selection, teacher retention, taxation, material supplies, etc. All of those decisions are made by white people in the white community. Unfortunately, all of those decisions are also made by white people for the black community. So given this history of institutional racism in this country, there is no evidence to suggest that white people will voluntarily provide equality and access to black youth out of some benevolent spirit. So a reform is needed to ensure greater parental and community empowerment over the decision making aspects of their child's education (personal communication, 1999).

His analysis of the fundamental power relations, and institutional racism within public school systems, clearly articulates the essence of the argument for community control during the Black Power era in the latter part of the 1960s.

Joseph M. Cronin (1973) described the rationale for community control in this manner:

> Efforts to integrate the schools met with openly hostile resistance. . . . Black leaders, after five to ten years of struggle to eliminate *de facto* segregation, grew cynical in the

mid-1960s about the willingness of white leaders to move decisively. A new and younger group of activists, many of them veterans of the tense confrontations in the South (integrating lunch counters and universities or registering voters in the mid-60s), placed little trust in the white man's willingness to correct injustices. Better to try to take over their own neighborhood institutions—the stores, the schools, the community centers. Black men had better develop their own pride, prowess, and power because the white power structure would not yield (182–183).

Beginning in 1966, as some young organizers in civil rights groups became more radical, the issue of control and power became central to the ideological underpinnings of the movement. While there were many who understood these issues prior to the movement's shift in emphasis, others learned through their experience in the movement.

In order to gain community control of schools, decentralization of the public educational system was necessary, so that community members would have more input into school decision making. Decentralization dissects centralized administration into smaller, local districts (Cronin, 1973), which may share power among central administration, community leaders, school administrators, and teachers (Fantini, Gittell, and Magat, 1970). Community control, on the other hand, puts the majority of the power into the hands of the community. Events in New York during the late 1960s are instructive as they paralleled what was happening in Chicago.

Glance at New York

New York City's decentralization and community-control struggles highlight racial polarization, White middle-class cultural values versus Black working-class cultural values, and the United Federation of Teachers' (UFT) fight to maintain power within the status quo (Podair, 2002). The African-American Teachers Association, founded in 1964 as the Negro Teachers Association, was among the defenders of Black working-class culture. The ATA articulated their discontent with who ran the schools, the watered-down curriculum, and the question of intelligence and discipline of Black youth. Podair (2002) argued that White teachers' acceptance of the culture-of-poverty arguments that were pervasive in the 1960s, along with teachers' belief that low-income students were unlikely to achieve academically, caused their indifferent attitude toward the teaching of Black students. Teachers' beliefs about the inability of Black students to learn curtailed these students' educational potential. This was further compounded by the tracking system, which often left Black youth in the lowest tracks. Preston Wilcox's (1966) reprinted article in the *Negro Teachers Forum* articulated the limits of the educational system and the need for a change in power:

. . . . The present public educational system is not training the vast majority of youth in the ghetto to anything like the limits of their potential. If it is true that the public school system can do no more than it is already doing, then the communities of the poor must be prepared to act for themselves. The residents of the ghetto must seize the opportunity to assume a leadership role in the education of their own children. . . . (p. 3)

The ATA's defense of poor African Americans was directly at odds with the UFT, whose White membership largely blamed students for their failures. The UFT grew into a powerful bureaucracy in the 1960s and became co-manager of the educational system (Podair, 2002; 1994). The UFT had built a civil-service system with what they claimed to be racially neutral, meritocratic exams. These exams, however, served as gatekeepers to career advancement as African Americans had more difficulty passing the exams. When New York City's experimental districts were created through funding from a Ford Foundation grant, the planning for the district effectively bypassed the UFT and the school superintendent. Without their input in the planning, the governing board was given power to hire and fire personnel without the approval of the Board of Education or the UFT. Made up of community members and headed by Rhody McCoy, the governing board sent letters to a group of 19 White UFT teachers and administrators transferring them (Berube and Gittell, 1968). Their transfers precipitated three UFT strikes between September 9 and November 17, 1968. The transferred school personnel were reinstated on November 19, 1968. The strikes led to the end of the Ocean Hill–Brownsville experimental district. The governing board also hired principals who had not met the specified qualifications for principals. The Council of Supervisory Associations, an administrative union, filed a lawsuit, and the UFT supported the suit. New York's highest court upheld the experimental principal appointments, but set parameters for future appointments that were more consistent with the existing policies (Podair, 2002).

When the governing board hired "unqualified" principals and transferred 19 teachers, the UFT lashed out at this challenge to the bureaucratic process they had created. Had the UFT had its way in the planning of the experimental districts, it is doubtful that community control would have resulted from the decentralization experiment. The UFT's initial plans called for the continuation of the status quo. Podair (2002) captured the power struggle in the following statement: "Community control threatened the labor edifice [Albert] Shanker and the UFT had constructed, one that would crumble without centralized control of schools" (p. 44). The centralized control had afforded many groups power, and their desire to maintain that power went beyond their concern for Black and Puerto Rican youth.

Farragut High School

Background

Farragut High School, located in the South Lawndale community on Chicago's West Side, serves residents from both the North and South Lawndale communities. With the second migration of southern Black migrants into Chicago after World War II, the West Side's Black population expanded, replacing many of the Jewish and immigrant communities that had once lived in those areas (Hirsh, 1983). The community the school served had a 91.2 percent White population and an 8.6 percent Black population in 1950. By 1960, only 35.3 percent of the Whites remained in the area while the Black population increased to 64.4 percent. Farragut's school statistics indicated the continued expansion of the Black population (Board of Education, 1966). In 1963, the school's population contained 80.1 percent Black students. By 1968, the school had 91 percent Black students (Board of Education, 1968b). As Farragut's Black student population increased, so too did its Black teacher population. In 1968, 43.2 percent of the teachers at Farragut were Black (Board of Education, 1968a).

According to Anders (1971), Farragut was plagued with gang problems, high absenteeism, and student and teacher disorder. As the population shifted to majority Black, Anders wrote, "The white administration and many of the teachers were unprepared for and threatened by the change, the new sounds, the constant movement. Some teachers were frankly not interested in providing education for Black city kids" (pp. 67–68). The lack of preparation for the shifting population and the attitudes toward Black students led to some of the disorders in the school.

Farragut High School was the only school where temporary success with community control occurred. The political atmosphere in Chicago led to some acquiescence. Although city and school officials opposed the individual school and citywide demonstrations, the central school authorities were more willing to grant the demands of community-control advocates than they were willing to grant to advocates of desegregation, because community-control demands did not necessarily threaten White middle-class flight. Protests took place at Austin and Harrison High Schools where there were still sizable numbers of White students. However, those schools were in areas where racial transition from White to Black was already occurring at an alarming rate; but the majority of the schools where students and teachers had sustained protests were already 90 percent, or more, African American.

While the Black Teachers Association, a subset of the Chicago Teachers Union, challenged the racism in the CTU, the struggle at Farragut showed some interracial cooperation. There were a number of sympathetic White teachers who assisted in the ouster of the school's White principal. The White district superintendent also served as a broker between the teachers and the central administration, making the ouster of the principal a reality that would be unchallenged for more than a year. Without a doubt, the actions of Black teachers at Farragut made community control possible; but it is debatable whether they would have been able to successfully oust the principal without the district superintendent's actions.

Martin Luther King Jr.'s assassination on April 4, 1968 was the impetus that led to the activities at Farragut. The next day Stokely Carmichael called a press conference in Washington D.C. The *Chicago Tribune* (1968a) reported that Carmichael declared:

> I think white America made its biggest mistake when she killed Dr. King. She killed all reasonable hope. . . . When white America killed Dr. King, it declared war on us. . . . We have to retaliate for the execution of Dr. King. . . . Our retaliation won't be in the courtroom but in the streets of America. I don't think we have any other alternative to retribution. (p. 9)

When asked by a White reporter if he feared for his own life, Carmichael replied, "To hell with my life—you should fear for yours." Carmichael's words captured the angry spirit of the rebellions that took place nationwide. On April 5, 1968, students gathered in the Farragut's auditorium seeking consolation after King's assassination on the previous day. Principal Joseph Carroll demanded that students go to class once the bell rang, but students yelled at Carroll in defiance. Hannibal Afrik, who would become the leader of the Farragut movement, told the students to go home to eliminate a potentially volatile situation. A White Farragut teacher was quoted in the *Chicago Tribune*: "We had to get out of there. The Negroes took over" (*Chicago Tribune*, 1968b, p. 4). The students left and no doubt some either witnessed or participated in the rebellions that occurred on the West Side of Chicago. The rebellion left Black areas of Chicago in flames. The National Guard had to be called in to quell the disturbances.

King's assassination and Carroll's reaction served as a turning point in Afrik's life. For him, Carroll stood as a symbol of the cultural insensitivity of racist institutions. He made up his mind that Carroll had to go because the principal was a part of the problem that existed at Farragut. Afrik was a biology teacher who had migrated to Chicago in 1957. He received a biology degree from Central State University in Wilberforce, Ohio, in 1955. While working as a biochemistry researcher at the University of Illinois at Chicago Medical School, he had access to high-school students touring the facility. He noticed how little students in general knew about science and how much less Black students knew. Wanting to make a difference, he began substitute teaching once a week. After attending the March on Washington in 1963, he decided to teach permanently and to help Black students become scientific achievers (Afrik, personal communication, March 16, 1999).

Afrik completed his master's degree at Chicago Teachers College and began teaching as a Full Time Basis substitute (FTB). It took him three attempts to pass the Board of Education certification, which was separate from the state certification (Afrik, personal communication, March 16, 1999). The certification included a written as well as an oral exam. Many Black teachers who managed to pass the written exam often failed the subjective oral portion of the exam because of their southern dialect, and at times, their political affiliation (Anderson, 2002). A large number of the Black teachers in the system were uncertified, and therefore some of those FTBs who protested to improve the education of Black youth risked their jobs. A number of FTBs were fired for their participation in demonstrations against the school system and for their radical political stance. Although students and community members protested their firing, their temporary status left them without recourse. A group called the Concerned FTBs organized sick-ins and wildcat strikes in an attempt to gain permanent status within the system. The CTU did little to assist them with their struggle (Danns, 2003b).

Afrik noted that many of the teacher-training programs did not provide pre-service teachers with an adequate education to teach in inner-city schools. Those wanting to be teachers had to overcome numerous obstacles to be eligible for higher education, and then were held to the same standards as White candidates who were better prepared. Afrik insists that there are three undeniable features of public education in this country: it is based on White male nationalism; has relegated Blacks to inferior education; and was never intended to provide equal opportunity to Blacks. He argued that, "The masses of our people in this country, in spite of their inherent intellectual capacity to learn were systemically deprived . . . from having an equal opportunity" (Afrik, personal communication, March 16, 1999).

Afrik believed that the following school reforms were needed: guarantees that Blacks have equal opportunity, relevant materials, improved teacher preparation, community control of schools, and accountability of elected officials to maintain equality. His analysis of educational problems illustrated his concern for Black students as well as his understanding of many of essential reforms needed to improve the educational system. Afrik noted that as he entered the teaching profession, the prevailing sociological theory of the day cast Blacks as victimized, culturally deprived, disadvantaged, and uneducable (personal communication. March 16, 1999).

Incensed by questionable social theory and the events unfolding before them, Afrik and other Farragut teachers organized during the summer of 1968. Other groups on the West Side, where Farragut is located, conducted educational conferences. Parents held a conference in May 1968 to discuss the inequalities in Black schools and the inadequate preparation of Black high-school graduates. In an August 1968 Model Cities' conference, teachers and administrators in the West Side's North Lawndale School District 19 discussed the numerous problems that existed in those schools. Both conferences highlighted the failure of the curriculum to keep up with the changing communities. These activists and educators insisted that relevant curriculum would be one of the necessary solutions to the problems facing West Side youth. Prior to the 1968 conferences, communities organized to oust principals at Jenner, Attucks, and Crown Elementary Schools because they were not meeting the needs of Black students (Danns, 2003a).

The activism indicated a definite call for improvement at Black schools, rather than desegregation as civil rights activists had fought for. However, not all Black activists in Chicago were willing to abandon desegregation. African Americans in the Austin community rallied in support of Superintendent James Redmond's 1967 busing proposal, which was mainly to relieve overcrowding, and secondly to acquire desegregation. Nonetheless, the more dominant belief in the late sixties was that community control of Black schools would be a better avenue for equalizing education. As one activist noted in a *West Side Torch* interview on busing, "My child can get as good an education sitting beside black as beside white" (*West Side Torch*, 1968b, p. 4).

Farragut Teachers' Struggle

Farragut teachers met during the summer to create the "Black Manifesto." Lois Travillion, a teacher who participated in the organizing, noted that Farragut students were being shortchanged and tracked into the lowest educational tracks. She questioned the low expectations for Black students, and believed that there was a sense that teachers just needed to keep Black students under control in order to keep the school's name out of the press (Travillion, personal communication, March 15, 2000). Teaching Black students was secondary to controlling their actions. The issue of controlling students' behavior was common. Hirsh High School students walked out of school two days before King's assassination, protesting an "Operation Snatch" policy, which allowed teachers to seize tardy students and hold them in their class the entire period even if the students did not belong in that class. Their absence from class would be charged as a cut (*Chicago Defender*, 1968d, p. 3). The "Operation Snatch" policy was more concerned with discipline than education. Disciplinary issues became part of the concern Black activists had with the school system, and they demanded more control in the process to change the way discipline was administered.

On September 3, 1968, as students returned to schools from summer break, Farragut teachers called a press conference and announced their "Black Manifesto" to the school administration (*Chicago Defender*,1968a). The creation and announcement of the manifesto was in itself defiant. The *Chicago Defender* quoted Afrik stating that, "This is an act of black determination and represents the first time that black teachers have organized within a school and presented their program to the local and district school organization." He added that the community support of the teachers "signifies the peak of black pride and is destined to achieve positive educational improvement at our school" (*Chicago Defender*,1968a, p. 10).

In the Black Manifesto, teachers demanded a Black administrator and a Black administrative assistant in the area of discipline, both to come from within the staff. They demanded that the Afro-American history course be expanded to one year, with one semester dedicated to African culture. They also demanded the "immediate inclusion of 'black' contributions in every subject by each faculty member" through the use of supplementary text materials, class discussions, lectures or audiovisual aids. The manifesto insisted that department chairs evaluate their curriculum, and that support staff such as counselors, school nurses, psychologists, teacher aids, library staff, custodians, and engineers "submit recommendations for improvement of their services in relation to the educational programs." In terms of the administrators, the manifesto demanded that they evaluate existing resources and utilize community resources to improve the instructional materials and equipment, reduce the dropout rate, create a re-enrollment program, mandate in-service educational programs, be more fiscally accountable for school funds in order to finance creative projects, and create a liaison position to elementary schools to ensure the proper preparation of incoming freshmen. Other demands dealt with relieving overcrowding, updating the facilities, and granting Black businesses contracts with the school. The Black Manifesto dealt with the fundamental educational problems that existed within Farragut High School, as well as calls for culturally relevant education and Black school leadership.

Farragut teachers were determined that their demands for school reform would not be mere suggestions for change, but that they would struggle to make sure the demands were implemented. Afrik called the demands "non-negotiable." The demands had deadlines, many of which were September 30, 1968. The majority of Black teachers at the school signed a petition to show unity among the Black faculty. The principal tried to ignore the demands, but

Afrik insisted that if the demands were not met, Farragut would no longer be open as a public school (Afrik, personal communication, March 16, 1999).

Lois Travillion recalled that the Farragut teachers agitated by pressuring the school administration. They marched around the building and conducted other forms of protests (Travillion, personal communication, March 15, 2000). As the September 30 deadline approached, Afrik told the press that the teachers would begin evacuating the school if their demand for a Black assistant principal was not met. He was quoted in the *West Side Torch* as saying: "We will evacuate all black teachers, teacher aides, staff members, civil service employees, and students from the school and if necessary, establish black schools to educate our children until our demands are met" (*West Side Torch*, 1968a, p. 2). Principal Carroll still refused to meet the demands. However, his superiors moved to create a new assistant principal position at Farragut, which set precedence for other Black high schools as well. There were four existing assistant-principal positions; so instead of replacing any of the assistant principals already in position, a new fifth position was created (Afrik, personal communication, March 16, 1999; Joseph Rosen, personal communication, June 15, 2000). Arleen J. Hunter became Farragut's first Black assistant principal (Board of Education, 1968a). She was a Farragut teacher with two master's degrees and had been an assistant to Carroll.

Carroll continued to drag his feet instead of meeting the teachers' demands. The only demands met were for the Black assistant principal, disciplinarian, and counselors. In December 1968, teachers conducted a two-day "teach-in" to protest Carroll. Fifty-five teachers, including 15 White teachers, brought their students to the auditorium, renamed Black Liberation Hall, and the students were taught Black history, literature, and poetry (*Chicago Defender*, 1968c, p. 3). Although Carroll was not in attendance at the teach-in, District Superintendent Joseph Rosen attended and called it, "a wonderful dialog between teachers and students" (*Chicago Defender*, 1968b, p. 1). Rosen further stated that he did not understand why Carroll had not met the rest of the demands. Assistant Principal Joseph Krob stated that the demands were reasonable, but the timeline for meeting them was unrealistic.

White teachers at Farragut, led by English teacher John Moscinski, formed the Concerned Teachers Organization, and they assisted in acquiring 140 signatures calling for Carroll's ouster. *Chicago Today* reported Carroll's insistence that he would only leave if school personnel decided that he should go (*Chicago Today*, 1969a). White teachers were supportive of ousting Principal Carroll because his leadership led to low teaching morale, high teacher absenteeism, and teacher transfers. Anders (1971) wrote of Carroll:

I often watched him as he strode back and forth in his glass office, arms behind his back head down, giving orders. He did not know me, nor most of the faculty, by name, unless someone had gained a reputation for tardiness or a sloppy record book. He talked on the phone a great deal and some days the only proof of his existence was the sound of the toilet flushing in his office. . . . When a few concerned teachers at Farragut approached him with ideas for new programs, requests for better materials, he always smiled, nodded several times in agreement, and said "OK," and did nothing (pp. 72–73).

Despite the assistance of White teachers, Black teachers were considered a disruptive minority.

In the spring of 1969, States Attorney Edward Hanrahan, who orchestrated the cover up of the assassination of Black Panthers Fred Hampton and Mark Clark on December 4, 1969 (Cohen and Taylor, 2000), called Farragut teachers before a grand jury for an investigation of Chicago school violence. Only seven teachers from Farragut's Black Teachers Association were questioned, despite the violence at other schools (Afrik, personal communication, March 16, 1999). Afrik recalled that informants warned him that the grand jury was actually called to incriminate him through the use of other teachers. Hanrahan said he was investigating Black radicals on the schools' payrolls who were inciting violence among students. He insisted that, "What we are trying to do is uncover any crimes in which . . . we can develop a basis for prosecution then prosecute" ("Grand Jury Calls 7 Farragut Teachers," 1969). Afrik was questioned regarding a letter he had written to Carroll, which Hanrahan intended to use to incriminate him (Anders, 1971).

Although no one was indicted, the grand-jury investigation showed that city officials were seriously concerned about the teachers' demands for quality education, school reform, and community control. The teachers' struggle was courageous because they risked their jobs and possibly more as the city was tightening up on "disturbances" since the rebellions after King's assassination on April 4, 1968, and the National Democratic Convention protests in the late summer of 1968. The teachers' dedication and commitment was noticed, so tactics such as the grand jury and police intelligence investigations were devised to stop their struggle.

A gang shooting in the lunchroom in February 1970, and Carroll's decision to not support a security meeting, led those who were fed up with the conditions at the school to call a meeting. On February 19, 1970, parents, teachers, and concerned community members met to discuss their grievances (Anders, 1971). Community organizer Ida "Ma" Fletcher, a school lobbyist whom Rosen said could get things done when others could not (Rosen, personal communication, June 15, 2000), led the meeting and called for a vote

192 | *Black Protest Thought and Education*

to oust Carroll. Of the 170 people present, about 150 voted to oust Carroll (Anders, 1971). Rosen informed Carroll of the vote, but Carroll was hesitant to leave. Rosen contacted his supervisor and insisted that Carroll had to go because he was an ineffective principal. Carroll was reassigned (Rosen, personal communication, June 15, 2000).

A Black counselor, Larry Flournoy, was installed as the school's acting principal. Parents, students, and teachers served on a School Policy Committee that ran the school. The School Policy Committee met the demands from the Black Manifesto. Teachers unwilling to submit to the changes after Carroll's ouster transferred to different schools (Anders, 1971). Farragut, in effect, had a community-controlled school for one year. But as with events in New York, the Principal's Club, an administrators' union, filed suit to garner the position that was filled by an "unqualified" person. Rosen had Flournoy take the principal's examination, but Flournoy failed the exam (Rosen, personal communication, June 15, 2000). Farragut's community-controlled school lasted until August 1971. The School Policy Committee capitulated once they were guaranteed the selection of each new principal (Afrik, personal communication, March 16, 1999). Elisha William Walker became principal August 25, 1971 (Board of Education, 1971–1972).

The teachers demanded educational reforms so that students could reach their highest achievement, while also demanding cultural changes in the curriculum to reflect the contributions of people of African descent. They demanded Blacks be placed in leadership positions in the school, ousted the principal, and then instituted community control of the school. Their struggle was a part of a larger struggle in Chicago during the Black Power era in which teachers, students, parents, and community organizations sought control of their schools and sought reforms, which they hoped would heighten Black students' educational opportunities. Principals were ousted, busing denounced, demonstrations conducted, and manifestos issued, not only as a critique of an inadequate educational system, but also in protest of the institutional racism that maintained such a system. Black teachers concerned with racism within the school system and the Chicago Teachers Union, organized to create a separate union (Landwermeyer, 1978) and, in 1969, they kept Black schools open during a teachers' strike (Washington, 1969). The actions of Farragut teachers, along with student activists and community organizers, led to increased African American history courses, curriculum more relevant to the needs of students, more Black administrators, the creation of an outpost for the reenrollment of dropouts, and the power to choose the Farragut principal. It also led to a change in the atmosphere of the school and higher teacher and student morale.

Conclusion

Centralized educational bureaucracy essentially took control of public schools away from local communities, without a real desire to meet the needs of those communities. African Americans, who were marginalized as a result of centralization, sought educational equality through desegregation, without demanding changes in the power structure that created and maintained the inequalities in the first place (Shujaa and Afrik, 1996). As the organizers in the Civil Rights Movement began to further contend with issues of power, the cry for Black Power was increasingly heard. More radical organizers insisted on Black control of Black communities. They hoped that community-controlled schools would be a liberating force. This directly challenged centralized schools and the bureaucratized authorities that clung to power.

The Farragut High School struggle stood as an example of teachers trying to work from inside the educational system to increase community control. After two years of struggle, they recognized that they would have to take over the school and implement the demands that the principal had ignored. Centralized control implies that the school administrators know what is best for students, in spite of their failure to adequately educate people of color. Hiding behind a system of credentials and certification, which supported the illusion of meritocracy, powerful school bureaucracies fought to maintain their existing power even when that power was challenged. That is what was learned from the cases in New York City and Chicago. In New York, the United Federation of Teachers used professional standards and workers' rights as leverage to overthrow the decision making of the local governing board. In both cities, the administrative unions sued or threatened to sue to obtain positions occupied by "unqualified" personnel. The decisions of the local community and Black teachers could not possibly be "legitimate" because institutional procedures were not followed. Securing institutional procedures and maintaining control was more important than meeting the needs of the students.

This chapter illustrated the commitment of Black teachers at Farragut to the educational success of their students. Their realization—that those in control at their school prevented students' educational success—meant they had to be willing to risk their livelihood to change the power relations at their school. The support from parents and community leaders solidified a base from which the teachers could operate. Afrik spoke of the kind of commitment needed to make changes:

> If we are serious about the education of our children, there is no sacrifice too great for our youth. . . . If we're going to be serious about the education of our children, we

do what Malcolm said. We will do whatever it takes by any and all means necessary. And when white . . . policy makers realize our commitment, reluctantly and begrudgingly they will capitulate, but only when they are convinced that there will be no compromise in our commitment for our children. (personal communication, March 16, 1999)

The unfortunate reality is that while the commitment Afrik speaks of is essential in creating changes within society, without the power to maintain decision-making aspects of change, the system's institutional balance is weighted in favor of those who truly have control in that system. But had it not been for the commitment of people such as the Farragut teachers and others during the 1960s and 1970s, would I and other scholars of color be in the position to write about their stories?

References

Anders, E. (1971). Everybody run Farragut. Courtesy of Hannibal Afrik, publisher unknown, pp. 67–95.

Anderson, A.B. and G.W. Pickering (1986). *Confronting the color line: The broken promise of the Civil Rights Movement in Chicago.* Athens: University of Georgia Press.

Anderson, J.D. (1988). *Education of Blacks in the South, 1860–1935.* Chapel Hill: University of North Carolina Press.

Anderson, J.D. (2002). Discussion at the American Educational Studies Association Conference in Pittsburgh, PA.

Berbube, M.R. and M. Gittell. (1968). *Local control in education: The Demonstration school districts.* New York: Praeger Publishers.

Board of Education (1971–1972). *Proceedings* (July 1, 1971–June 30, 1972). Chicago: Author.

Board of Education (1968a). *Racial survey: Administrators and teaching personnel* (September 20). Chicago: Author.

Board of Education (1968b). *Student racial survey* (September 20). Chicago: Bureau of Research Development Special Reports.

Board of Education (1966). *Observation count by teachers* (October). Chicago: Author.

Chicago Defender (1968a). Farragut teachers issue demands (September 4), p. 3, 10.

Chicago Defender (1968b). Farragut teachers stage all-day teach-in, threaten more action (December 21–27), p. 1.

Chicago Defender (1968c). How Farragut teachers won big victory (December 24), pp. 3.

Chicago Defender (1968d). Student walkout closes Hirsh High School: Principal to meet today to discuss complaints (April 3), p. 3.

Chicago Today (1969a). Black teachers helm at Farragut High School (May 16).

Chicago Today (1969b). Board member admits school integration failing. (April 30).

Chicago Tribune (1968a). Must avenge King's death: Carmichael (April 6), p. 9.

Chicago Tribune (1968b). Report 9 Slain in Rioting: 3000 Guardsmen Patrolling Streets, Daley Pleads for an End to Violence (April 6), p. 4.

Cohen, A., and E. Taylor (2000). *American pharaoh: Mayor Richard J. Daley, his battle for Chicago and the nation*. Boston: Little, Brown and Company.

Cronin, Jim. (1973). *The control of urban schools*. New York: The Free Press.

Danns, D. (2002). Black student empowerment and Chicago school reform efforts in 1968. *Urban Education*, 37 (November), 631–655.

Danns, D. (2003a). Chicago high school students' movement for quality education, 1966–1971. *Journal of Negro Education*, 88 (Spring), 138–150.

Danns, D. (2003b). *Something better for our children: Black organizing in Chicago public schools, 1963–1971*. New York: Routledge.

Fantini, M., M. Gittell, and R. Magat (1970). *Community control and the urban school*. New York: Praeger Publishers.

Grand jury calls 7 Farragut teachers (1969). Newspaper clipping from unknown source.

Havemann, J. (1968). Student boycott leaders tell demands to school board. *Chicago Sun-Times* (October 31), pp. 3, 40.

Hirsh, A.R. (1983). *Making the second ghetto: Race and housing in Chicago, 1940–1960*. Chicago: University of Chicago Press.

Landwermeyer, F.M. (1978). Teacher unionism, Chicago style. Ph.D. dissertation, University of Chicago.

Payne, C.M. (1995). *I've got the light of freedom: The organizing tradition and the Mississippi freedom struggle*. Berkeley: University of California Press.

Podair, J. (2002). *The strike that changed New York: Blacks, whites and the Ocean Hill–Brownsville crisis*. New Haven: Yale University Press.

Podair, J. (1994) "White" values, "black" values: The Ocean Hill–Brownsville controversy and New York City Culture, 1965–1975. *Radical History Review*, 59 (Spring), 36–59.

Ralph, J. (1993). *Northern protest: Martin Luther King Jr., Chicago, and the Civil Rights movement*. Cambridge, Mass.: Harvard University Press.

Shujaa, M.J., and H.T. Afrik (1996). School desegregation, the politics of culture and the Council of Independent Black Institutions. In M.J. Shujaa, ed., *Beyond desegregation: The politics of quality in African American schooling* (pp. 253–268). Thousand Oaks, Calif.: Corwin Press, Inc.

Tyack, D. B. (1977). City schools: centralization of control at the turn of the century. In J. Karabel & A.H. Halsey, eds., *Power and ideology in education* (pp. 397–411). New York: Oxford University Press.

Tyack, D. (1974). *The one best system: A history of American urban education*. Cambridge, Mass.: Harvard University Press.

Vrame, W.A. (1970). A history of school desegregation in Chicago since 1954. Ph.D. dissertation, University of Wisconsin, Madison.

Walker, V.S. (1996). *Their highest potential: An African American school community in the segregated South*. Chapel Hill: University of North Carolina Press.

Washington, S. (1969). Inner city teachers defy union's order to strike. *Chicago Sun-Times* (May 23), pp. 1, 52.

Watkins, W.H. (2001). *The white architects of black education: ideology and power in America, 1865–1954*. New York: Teachers College Press.

West Side Torch (1968a). Farragut teachers plan if demands not met (September 19–October 3), p. 2.

West Side Torch (1968b). Westside Speaks on Busing (February 6–March 2), p. 4.

Wilcox, P. (1966). The controversy over I.S. 201: One view and a proposal. *Negro Teachers Forum*, 1 (November).

Chapter Nine

DAVID STOVALL

Critical Race Theory as Educational Protest

POWER AND PRAXIS

> Theory ought not to be a fetish. It does not have magical powers of its own. On the other hand, theory is inescapable because it is an indispensable weapon in struggle, and it is an indispensable weapon in struggle because it provides certain kinds of understanding, certain kinds of illumination, certain kinds of insights that are requisite if we are to act effectively.
>
> —Cornel West, *Conversation with bell hooks*

In order to provide proper context for the title and aforementioned quote, the following document should be read as a broadly based application of the tenets of Critical Race Theory (CRT) to urban public education. CRT is educational protest, as well as scholarship intended to provide new insight and opportunity for educational praxis. Rooted in legal, social, historical, and philosophical ideology, the purpose of CRT could be interpreted as twofold: to identify White supremacy in education; and to develop praxis to counter its hegemony. CRT is not the "end-all-be-all" in creating antiracist education. Instead, it should be included in the array of epistemologies that address issues of race and racism in education.

This chapter asserts that protest should not be confined to civil disobedience. Rather, it should be viewed as a protracted effort in the struggle to address the needs and concerns of Black students. Current discourse does not give protest such ideological consideration. Historically in many African American communities, protest has been crucial to the development of constructive responses to the vestiges of racism. The following account should be read in similar fashion. Although its means are dynamic and situational, protest remains rooted in an ideological stance against racism and injustice.

Explaining Critical Race Theory

Although introductory in terms of utility, CRT should be understood as a call to work. CRT is a theory, but it also operates as a "weapon in struggle" by providing tools with which to address the concerns of African Americans in education. It strays from traditional theoretical concepts in that, within CRT, analysis is derived from the participation of the scholar in concerted efforts to eliminate oppressive educational conditions. Although some may read the previous statements as suggesting CRT as a hybrid of grounded-research and postmodern theory, the summation would not be accurate. Instead, it embraces both concepts, as do critical-race feminism, queer theory, and other frameworks, as contributors to the development of CRT as a field of scholarship and praxis. Its difference lies in the attempt to amalgamate the contributions of people of color in the fight against racism. Most recently, the various contributors to CRT have made the attempt to identify and create interdependencies between groups of color. In short, CRT stems from a simple understanding: racism is persistent in the lives of people of color in the United States. Due to social and historical developments, each group has a unique contribution to make to the discourse of CRT. And each of these ways of understanding intersects with a discussion of White supremacy. The concept is not "we are the world," but "we all are catching hell from racism." Each contribution is unique. Instead of staking claims as to which group's knowledge and experience is more authentic or valuable, CRT incorporates narrative as the "tie that binds." As individual experiences (narratives) are collected and understood to demonstrate common themes, the job of the critical-race theorist is to critically assess the thematic trends in relationship to a discipline or disciplines. Through the lens of this collection of disciplines, "intersectionality" serves to articulate the experiences of people of color with racism.

It is also important to note in the beginning of this text that CRT does not propose another woe-is-me approach to the current state of public education. Instead, it offers the recognition of a society that has "racialized" groups, subsequently giving advantage to one over the other. Critics of CRT argue this new inquiry to be part and parcel of a "postmodern" liberal ideology that "plays the race card" and ignores the current "reality" of improved race relations. In response, and to set the record straight, it must be noted that the disadvantages of racism in educational and other settings are well documented (e.g., Watkins 2001, Ladson-Billings 1998, Du Bois 1994, West 1993, Walker 1993, James 1968, Williams, 1972). However, current media has largely ignored the daily reality of police brutality, gentrification, disproportionate sentencing in the criminal justice system, decreasing access to health care, and the urban drug trade. CRT is not a plea for "understanding." Rather, it is a response aimed at changing the realities of the public institutions, including education. Not just in the ideological sense, but also as an active engagement in praxis, real change will confront the reality of public education as an often-debilitating environment for children of color.

In protest of the current conditions of urban public education, its intention is to provide a radical constructive critique—*radical* because CRT in this sense is not a tool of educational reform. Where a reform effort may propose a change from within or a change of existing structures, CRT suggests a concerted effort, from those negatively affected by the current system, to determine their own needs and responses. In opposition to current forms of scholarship, the role of the researcher is secondary—not in the sense that the findings are not communicated throughout the academic community, but rather because the efforts of those affected are central to the creation of new approaches to education. Echoing sentiment expressed in Yamamoto's (1997) "Critical Race Praxis," the call in this article is for race theorists to "spend less time on abstract theorizing" (p. 873), and more time on community-based educational efforts. The suggestion for power and praxis lies in the tenets of CRT as a continuation and expansion of the numerous attempts to address the educational concerns of African American students. While it is postmodern in its emphasis on situational knowledge and in other ways, it does not face the usual critiques of postmodernism as being disconnected or stagnant. Rather, CRT has challenged scholars to venture "outside the box" to forge alliances throughout various disciplines. Although a critique, it does not dismiss itself from the historical lineage of the various scholars (Woodson 2000, Foster 1997, Delpit 1995, Shujaa 1992) who have identified White supremacy as a crucial element in the structure of urban public education.

In providing critical analysis of education from the perspective of Black protest, it is important to situate ourselves in ideology and history. A colleague and dear friend always engages me with the question, "Were public schools ever meant to work?" And although my initial response is a resounding, "No," I must revisit her question and ask my own question: "Work for whom?"

Understanding racism as endemic to the United States, CRT can be integral to the identification of the intricate relationships in the urban-school setting. Providing a format with which to locate the function of racism in education, CRT provides the ability to:

1. Name and discuss the pervasive daily reality of racism, which disadvantages people of color.

2. Expose and deconstruct seemingly colorblind or race-neutral policies and practices, which entrench the disparate treatment of non-White persons.
3. Legitimize and promote the voices and narratives of people of color as sources of critique of the dominant social order that purposefully devalues them.
4. Revisit civil-rights law and liberalism to address their inability to dismantle and expunge discriminatory sociopolitical relationships.
5. Change and improve challenges to race-neutral and multicultural movements in education, which have made White students' behavior the norm (Ladson-Billings 1998, p.16)

Although most of the five statements are seemingly light in the hopes of what CRT hopes to accomplish—naming, exposing, giving voice, reanalyzing—they are weighty in terms of what is to be done. Amid common responses to educational-reform efforts, CRT supports the claim that critique is not enough. In order to address the current state of urban education, there must be new systemic and external efforts to address the needs and concerns of students, parents, and teachers. For many, this statement may appear too broad. In terms of creating a space for CRT to flourish, it needs enough space to incorporate tenets from various disciplines. The idea is not to imply a site-specific model for educational change, but to declare the intersection of disciplines in CRT as necessary to the development of new approaches.

Compiling Relevant Research

The work of education scholar William Tate (1997) provides a comprehensive account of the education literature dedicated to CRT. The contribution enforces CRT as an amalgamation of research paradigms used to address race in public education.

Identifying what is most important to the "hybrid" nature of the discipline, Tate cites the inclusion of real-life experiences, recorded as narrative, as the crucial link between research interests. Regarding education, he incorporates Calmore's (Calmore in Tate 1997) argument that CRT:

> . . . challenges the universality of White experience/judgement as the authoritative standard that binds people of color and normatively measures, directs, controls and regulates the terms of proper thought, expression, presentation, and behavior. As represented by legal scholars, CRT challenges the dominant discourses on race and racism as they relate to law. (Tate 1997, p. 197)

Legal importance notwithstanding, CRT's insights can also be directly applied to education in terms of the application of standards and disciplinary measures in the school setting. Although still rarely used in educational paradigms, CRT provides space in which to observe the workings of racism through close attention to stories.

In addition to previously mentioned "tenets" of CRT, Tate asserts the theory's ability to highlight three identifiable assumptions of the White male paradigm, which assumes that:

1. The white middle-class American (male) . . . is the standard against which all others are compared.
2. Instruments used to measure differences are universally applied across all groups.
3. Although we need to recognize social class, gender, cultural orientation, and proficiency in English, these and other factors are ultimately extraneous and can later be ignored (p. 215).

Unfortunately, in addition to the qualities mentioned in the third point, many scholars have argued cultural relevance as "extraneous" and unnecessary for urban public curricula. In response, Tate alludes to Aleinkoff's 1986 critique of colorblind policy. In Aleinkoff's interpretation, policy "requires color consciousness—one must notice race in order to tell oneself not to trigger the usual mental processes that take race into account" (Aleinkoff in Tate 1997, p. 214). This refutes the often-used phrase, "When I see a person I don't see race."

CRT's Departure from Critical Legal Studies

Focusing on CRT's break from Critical Legal Studies (CLS), its source framework, Tate cites the development of CRT as a critique of the "liberal" nature of the earlier paradigm, CLS. In Aleinkoff's view, CLS did not take into account a primary contributor to the inequity paradigm, race. According to the work of Derrick Bell, the role of the civil-rights lawyer was not simply to deliver an interpretation of the legal rules, but to "fashion arguments that might change existing laws" (Tate 1997). To the CRT scholar, CLS is idealistic; it does not take into account the primary sources and structures that contribute to an unjust society. Instead, CLS focuses on addressing the class disparities, perpetuated by conservative interpretations of government policy. An education parallel would be a CLS examination of the Department of Education's 1983 report "A Nation at Risk." Rather than critiquing the report for the negative effects of high-stakes testing, encouraged by its recommendations on inner-city populations, the report would focus solely on which schools would be afforded the funds to enable them to become successful. Race would not be examined as a factor in the review of how the recommendations were implemented, or which children were most affected as a result. Although both interpretations have something to offer, one cannot exist in absence of the other. In other words, a class analysis is not valuable outside of a race analysis. Critical race scholars hold that "racism will not be understood or go away." Critical legal scholarship is correct in recognizing that "legalisms are indeterminate and the law reflects the interest of the power structure" (Tate 1997, p. 216). However, CRT strengthens the argument through the idea that social reality "is constructed by the creation and exchange of stories about individual situations" (ibid.). Narrative, in creating such an exchange, is the agent that fuses history, sociology, education, philosophy, gender studies, and legal scholarship. It expands the scope of CLS through the addition of race.

Bell's (2000) Interest Convergence Theory captures the previous idea. Through interpretation of recent civil-rights decisions, Bell believes the most important question confronts "whether the debilitating effects of racial discrimination can be remedied without requiring Whites to surrender aspects of their superior social status." As an example, many urban public schools have incorporated diversity programs without actually consulting the "underrepresented" groups these programs are intended to serve. Teams of researchers are brought in to give suggestions as to what steps schools should make to give voice to students of color. Unfortunately, both examples often result in superficial outcomes, especially when change might mean a loss of power for Whites. Using *interest convergence* to analyze educational policies like "zero-tolerance" reveals it, and many other policies, to represent little more than an attempt by administrative bodies to maintain the status quo under the façade of equal treatment. Nevertheless, administrators continue to enact inhumane policies as "fair treatment." In the well-known example of the seven African American boys in 1999 who were expelled from a high school in Decatur, Illinois, for fighting, the argument was that violation of the policy dictated the severe punishment. Little information was released as to what "zero-tolerance" might mean in this and other schools, how it would be enforced, and whom it would affect; the interests of the power structure were served through the application of policy without collective understanding or discussion. Tate (1997) notes that:

> . . . reality is not fixed. . . . Rather, we construct it through conversations, through our lives together. Racial and class-based isolation prevents the hearing of diverse stories

and counter stories. It diminishes the conversations through which we create reality [and] construct our communal lives. (p. 218)

Education, like any human interaction, is a set of relationships between groups. CRT, in this and other fields, calls for critical analysis of such relationships to reveal how power structures impede the ability of specific groups to address their needs and concerns. Colorblindness is an illogical concept in a society "in which specific groups have been treated differently historically and in which the outcomes of this differential treatment continue into the present" (p. 219). CRT provides the insights necessary to support antiracist and social-justice initiatives in education (Noguera 2003; Satterthwaite, Atkinson, & Gale 2003; Ayers, Quinn, & Hunt 1999).

Returning to the importance of narrative, Tate notes Bell's contribution in an explanation of the attraction of narrative:

> . . . it corresponds more closely to the manner in which the human mind makes sense of experience than does the conventional, abstracted rhetoric of law. The basic thrust of the cognitive process is to employ imagination to make meaning out of the embodied experience of the human organism in the world. In its prototypical sense as storytelling, narrative proceeds from the ground up. In narrative, we take experience and configure it in a conventional and comprehensive form. This is what gives narrative its communicative power; it is what makes narrative a powerful tool of persuasion and therefore, a potential transformative device for the disempowered. (p. 228)

Instead of "abstracted" theoretical constructs that often confuse and misinterpret findings, narrative provides a space for specific stories to be told by those who experienced the narrative events. As scholars began to engage in the production and collection of narratives, a progression occurred, from its early application to legal decisions, to later analyses of educational policy.

In concert with critical studies in the humanities and social sciences, CRT invites politicized discussions of race via examination of common trends in narrative. To Delgado and Stefancic (2001), CRT scholarship is characterized by:

1. Insistence on "naming our own."
2. Belief that knowledge and ideas are powerful.
3. Readiness to question basic premises of moderate or incremental civil-rights law.
4. The borrowing of insights from social science on race and racism.
5. Critical examination of the myths and stories powerful groups use to justify racial subordination.
6. Contextualized treatments of doctrine.
7. Criticism of legal liberalism.

8. An interest in structural determinism—the ways in which legal tools and thought-structures can impede law reform. (Delgado & Stefancic 2001, p. 218)

Delgado and Stefancic argue that CRT is inclusive scholarship. By focusing on "naming our own," they confront the exclusion of people of color in legal scholarship. In critiquing CLS and legal academia, Delgado and Stefancic address exclusion as a historical phenomenon. Similar to Bell's account in *Race, Racism and American Law* (2000), CRT's characteristics are rooted in analysis of legal decisions. The dominant discourse is argued to be a "homeostatic device by which our society ensures that most race-related reform will last a short time" (p. 223). CRT, in opposition to mainstream discourse, confronts the notion that equality has been achieved and present policy should move "beyond" issues of race. Despite criticisms, the concept is not as radical as one may believe. Similar to works concerning multicultural education (Takaki, 1994), the idea is to include the contributions of people of color, to provide a factual account of history and culture in the United States. Education, in its development and implementation, is inclusive of this dichotomy through legal decisions and interpretations of race. Tate, in response to CRT critic James Banks, notes that "educational systems are built on laws, policies, and folkways requiring macro-level analyses that overlap with micro-level issues such as curriculum and pedagogy" (p. 219). Crucial to synthesis of the various "folkways" in education, CRT attempts to engage in subject-matter alternatives to the "master narrative" (Takaki 1994). If conventional history is written by the winners, CRT is written by the oppressed.

Crenshaw (in Crenshaw et al. 1995) expands the concept. For her, racism, as hegemonic practice, transcends the boundaries of scholarship traditions and is pervasive. The sheer power of the race concept transcends the failure of CLS to recognize its "liberal" interpretation of legal paradigms. A parallel can be drawn with education:

> Black people do not create their oppressive worlds moment to moment, but rather are coerced into living in worlds created and maintained by others. Moreover, the ideological source of this coercion is not liberal legal consciousness, but racism. If racism is just as important as, if not more important than, liberal ideology in explaining the persistence of White supremacy, then the critic's single-minded effort to deconstruct liberal legal ideology will be futile (Crenshaw et al. 1995, p. 230).

Arguably, the most crucial element to the development of CRT as legitimate analysis of current educational structures is the recognition of White supremacy. Invoking earlier sentiment, Tate eludes to the political element of CRT through Crenshaw's call for "a distinct political thought that is the product of the lives and conditions of Black people" (Crenshaw et al. 1995).

CRT as a theoretical construct incorporates the concept of intersectionality. Intersections "provide insights into the lives of those at the bottom of complex layers of social hierarchies to determine how the interactions with each hierarchy influence the dynamic of another" (p .232). The façade of objective educational standards through testing is identified as problematic through the disproportionate number of African American and Latino students retained in elementary grades. Coupled with the disproportionate number of said groups in special education, CRT provides a critique of a structure that holds, at its genesis, the belief of the inherent failure of people of color. Simply put, CRT sheds light on the complexity of racism. CRT, as a discussion of such intricacies, gives credence to both group and individual phenomena in the process. Utilizing its tenets provides insight to examine the simultaneous operation of group and individual dynamics. For the CRT in education, the question is:

> . . . not so much whether or how racial discrimination can be eradicated while maintaining the vitality of other interests linked to the status quo such as federalism, tradition values, standards, establishing property interests, and choice. Rather, the new question would ask how these traditional interests and cultural artifacts serve as vehicles to limit and bind the educational opportunities of students of color. (Crenshaw et al., p. 234)

The challenge becomes:

> . . . to find theoretical frameworks that allow for an expansive examination of race that moves beyond those associated with the inferiority paradigm. Such inquiry must begin with the recognition that this paradigm is a tool for the maintenance of racial subordination. The defining element of CRT suggests that this theoretical perspective can provide novel and innovative ways of exploring educational policy, research and practice. (p. 236)

Continuing the sentiment, Gloria Ladson-Billings (1998) provides crucial insight to the necessity of CRT through the idea that "thinking of race as solely objective denies the problematic aspects of race." By reinforcing the relationship of the law to education, we often find policies "designed to proscribe the contours of education" (Ladson-Billings 1998, p. 16). Programs aimed at diversity are suspect as a "sanitation" of the language of the Civil Rights Movement. The idea of multicultural education holds that "we're all immigrants and need to rise above immigrant status despite the various histories of specific groups and forced immigration" (p. 18). As a result, students of color are made to feel guilty for historical persecution and are expected to "rise above" immigrant status like every other group. For this reason, many attempts at multicultural education are inefficient in the production of relevant curricula. In response, CRT exposes racism while providing "radical proposals for addressing it" (p. 22). The nature of such proposals creates bold and unpopular decisions that CRT deems necessary. Excuses are not popular. If racism is endemic to the society and its evils are known, there is no excuse for not participating in praxis to change such realities.

Critical Race Praxis

The waters become murky when scholars engage in a deconstruction of mainstream discourse and propose a call to work. If we were to engage in the "objective" model of qualitative research, we would only propose suggestions for future research. However, in the case of CRT, the idea is to engage praxis as a necessity.

Again borrowing from legal scholarship, Eric Yamamoto (1997) argues for a critical-race praxis enabling lawyers to address "color-on-color" racial conflict in addition to White racism. The combination of the two prompts the author to suggest a race *practice* (p. 873). Such practice consists of establishing legal clinics, working in conjunction with community organizations, guiding student activists, establishing relationships with sympathetic politicians, and drafting ordinances and laws to address race-based inequity.

The same should be done in education. Professors should establish critical courses on teaching and administration, create and maintain alternative certification initiatives, support the recruitment and retention of people of color in teacher-education programs, and contact external grassroots organizations that may work with schools to get preservice and incoming teachers on board. While not a complete laundry list of what needs to be done, the previous serve as possible opportunities to include CRT as an integral component in teacher education.

By shifting thought into action, CRT shifts into academic activism in terms of incorporating ideological stances to address practical issues. Although resembling a classical "top-down" theoretical approach, CRT challenges the existing paradigm to the tune of "action researchers" who place theoretical assumptions as secondary to the experiential knowledge of the groups in question.

An example of the aforementioned would be the development of a small-schools multiplex in Chicago, scheduled to open in the fall of 2005. The school, originally promised to a predominantly Mexican American community in the early 1990s, never came to fruition. However, in the same historical moment, four new selective-enrollment magnet schools were being built in gentrifying or affluent areas with a rapidly increasing or stable White population. The Mexican American neighborhood remains working class and low income. When it came time for them to get their school, the central office of Chicago Public Schools (CPS, hereafter) said there was no money left to build the community high school. Feeling slighted by the central office of CPS, concerned community members staged a 19-day hunger strike. Not wanting the negative press in a system riddled with internal problems and external pressures, CPS agreed to construct the Little Village High School Multiplex. The building will house four small schools, while sharing athletic teams and other extracurricular activities. Determined by the community at large, the four schools will be the School of Social Justice, the School of World Languages, the School of the Arts, and the School of Math and Technology. As a member of the curriculum team, we have the responsibility to engage young people (in this case Mexican American and African American students) in the process of community engagement for social change.

In addition to the hunger strike, the process remained a contested one in the development of school infrastructure. The high school planning team (a coalition of hunger strikers, community members, and educators) was required to comply with the various local, state, and federal mandates to be monitored by CPS. One of these compliances was with a federal desegregation ordinance placed on CPS in 1982. With the Little Village neighborhood at over 95 percent Mexican American, CPS mandated the high school be at least 30 percent African American. The planning team has contacted community members in a neighboring African American community to become part of the high school development process, and we are currently engaged in a potential "color-on-color" conflict. Factions from the original hunger strikers have voiced that they don't want African Americans in the high school because they were not involved in the initial struggle. African Americans don't want to be the fringe group brought in under a federal mandate. Some Mexican American community members are opposing the proposed School of World Languages and worry if their children will suffer from further isolation. CPS on numerous occasions has attempted to move their own agenda forward in the attempt to propose a structural model entirely different than the original model proposed by community members.

In the attempt to be proactive, the high school development team (myself included) is engaged in critical-race praxis. Coupled with the intraracial issues, the group is receiving pressure from the central office to comply with mandated requirements. Opposed to reactionary-impulse responses, the planning committee has developed a structure of community accountability where both neighborhoods will be represented on a board that will monitor the day-today functions of the high school, and report them to the community at various outlets (i.e., block club meetings, community organization meetings, church groups). There is an open policy for any concerned member to participate. The work ahead is immense, but the premise remains: if both communities do not engage the process of maintaining a functional, productive school, the powers that be *will* take over and impose their own agenda.

In their critique of racial dynamics in the United States, critical-race theorists should recognize, and work to alleviate, problems that lead to such tensions. Justice, as an "experienced" phenomenon, involves grappling with the "messy and conflictual racial realities" often absent from current literature (Yamamoto, p. 875). In developing praxis, the idea is to create a method to address these realities while engaging in antiracist practice.

Incorporating an intersection of theoretical constructs (i.e., poststructuralism, Marxist ideology, critical-race feminism), Yamamoto suggests four starting points of "race praxis inquiry": conceptual analysis, performative inquiry, material analysis, and reflexive action (p. 878). The concept approaches race praxis from an ideological stance. Implied are the assumed functions of White supremacy. Included in the construct is the effect of White supremacy, as an endemic reality, on communities of color in struggle against each other for resources. Performative inquiry involves the action necessary to enact a critical-race praxis. In the development of community-based initiatives, theoretical approaches are enhanced through experiential knowledge gained in the process. Based on his own experiences in the attempt to fuse grassroots and academic communities, Yamamoto observes possible tensions if theorists do not engage in praxis:

> One conclusion I draw from interactions with political lawyers and community activists is that theoretical insights about race and critical socio-legal analyses of particular controversies are unlikely to be meaningfully developed and translated for frontline anti-subordination practice unless theorists personally engage with the difficult, entangled, shifting realities of that practice. (p. 880)

The same could be said for educators and the tensions between professors and students. If both groups are politically charged and dedicated to the encouragement of critical praxis, it may very well become difficult for the students to grasp an instructor's intent, especially if the class is embedded with "high-end" theoretical constructs. If professors are involved in similar struggles, examples can be provided to help contextualize how racism operates in public schooling. From there, scholars can assist activists' work from an experiential knowledge base.

This line of reasoning incorporates both material and reflexive properties of race practice. Borrowing from Yamamoto and replacing "law" with "education," critical-race praxis can embrace the idea that schools do not necessarily define what is just for racialized communities (p. 885). Engaging in an "inquiry into racial group agency and responsibility," he also suggests an interracial praxis that identifies the complex relationships racial groups may experience with each other in battling oppression. Each racial group may have particular relationships within themselves and with other groups, depending on the situation. Urban schools exemplify such relationships, depending on the racial composition of the community being served.

In terms of the culture of schooling, some scholars have argued for the connections of CRT to emancipatory pedagogy. Marvin Lynn (1999) argues that urban schools are not "created with the intent of being spiritually, emotionally, and intellectually emancipating" (Lynn 1999, p. 607). Instead, they are promoted and utilized as a system of order and control.

Through the examination of African American pedagogy, Lynn cites the work of Ladson-Billings to highlight the process of "culturally relevant" teaching as a process that places emphasis on culture, while "facilitating the development of basic skills that will allow the students to successfully navigate the White world" (p. 608). Similar to the tenants of Afrocentricity, Lynn expands the concept into CRT to incorporate issues of "race, gender, and class oppression" (p. 609).

After collecting narrative from teachers on how racism is embedded in the culture of schooling, Lynn's findings were striking. The overwhelming majority of teachers felt that racism was unavoidable in the urban educational setting. Following the analysis, Lynn concluded that "one cannot not prioritize one facet of his or her identity over another because it creates a false dichotomy that negates the fact that we all live our daily lives as race, classed, and gendered subjective entities" (p. 619).

So Now What?: Putting CRT to Work

When looking at the plight of urban schooling, it becomes a challenge to not develop a defeatist attitude. Nevertheless, the reality is that most African American children are being served in the public setting. Teaching is not an easy profession. Administrators don't have it that great either. However, it does not absolve either group from possible participation in a dangerous system of control and subordination.

Additionally, academics should not be granted immunity. It can be simple to sit back and provide commentary on the various relationships and inequalities in public schools. Despite the fact that few are writing about the function of racism in public education, it is ridiculous to rest on our laurels. We might have a little trouble in collecting data and conducting interviews, but it is nothing like being in a classroom in a school under probation, with mandatory testing standards, and students that may not have eaten before coming to class. I know it's wrong to compare oppressions, but we must respect the environment of concerned teachers and administrators.

Pragmatically, it's impossible to make the statement that "all teachers are bad." However, it is possible to report that most urban systems of education perform at substandard levels in relation to the education of African American students. It is also correct to say that urban education, as a system, supports a belief in the inherent inability of African American students to perform in school (Lipman 2004, Gould 1996, Spring 1980). When their success and completion are viewed as contrary to the norm, there is a problem. In order to counter such absurdity, CRT creates a space to dispel such ideas. Through discourse, narrative, and practice, teachers, students, administrators, and parents are given the opportunity to address the function of racism and how it impedes their daily ability to function in school.

Nevertheless, writing is not enough. We must engage in praxis that not only deconstructs the negative realities of the public school, but also supports the models that have proven effective in providing students with an education that reflects their self-worth and importance to the world. It is not easy. Academics have to deal with the fact that critical analyses of racism are viewed as questionable in many circles. Teachers' battles include securing preparation time, pressure from administrators, high-stakes testing, and "Gestapo-like" discipline codes. Administrators deal with pressure from superintendents, local school councils, and bureaucratic hierarchies. Parents don't receive necessary information from schools concerning policy and procedures, interact with nepotistic school councils, and encounter shady education bureaucrats. And students have to deal with it all. If we say we are concerned about the role education has in the lives of Black people, we must take the giant leap into becoming both critical and creative.

References

Ayers, W., T. Quinn, & J.A. Hunt (1999). *Teaching for social justice*. New York: Teachers College Press.

Bell, D. (2000). *Race, racism and American law* (4th ed) Boston: Little Brown Publishers.

Brooks, R.L. (1990). *Rethinking the American race problem*. New York: Roman & Littlefield.

Crenshaw K., N. Gotanda, G. Peller, & K. Thomas (1995). *Critical race theory: The key writings that formed the movement*. New York: The New Press.

Delgado, R., & J. Stefancic (2001). *Critical race theory: An introduction*. New York: New York University Press.

Delpit, L. (1995). *Other people's children: Cultural conflict in the classroom.* New York: The New Press.

Du Bois, W.E.B. (1994). *The souls of black folk.* Mineola, N.Y.: Dover Publications.

Foster, M. (1997). *Black teachers on teaching.* New York: The New Press.

Gould, S.J. (1996). *The mismeasure of man.* New York: W.W. Norton and Co.

James, C.L.R. (1968). *The black jacobins: Toussaint L'Overture and the San Domingo Revolution.* New York: Vintage Press.

Ladson-Billings, G. (1998). Just what is critical race theory and what's it doing in a nice field like education? *International Journal of Qualitative Studies in Education,* 11(1), 7–24.

Lipman, P. (2004). *High stakes education: Inequality, globalization, and urban school reform.* New York: Routledge-Farmer.

Lynn, M. (1999). Toward a critical race pedagogy: A research note. *Urban Education,* 33 (5), 606–627.

Noguera, P. (2003). *City schools and the American dream: Reclaiming the promise of public education.* New York: Teachers College Press.

Satterthwaite, J., E. Atkinson, & K. Gale (2003). *Discourse, power, resistance: Challenging the rhetoric of contemporary education.* Staffordshire, England: Trentham Books.

Shujaa, M. (1992). Education and schooling: You can have one without the other. In Shujaa, M., *Too much schooling, too little education.* Trenton, NJ: Africa Free Press.

Spring, J. (1980). *Educating the worker-citizen: The social, economic, and political foundations of education.* New York: Longman Publishers.

Takaki, R. (1994). *A different mirror: A history of multicultural America.* San Francisco: Back Bay Books.

Tate, W. (1997). Critical race theory and education: History, theory, and implications. *Review of Research in Education* 22, 195–247.

Walker, D. (1993). *David Walker's appeal, to the coloured citizens of the world, but in particular, and very expressly, to those of the United States of America.* Baltimore, MD: Black Classic Press.

Watkins, W. (2001). *The white architects of black education: Ideology and power in America, 1865–1954.* New York: Teachers College Press.

West, C. (1993). *Race Matters.* New York: Beacon Press.

West, C. (1999). *The Cornell West reader.* New York: Basic Books.

Woodson, C.G. (2000). *The miseducation of the negro.* Trenton, NJ: Africa World Press.

Williams, C. (1972). *The destruction of black civilization.* Trenton, NJ: Africa World Press.

Wing, C., ed. (1997). *Critical race feminism: A reader.* New York: New York University Press.

Yamamoto, E. (1997). Critical race praxis: Race theory and political lawyering practice in post–Civil Rights America. *Michigan Law Review,* 95 (7), 821–900.

Contributors

DIONNE DANNS received her Ph.D. in Educational Policy Studies in 2001 from the University of Illinois at Urbana-Champaign. She is currently a visiting assistant professor at the University of Illinois at Chicago. Danns's first book, *Something Better for Our Children: Black Organizing in Chicago Public Schools, 1963–1971* was published in Routledge's dissertation series. Her research interests include history of African American school reform efforts in Chicago and student and teacher activism.

BEVERLY M. GORDON, Ph. D. Univ. of Wisconsin, Madison, is an associate professor of curriculum studies in the Social and Cultural Foundation Program, School of Educational Policy and Leadership at Ohio State University. She teaches curriculum studies, African American education, and pedagogy. Her articles and chapters have appeared in *Educational Policy*, the *Journal of Negro Education*, *Urban Review*, the *Journal of Education*, *Theory into Practice*, *Handbook on Research on Multicultural Education*, the *Congressional Black Caucus* and numerous books. She served the American Educational Research Association as program chair and president, Research Focus on Black Education SIG; affirmative action chair, Divisions B and G; program chair, Committee On the Role and Status of Women in Educational Research and Development; vice president, Division G; and chair, Faculty of Color in Education Committee.

EILEEN M. HAYES is assistant professor of music (ethnomusicology) at the University of North Texas. She received her Ph.D. from the University of Washington in 1999. Hayes's areas of interest are music and nationalism, gender and music, black critical thought, and African American Music. She has presented papers at conferences of the Society for Ethnomusicology, College Music Society, and Feminist Theory and Music. Forthcoming publications include chapters in Maultsby and Burnim's *African American Music: An Introduction* (Routledge Spring 2005) and *More Than the Blues: Critical Perspectives on African American Women Musicians*, an anthology Hayes is coediting with Linda Williams (University of Illinois Press).

ANNETTE HENRY is associate professor in curriculum/policy studies, College of Education, University of Illinois at Chicago. Her scholarship examines Black women teachers' practice, feminist theory, critical pedagogy, cultural studies, second language/dialect education, Caribbean students, qualitative research methodologies, narrative research, classroom research, and collaborative outreach to urban schools. She is author of *Taking Back Control: African Canadian Women Teachers' Lives and Practice.* (SUNY, 1998). Her publications appear in the *Canadian Journal of Education; Curriculum Inquiry; International Journal of Qualitative Studies in Education; Anthropology and Education; Race, Ethnicity and Education; Journal of Negro Education; Urban Education;* and *Theory into Practice.* Her awards include National Academy of Education Post-Doctoral Fellowship (1996–1998), Scholar of the Year Award at the AERA Black Education SIG (1997), and the Jason P. Millman Promising Scholar Award in 1998 (Cornell University). She is currently associate editor and book review editor for *Race, Ethnicity and Education* and coeditor of the *Handbook of Social Foundations in Education.* Mahwah, NJ: Erlbaum (in preparation).

HAROON KHAREM is an assistant professor in the School of Education at Brooklyn College. He is the author of journal articles and book chapters on African American history and racism. Professor Kharem collaborates with other professors at Brooklyn College to professionally develop community teachers.

SIDNEY J. LEMELLE is professor of history and Black studies at Pomona College (Claremont, CA). He has written widely on topics related to Africa and African Diasporan History. With Robin D.G Kelley he has coedited *Imagining Home: Class, Culture and Nationalism in the African Diaspora* (1994). He is currently completing a soon to be released book *The Vinyl Ain't Final: Globalization and Localization of Black Popular Culture,* coedited with Dipa Basu (Pluto Press, 2005). Professor Lemelle has also taught at the Claremont Graduate University, the University of California at Los Angeles, and the University of Dar es Salaam, Tanzania.

DANIEL PERLSTEIN is a historian at the University of California Berkeley's Graduate School of Education. His work focuses on the interplay of democratic aspirations and social inequalities in American schools. Among his recent writings are *Justice, Justice: School Politics and the Eclipse of Liberalism* (New York: Peter Lang, 2004).

SANDRA RICHARDS is a doctoral candidate in the School of Educational Studies at Claremont Graduate University (CGU). In addition, she recently earned a certificate in Africana Studies, a joint program of the Intercollegiate Department of Black Studies (DBS) of The Claremont Colleges and CGU. Her research focuses on Caribbean (Black) education, Diaspora studies, critical pedagogy, and educational development in underserved regions. Currently, Ms. Richards is examining educational and vocational training programs in Jamaica's youth homes. Her dissertation seeks to use emergent theory to develop greater insight into the educational experiences of youths who live in conditions of marginality and exclusion from the economic mainstream. Through liberating education, Ms. Richards strives to secure a future for some of the most vulnerable children of Jamaica and to contribute to improved conditions of economic well-being for Black people throughout the African Diaspora.

DAVID STOVALL is an assistant professor of policy studies in the College of Education at the University of Illinois at Chicago. His current research interests include social justice and education, critical race theory, youth and community development, and youth culture. In the attempt to engage theory through practice, he is currently involved with a high school development project.

WILLIAM H. WATKINS was born in Harlem, New York, and raised in south-central Los Angeles. A former high school teacher, he completed his Ph.D. in 1986, University of Illinois at Chicago. Bill served on the College of Education and Black Studies faculties at the University of Utah before returning to the College of Education at the University of Illinois at Chicago in 1995. Bill is the author of *The White Architects of Black Education* (Teachers College Press, 2001), and lead editor and contributor to *Race and Education* (Allyn & Bacon, 2001); he has contributed numerous articles, chapters, essays, and reviews in scholarly journals, books, encyclopedias, and the popular press. Bill is past President, Society for the Study of Curriculum History; and past president, Research Focus on Black Education SIG, AERA. Bill has presented papers and lectured widely throughout North America, Mexico, Africa, Europe, Asia, and Australia. His life's work is dedicated to equality, social justice, and peace.

JOY ANN WILLIAMSON is an assistant professor of the history of education at Stanford University's School of Education. Her work focuses on the intersection of social movements and higher educational reform during the middle twentieth century with a particular focus on African Americans.

Index